INSIDE
the
SESSION

INSIDE
the
SESSION

What Really Happens in Psychotherapy

Paul L. Wachtel

American Psychological Association • Washington, DC

Published by
American Psychological Association
750 First Street, NE
Washington, DC 20002
www.apa.org

To order
APA Order Department
P.O. Box 92984
Washington, DC 20090-2984
Tel: (800) 374-2721; Direct: (202) 336-5510
Fax: (202) 336-5502; TDD/TTY: (202) 336-6123
Online: www.apa.org/pubs/books
E-mail: order@apa.org

In the U.K., Europe, Africa, and the Middle East, copies may be ordered from
American Psychological Association
3 Henrietta Street
Covent Garden, London
WC2E 8LU England

Typeset in Goudy by Circle Graphics, Inc., Columbia, MD

Printer: Edwards Brothers, Inc., Ann Arbor, MI
Cover Designer: Mercury Publishing Services, Rockville, MD

The opinions and statements published are the responsibility of the authors, and such opinions and statements do not necessarily represent the policies of the American Psychological Association.

Library of Congress Cataloging-in-Publication Data

Wachtel, Paul L., 1940-
 Inside the session : what really happens in psychotherapy / Paul L. Wachtel. — 1st ed.
    p. cm.
 Includes bibliographical references and index.
 ISBN-13: 978-1-4338-0940-8
 ISBN-10: 1-4338-0940-0
 1. Psychotherapy. 2. Psychotherapy—Case studies. I. Title.

 RC480.W266 2011
 616.89'14—dc22
                                        2010035701

British Library Cataloguing-in-Publication Data

A CIP record is available from the British Library.

Printed in the United States of America
First Edition

doi: 10.1037/12321-000

For Karen and Sameer, Kenny and Margaret

CONTENTS

PREFACE

The literature of psychotherapy is filled with clinical examples. But it contains relatively few word-by-word accounts of entire sessions. Examples are, by their very nature, *chosen*. That is their strength—they are chosen because they are apt, because they are viewed by the author as illustrating or illuminating a particular point especially well. But that is also their weakness. The very fact that they are chosen should make us cautious. In selecting what fits, what illustrates, what exemplifies, one is almost necessarily excluding what *does not* fit. This is not because of any malign motive on the author's part but simply because the very nature of perception and memory is such that we smooth out the rough edges and see and recall what fits well in our schemas. We try, in presenting examples, to separate the chaff from the wheat, to focus on figure, not ground. But the question of what is the chaff and what is the wheat, what is figure and what is ground, is perhaps the most crucial contested territory of all. If we wish to understand why people of intelligence and good will can at times hold such strikingly different views of the therapeutic process or of what makes for effective therapeutic change, there is probably no better place to start than to ask, for each, what is chaff and what is wheat; what do you notice, focus on, build your theories and views around; and what do you cast to the periphery as largely irrelevant or distracting?

My point is not that clinical examples are not useful. I have employed clinical examples in abundance in my writing over the years. One of my books, *Therapeutic Communication* (P. L. Wachtel, 1993; new edition in press) is *very largely* composed of examples specifically chosen to illustrate a range of points about helpful and not so helpful ways to phrase our comments to the people we work with, and I spent a lot of time choosing "just the right ones." Clearly I believe there is a place—a valuable place—for such a way of illustrating and clarifying one's ideas. But one gets a very different picture of the clinical enterprise from *un*selected examples, and this book is rooted in this second approach.

I present here complete transcripts of three sessions, along with my comments that depict how I was thinking and feeling from moment to moment as the session proceeded. In contrast to the approach of presenting particularly apt examples, the essence of this book, one might say, is that it presents what is apt and what is inapt alike, in unselected fashion, and lets *the reader* decide what is apt and what is not. Moreover, I have refrained from selecting not only by presenting the sessions unexpurgated, as it were, but also by virtue of the sessions themselves being unselected. That is, I did not delve into a vault of session tapes looking for "the good ones." Rather, the book originated with my being invited to make a DVD demonstration session for a series being produced for the American Psychological Association as part of their video series, "Systems of Psychotherapy." The standard procedure for this series is for the therapist to fly to Chicago, meet for a single session each with four different patients who have been recruited by the producers, and then select which of the four sessions was most representative of his or her work. As it turned out, when I arrived in Chicago I found out that only two patients had been recruited on that particular occasion. Moreover, to add to what at the time looked like a formula for disappointment, at the end of the session with Louise (Chapter 3), the director came into the room and said, "I have bad news for you." There had been a problem with the sound, he told both me and Louise; would we be willing to do a second session right then and there? So as it turned out, I conducted three sessions that day, two with Louise (Chapters 3 and 4) and one with Melissa (Chapter 5). Had there been only the two sessions, I might not have thought to do this book. But the technological glitch (which turned out not to be a problem when I actually listened later to the video) afforded the opportunity for a second session with Louise, and somehow the three sessions became the critical mass that led to this book. No selection among sessions was necessary or occurred. I taped three sessions and I present three here.

This book is written both for the student or beginning therapist and for the experienced practitioner. For the beginning therapist, it is my hope that the book will enable you to look over my shoulder and see not only what I did in the course of a session but how I was thinking; what I was experiencing; *why* I did what I did; and, importantly, when, on reflection, it seems to me that I missed an opportunity or made an error. Students do not usually have access to the feelings and thoughts, much less the mistakes and missed opportunities, of experienced clinicians as they participate in their sessions. Usually, the experienced clinician is in the role of supervisor, and it is the student who reveals her thoughts and feelings and risks exposing her foibles. In this book, my aim is to reverse this, to permit the student not only to observe my work but to hear as well about my thoughts and feelings as I proceed through the session and to have sufficient data about both to make her own judgments.

For the experienced clinician, too, my aim is for you to be inside my mind as I sit in the sessions with the patient, as well as when I think about the session afterward and think more generally about the nature of psychotherapy and the therapeutic process. Most of us in the profession do not have sufficient opportunity to look over the shoulders—and into the minds— of our colleagues; psychotherapy is usually a relatively lonely profession once one begins to practice on one's own. I hope in a small way to contribute to breaking down that isolation by sharing my own work verbatim along with as much detail about my thought processes and feelings in the session as I can recapture. I aim as well—both in the theoretical chapters and in the commentaries that are presented in conjunction with the transcripts of the sessions— to raise a range of probing questions about how psychotherapy works and how it should be practiced. The book takes a fresh look at a variety of assumptions that have guided clinical theory and practice and aims to present an articulated, integrated account of the therapy process based on many years of clinical experience as well as careful attention to the research literature. The work presented in this book derives from an integrative perspective that draws in different ways from the psychodynamic, cognitive–behavioral, systemic, and experiential traditions, and in the very process of doing so, it simultaneously affirms and challenges many of the assumptions and comfortably familiar ways of working of each.

SOME NOTES ON LANGUAGE

Language is, of course, what makes us human, and it is probably the most important tool of the psychotherapist. But it is also a potentially divisive force in our lives, a means whereby groups of people differentiate themselves from each other in ways that, on the level of nations and ethnic groups, can be tragic, and that even with regard to the differences in theoretical orientation in our own field can be highly problematic. As someone who, as an integrative theorist and therapist, has had to be able to communicate closely and regularly with therapists of diverse orientations and, in turn, to try to enable them to see the value in ideas from those of other orientations, I have been struck repeatedly by how language can be an *obstacle*, how (differently for therapists of different orientations) some terms become excessively valued buzzwords and others become X-rated offensive terms that make it difficult for them to be heard. At times it has seemed to me that the overvaluing of one's own language and the chalk-on-a-blackboard experience of the other orientation's language is most intense when both sides are actively working not to see affinities in their ways of thinking or practicing.

I do not intend here to take on this huge can of worms. I have tried through much of my writing to explicate some of the ways in which therapists of different orientations have been approaching rather similar ideas through rather different language (see especially P. L. Wachtel, 1997). My point in doing so is not to claim that they are really all the same. There would be little value to an integrative therapeutic approach if the elements one was trying to integrate were actually all the same. There are *very significant* differences between the ideas and ways of working that derive from each of the major orientations in our field, and the aim of my integrative efforts has been to capitalize on those differences, to create a therapeutic framework within which those differences can be brought to bear to yield a whole that is more than the sum of its constituent parts. A brief account of that integrative framework will be presented in Part I of this book, Grounding Assumptions and Principles, and its expression in the clinical setting will be evident in the sessions and commentaries in Part II, The Sessions. I want here, in this preface, simply to highlight two rather specific linguistic issues that are strongly capable of dividing us or rendering us unable to hear each other and to alert the reader to my own particular approach to negotiating these dangerous shoals.

The first linguistic issue is one that is not specific to the world of psychotherapy but is a significant fault line, so to speak, in our culture at large. For several decades now, socially aware users of the English language have struggled to find a way to transcend the linguistic habits that for so long rendered women invisible when the language expressed generic statements about human beings (from grand pronouncements about "mankind" to simple statements such as "Every writer should keep his language simple").[1] The problem is that it is difficult for a writer to keep his or her language simple when his or her ideas are complex enough that he or she uses many subordinate clauses in his or her sentences. Yes, I intentionally made the last sentence almost impossible to read without getting a stroke; but I did so to illustrate the challenges that a less sexist use of language can present.

---

[1]Not every language presents the same issues as English. The gender-free Spanish word *su* (which can mean "his" or "her") or the German word *Man*, which in its context is less off-puttingly academic than the English word *one*, make life easier in at least this respect for writers of those languages. Each language presents its own specific challenges.

Every author must find his or her own solution to the problem (as I did here in a sentence that was less daunting). In this book, my primary solution is to assign feminine pronouns (*she, her, hers*) to generic statements about therapists and masculine pronouns (*he, him, his*) to generic statements about patients. If the reader is alerted to this, it will make reading clearer and easier and, by differentiating genders in the two roles, also render some sentences clearer (Compare "when the patient tells his story to the therapist, she listens attentively" to "when the patient tells her story to the therapist, she listens attentively." In the latter version, it can be confusing on first take which *she* is which.) This differentiation of the pronouns for patient and therapist is the solution I have used in most of my books on clinical matters, and it has generally worked well. But here I also want to alert the reader to a further wrinkle. As it turns out, the two patients seen in these sessions (more about the word *patient* in a moment) were both women, and the therapist was a man. Consequently, in this book, on those occasions when I have been talking specifically about Louise or Melissa a sentence or two before and then make a statement that is more of a generalization about people in general, I have sometimes cast my generic statement in feminine pronouns even though I am not referring to the generic therapist role. That is, the general rule I just stated (patient masculine, therapist feminine) is not followed in every instance. Just as people in general come in both masculine and feminine forms, so too do my own generalizations sometimes get cast in feminine pronouns and sometimes in masculine pronouns. Moreover, in some simpler sentences, I do employ the by now familiar "his or her" form. I am confident that my references will be clear to the reader, but I am spelling out my strategy for negotiating these linguistic challenges because it is somewhat different from what some other people have chosen.

The second linguistic issue to which I want to call the reader's attention involves the words *patient* and *client*. In some sectors of the therapeutic community, the word *patient* is the preferred term; in others, *client* is generally used. This presents few problems when engaging in discourse within one's own reference group, but as an integrative theorist and therapist, I have done many workshops in which I have presented to "mixed company." On those occasions, I have been struck by what strong reactions people can have to the use of one term or the other. The term *client*, preferred both by cognitive–behavioral therapists and (of course) client-centered and other humanistic–experiential therapists, was introduced as an alternative to *patient* because the latter seemed to evoke a "medical" model and because, to those who preferred *client*, the term *patient* seemed to cast the individual coming to therapy as someone with psychopathology, rather than simply as a human being struggling with human problems.

Now, one of the human problems with which *I* struggle is that I was raised on the term *patient*, and so it is the term that comes most naturally to me. Because I did not want my linguistic usage to turn people off to the substance of what I was saying, for a number of years I would begin my workshops with a rather apologetic reference to my linguistic habits and ask those in the audience who were more comfortable and familiar with the term *client* to bear with me (and—almost—to forgive me). Then one day, a workshop participant gave me, and all of the other attendees, a fascinating lesson in etymology that has eliminated the apologetic tone to my explanations (but, as the reader can see, not the sense that I must alert the reader to this issue and "explain myself"). It turns out that the Latin roots of the word *patient* lie in words connoting "one who suffers," whereas the roots of the word *client* point to "one who depends." Indeed, *client* derives from the Latin *cliens*—freed (Roman) slaves who are still dependent on their masters. Thus, one can make a strong case that the word *patient* is more empathic with the person's suffering and the word *client* is unwittingly demeaning. Far from connoting the person's autonomy, his or her coming to the therapist as an equal, there is a linguistic taint, as it were, in the use of the word *client*, redolent of terms such as *client state*, a country with little or no real autonomy, dependent on a larger power.

For the reader who enjoys this kind of playful pedantry, Wikipedia, Google, and other web tools can provide an almost infinite gratification of this perverse taste. More substantively, there is serious reason to question, at this point in the 21st century, the assumption that the use of the term *client* by most cognitive–behavioral therapists reflects their insurgent challenge to the medical model. If it once made sense to view psychoanalysts as practicing from a "medical model" and behavior therapists as challenging that model, the situation is much more complex today, and in certain ways points in the opposite direction (P. L. Wachtel, 2010a). In any event, in this book I will mostly use the word *patient*. I hope that for those readers who have an aversion to that term, this playful digression has served to introduce a measure of desensitization.

More generally, I hope that both the theoretical and research considerations in Part I and the presentation of the sessions and my comments on them in Part II will also contribute to desensitizing readers to the important contributions of ideas from theoretical orientations other than that in which they were trained. The work we do is difficult enough without constraining ourselves with ideological blinders that prevent us from benefitting from observations—both those deriving from the clinical situation and those deriving from more systematic research—that can shed light from a different vantage point on the challenges we face.

* * * * *

Finally, I wish to acknowledge the able assistance of Vered Ronen, who helped enormously in the gathering of references and in placing my

Sanskrit identifications of relevant papers into good APA format. And, as a loving finale, I am delighted once again to acknowledge both the support I received from my wife Ellen throughout the process of writing this book and her perceptive comments on every chapter, usually begun while the paper was still warm from the printer. One of the joys of finishing the book is having more time to do all the things that have made our life together such a wonder.

I

GROUNDING ASSUMPTIONS
AND PRINCIPLES

1

PSYCHOTHERAPY AT GROUND LEVEL

It is easier—and safer for the therapist's reputation—to write *about* psychotherapy than to depict it directly. From 30,000 feet, the landscape looks orderly and the contours easy to grasp. But on the ground, things became much more uncertain. The experience of doing psychotherapy is, for almost all therapists, an experience that presents many moments (and often more than moments) of uncomfortable and unsettling ambiguity. The neat theories that can feel reassuringly definitive when encountered in classes or textbooks give way to a messy human reality that is much more enigmatic. Any therapist who claims that he or she confidently knows what to do most of the time probably isn't paying close enough attention to what is actually transpiring in the room.

The aim of this book is to present a *ground-level* view of the therapeutic process, complete with the confusion and unpredictability that are an inevitable part of that process. I aim to present in these pages the full transcripts of several sessions, along with a very detailed account of what I was thinking and feeling in the course of the sessions, what my intent was when I said (or did not say) certain things, and what my reflections were afterward regarding what I might have missed and how I might have responded differently. My aim is to present my work "warts and all" and to reflect on it in a way that I hope will be useful not only to students and beginning therapists but to clinicians with many years of experience as well. We have many presentations of therapy as it "should" be but fewer of how it is as it unfolds in real time, where foresight and hindsight may be widely divergent.

Although my writing on psychotherapy has often included numerous clinical examples, this is the first time that I have organized an entire book around the presentation of complete sessions. This means not just the "interesting" parts; not just the parts that "illustrate" something (one can only illustrate when one has some idea *what is being* illustrated); but the whole mess (or, from a more positive perspective, the whole arc)—the moments of feeling unclear, frustrated, even incompetent, and the moments when the skies clear and the direction in which to move becomes apparent. In combining this ground-level view with a presentation of my theoretical understanding of the process and of the patient, I hope to provide the reader with an educational experience of a sort that is not generally available.

One further feature of this book that may enhance its value for the psychotherapist is that a video of one of the sessions discussed here is available as a DVD (American Psychological Association, 2007) and provides an additional perspective on what is presented here. Psychotherapists who purchase and view the video can compare what is conveyed by the written transcript to what is evident when *watching* and *listening to* the session unfold. There are inevitably affective nuances and nonverbal dimensions of the transaction that are not captured by a transcript. Conversely, there are perspectives to be gained by the greater ease a printed transcript allows in going over the material repeatedly as well as by the examination offered here of the theoretical and clinical considerations that led to my interventions in the session. The two modes of presenting and addressing the session are complementary. Each makes its own unique contribution.

Regardless of whether the reader chooses to complement her experience by a viewing of the video as well, she will have the opportunity, in the pages that follow, to examine where I am the same throughout these three sessions and where I am different. It will be obvious that in certain respects my personal style and particular way of viewing things shapes what transpires in all three sessions, and at the same time, that I am in each instance responding to the unique features of the intersubjective field created by the two quite different individuals who share the room with me. Similarly, it will be evident that *within* each session, and thus even with *the same* patient, my responses and my experience vary considerably from moment to moment depending on the affective climate between us.

AN INTEGRATIVE RELATIONAL POINT OF VIEW

The theoretical perspective that guides the work presented in this book is rooted in more than 30 years of practicing from a point of view that brings together elements of psychoanalytic, cognitive–behavioral, systemic, and experiential approaches. It is rooted as well in my immersion in the significant evolution of psychoanalytic thought in recent years that has culminated in what is now known as the *relational* point of view in psychoanalysis (P. L. Wachtel, 2008). This newer version of psychoanalytic thought and practice is likely to be relatively unfamiliar to those readers who have primarily been trained in the other three orientations that contribute to the synthesis to which I just referred. The teaching of psychodynamic thinking in many training programs is frequently not only cursory, dismissive, and caricatured but often several decades out of date as well (Bornstein, 1988; Hansell, 2004; Redmond & Schulman, 2008; Westen, 1998).

It should be noted that the sessions presented here have enough elements that resemble features of cognitive–behavioral, systemic, and experiential approaches that they may feel more familiar to readers from those traditions than they might have anticipated; but it is my hope that these readers will be open to considering how the sessions also illustrate how new developments in the psychodynamic tradition can seamlessly complement their present approach and enable their work to achieve greater depth and clinical efficacy. To get the most out of this book, the nonpsychoanalytic reader needs to be alert both to the ways that the psychoanalytic aspects of the work are compatible with her own evolving clinical framework and sensibility and to the ways that the psychodynamic component adds something new to the mix, illuminating features of the clinical picture that the reader might otherwise have missed and introducing modes of intervention that valuably complement those already in her repertoire.

This does not mean that I am asking the reader to check her skepticism at the door. The psychoanalytic features of the work, and the theoretical assumptions on which they rest, must be subjected to the same rigorous evaluation as any of the other ideas and methods that constitute the contemporary therapeutic landscape. It is unfortunately true that for many years a large segment of the psychoanalytic community was disturbingly cavalier about the empirical foundations of psychoanalytic ideas (and indeed, there remains a subset of psychoanalytic thinkers with such attitudes today). But it is also true that psychoanalytic ideas and practices have been subjected to rigorous empirical examination to a considerably greater degree than is commonly appreciated and that their empirical foundation is in many respects quite as solid as that of the other theoretical traditions in our field (see, e.g., Blatt, 2008; Leichsenring &

Rabung, 2008; Levy & Ablon, 2009; Mayes, Fonagy, & Target, 2007; Shedler, 2010; Westen, 1998; Westen, Novotny, & Thompson-Brenner, 2004).

Needless to say, my arguments about the value of openness to unfamiliar ideas applies equally to the psychoanalytic portion of the book's readership. The same caricaturing of other theoretical orientations and modes of practice, the same tendentious "otherization," certainly occurs with as much regularity in psychoanalytically oriented training programs as in those of the other orientations. I thus offer this chapter's brief summary of my integrative perspective both to readers from my original home perspective of psychoanalysis, to enable them to see bridges to the vital contributions of innovative therapists of other orientations, and to therapists in the worlds of cognitive–behavioral, systemic, and experiential thinking to enable them to benefit from and to integrate a vital body of ideas and practices that they may have largely ignored up till now. Whatever the reader's home orientation, I hope that you will find both important ways in which what I am describing fits comfortably within your familiar frame of reference and ways in which it *stretches* your thinking. I hope as well that the session transcripts will illustrate how methods from "outside" of the orientation in which you were originally trained can be assimilated coherently into an evolving, increasingly comprehensive frame of reference.

THE CENTRAL ROLE OF ANXIETY

One way in which the version of psychoanalytic thought that guides the approach described here may feel surprisingly familiar and comfortable to cognitive–behavioral therapists is that it places a strong emphasis on the central role of anxiety in the difficulties that bring people to therapy and explicitly incorporates the concept of *exposure* in understanding how that anxiety is overcome (for more detail, see P. L. Wachtel, 1997, 2008). This emphasis on anxiety is consistent with a key reformulation in Freud's own thinking (Freud, 1926), a reformulation whose profound implications for the therapeutic process have generally not been well appreciated or understood in the psychoanalytic community (P. L. Wachtel, 2008). Whereas previously Freud had conceptualized anxiety as a product of repression, which he viewed as the more fundamental phenomenon, in 1926 he stated explicitly that he had been in error and that it was anxiety that underlay repression rather than vice versa. Since he had several times before this (e.g., Freud, 1914/1959) stated that the concept of repression was the "cornerstone" of psychoanalysis, he had, in effect, shifted the very cornerstone of his theory. If, as Freud later put it, "anxiety makes repression and not, as we used to think, the other way round," (Freud, 1933, p. 89) then it is anxiety that lies at the foundation of the entire edifice of psychoanalytic thought and is properly thought of as its cornerstone. This suggests that overcoming anxiety, even more than undoing repression, is the cornerstone of therapeutic change.

The reader should be aware, however, that although the clinical approach I am presenting in this book is centrally rooted in this reformulation, another implication of the perspective I am introducing is that Freud probably went too far in reversing his previous formulation. From the vantage point of the vicious circle conceptualization I will lay out in what follows (see also E. F. Wachtel & P. L. Wachtel, 1986; P. L. Wachtel, 1987, 1993, 1994, 1997, 1999, 2008), it is more accurate to state that the causal arrows run in *both* directions—anxiety leads to repression, and repression, in turn, leads to a variety of consequences that generate further anxiety.

It must also be noted that for some readers the term *repression* itself, even when removed from its position as cornerstone of the theory, is problematic. The concept of repression is often misunderstood as being primarily, if not exclusively, about experiences that have been "forgotten" but can later be recovered. A range of tendentious studies have "disproved" the concept based on this faulty understanding. A sounder understanding of the concept in the contemporary context would focus on the way the person can misrepresent his own experience. There are *many* possible constructions of what we are feeling or what we are up to (Hoffman, 1998, Neimeyer & Mahoney, 1995), and it is the way those constructions reflect not only what is actually happening but also how we *need* to see ourselves or the events of our lives that is the real focus of the contemporary concept of repression (or—to state the matter in a way more consistent with contemporary terminology—of the broader concept of defense). A more sophisticated understanding of these concepts makes it clear that they in fact converge quite considerably with the findings of research in the areas of social cognition and cognitive neuroscience.

IMPLICATIONS OF THE NEW UNDERSTANDING OF ANXIETY FOR CLINICAL PRACTICE

This fundamental shift in the foundations of the psychoanalytic vision should have resulted in corresponding fundamental shifts in psychoanalytic technique, since the practice of psychoanalysis had long been predicated on the idea that undoing repression was the most central therapeutic aim and the heart of the therapeutic process. But to a very great extent, when it came to therapeutic technique, this momentous shifting of the very cornerstone of the psychoanalytic approach remained an "unnoticed revolution" (P. L. Wachtel, 2008). What should have followed is a focus on how to diminish the *anxiety* that underlay the processes of avoidance and misconstrual that called themselves to the attention of Freud and other early analysts. Patients *did* persistently avoid noticing or acknowledging certain things about themselves and their relations to others. But that avoidance was not the problem in itself (though, apropos the vicious circle perspective I alluded to above and will elaborate later in this chapter, it further compounded the patient's difficulties in ways that need to be addressed in their own right). Closer to the heart of the problem was the anxiety and other painful affects that *motivated* the avoidance.

It needs to be noted that Freud did in many respects understand this underlying motivational foundation from the very beginning. Central to the idea of what he called "the defense neuropsychoses" (Freud, 1894, 1896) was the assumption that it was to avoid psychic pain that the patient put certain things out of his mind. But Freud's central identity as a *discoverer* of the hidden or not yet understood (see P. L. Wachtel, 2008) led him to emphasize instead the undoing of repression as the heart of the therapeutic process. Thinking of his work as much like that of the archaeologist who digs down beneath the surface to unearth precious clues and nuggets that reveal a hidden world, Freud viewed psychoanalysis most fundamentally as a process of uncovering what had been buried. Freud's central aspiration, as depicted by his biographer Ernest Jones (1961), was not as a therapist or healer but as a discoverer of the lost world of the unconscious mind. But the venue of his research was not the laboratory but the consulting room, and so it was essential to persuade himself that his focus on unearthing the buried contents of the unconscious was also, conveniently, precisely what would be of maximum benefit to his patients.

As I shall elaborate further momentarily, Freud was actually largely correct in assuming that his explorations of the patient's warded-off psychological experiences were curative. But the reason for this therapeutic effect had less to do with the patient attaining insight than with the patient's being *exposed*, in the process of exploring the warded-off thoughts, feelings, and intentions, to stimuli and experiences that had previously been fearfully avoided. Freud's discoveries about the nature of unacknowledged motives and thoughts, his ability to recognize disavowed intentions and the conflicted expression of feelings and attitudes in behavior that at first seemed to be about something quite different, helped to direct generations of therapists toward noticing phenomena and connections that might otherwise have been overlooked. Without his insights into the pervasive avoidance of awareness of certain powerfully important and determinative experiences, our therapeutic efforts would have been limited to surface complaints and to those objects of fear that the patient was already capable of identifying. To my mind, these latter efforts are often too crude to address much of what is presented by the large majority of patients in daily clinical practice—as opposed to patients narrowly culled for controlled trials (see Westen, Novotny, & Thompson-Brenner, 2004)—and it is for this reason that I believe that the methods of cognitive–behavioral therapy, as valuable as they are, need to be complemented by the understanding accrued from psychoanalytic inquiry. But I also believe that without a clearer understanding of just what *brought about* the improvements that resulted from psychoanalytic confrontations with previously unconscious thoughts or feelings, the therapeutic effort is likely to be inefficient and crude in a *different* way. What needed to be added to the earlier psychoanalytic understanding of the sources of therapeutic change—especially once it was understood that it was anxiety that underlay the patient's difficulties even more fundamentally than repression—was a clearer understanding of how anxiety is overcome. It is to this topic that I turn next.

EXPOSURE AND THE REDUCTION OF ANXIETY: A BROADER VIEW

Taking seriously the revised theory of the relation between anxiety and repression that I have just described implies some important modifications in psychoanalysis as a therapeutic modality, modifications that not only make psychoanalysis more humane and effective but also render it more compatible with developments in other therapeutic orientations. The two most important of these are (a) a confrontation with the question of *what does* lead most effectively to the overcoming of anxiety and (b) a series of shifts in the fundamental attitude of the therapist once her aim is seen to be to help the patient *become less afraid* of his feelings and experiences rather than one of *unmasking* those experiences or bringing to light what the patient has been hiding (from himself as well as from others). As I will elaborate shortly, these modifications in no way entail ignoring that people may misrepresent or hide important aspects of their experience, nor do they imply any less interest in helping people to understand themselves more fully and accurately. They do, however, point to important differences in how that self-understanding is to be pursued and what *other* therapeutic processes need to be linked to and combined with that increased self-understanding in order to be maximally helpful to the patient.

Turning first to the question of what enables people most effectively to overcome anxiety, there is by now a vast body of research suggesting that the most important factor is *exposure* to the experience that has been feared and avoided without the anticipated traumatic consequence. (see, e.g., Craske & Mystkowski, 2006; Deacon & Abromowitz, 2004; Foa, Huppert, Cahill, & Rothbaum, 2006; Foa & Kozak, 1986; Foa & Meadows, 1997; Keane, 1995, 1998; Zinbarg, Barlow, Brown, & Hertz, 1992). This conclusion has been drawn from hundreds, if not thousands of studies, ranging from laboratory investigations using nonclinical populations to controlled clinical trials. Up till now, the emphasis on exposure as a therapeutic process or modality has primarily been evident in the practice of cognitive–behavioral therapy, particularly in the realm of manualized treatments. But there is a far broader clinical potential for harnessing the impact of exposure in overcoming anxiety.

Treatments that are manualized and specifically targeted for specific symptoms or complaints have their place in the overall landscape of therapeutic approaches, but these narrowly targeted treatments also have significant limitations (see, for example, P. L. Wachtel, 2010a; Westen et al., 2004). A large portion of the patients who come to see therapists have difficulties that are not so readily categorized or targeted, and it will be apparent to the reader that they include the two people—Louise and Melissa—whose sessions are the core of this book. But in fact cognitive–behavioral and/or manualized and narrowly targeted treatments do not exhaust the potential applications of the research demonstrating the impact of exposure in overcoming anxiety. Careful attention to what actually transpires in psychodynamic treatments makes it clear that much of what goes on in these treatments entails a similar process of exposure, although both the modality or context of the exposure and the nature of the stimuli or experiences to which the patient is exposed can be quite different than in most cognitive–behavioral treatments (P. L. Wachtel, 1997).[1]

In cognitive–behavioral treatments, the focus has tended to be on exposure to external situations that are the explicitly identified targets of the patient's fears (bridges, dogs, airplanes, etc.), although increasingly there is also an emphasis on the patient's anxiety response to internal or proprioceptive cues that are part of the arousal pattern in which the patient is caught (e.g., Barlow, Allen, & Choate, 2004; Craske & Barlow, 2008). From this latter vantage point, it is not simply the external stimulus prompting the arousal pattern that must be targeted for exposure but the experience of anxiety itself; the patient must learn to gain some comfort with the internal somatic cues associated with anxious arousal rather than panicking and thereby escalating and perpetuating the problem.

These are causal dynamics that psychodynamic therapists need to (and often do) take into account. But dynamic therapists are usually also engaged in promoting the patient's exposure to still another class of stimuli, whether they are explicitly thinking of what they are doing in terms of exposure or not. The exposures that are most at the center of psychodynamic treatments tend to be to the stimuli associated with the patient's own wishes, thoughts, and representations of self and other.

It has, of course, traditionally been the assumption of psychodynamic therapists that it is the patient's lack of access to these thoughts and feelings

---

[1]Because most dynamic therapists do not think of what they are doing in terms of exposure, it is probably often the case that the exposure is less efficient than it might be if consideration were given specifically to the dimension of exposure—that is, how most effectively to bring about exposure to the thoughts and feelings the patient has been fearfully avoiding.

that is at the heart of his difficulties, and the therapy is very largely designed to bring them back into focus. The usual way of understanding this process, however, has been centered on ideas like interpretation and the promotion of insight; the patient needs to come to *know* and *understand* these aspects of himself in order to get better. This knowledge, of course, is not supposed to be a merely intellectual understanding, but self-*knowledge*, nonetheless, has been the key operating metaphor.

Certainly, as I discuss further later in this chapter, the promotion of increased self-knowledge and self-understanding remains of great concern and value (and is in fact pursued by therapists of almost all orientations, whatever terminology they use to depict the process). But something else is happening in successful psychodynamic treatments as well that is usually less well understood, or even noticed. In the process of promoting insight, of interpreting (and hence interrupting) defenses that keep the patient out of touch with his experience,[2] a successful psychodynamic therapy brings the patient *into closer contact with* the experiences that have been warded off. The patient thinks the thoughts and feels the feelings that he has previously avoided—or, put differently, he is *exposed* to them.

Depicting the process as significantly one of exposure provides an alternative perspective on what is happening in psychodynamic therapies, and it happens to be a perspective that highlights the more *experiential* nature of the therapeutic process. It is not a matter of mere words or knowledge, even "emotional" knowledge. Nor is it exclusively or even predominantly a matter of "interpretation." Interpretation and self-knowledge do contribute to the process, but something else that is very important is also involved. The process of change proceeds to a significant degree through *direct experience*. (For an interesting discussion of the experiential—rather than exclusively or primarily interpretive—element in the psychoanalytic process, see D. N. Stern, 2004; D. N. Stern et al., 1998; Lyons-Ruth, 1998, 1999. These authors, rather than thinking in terms of exposure, introduce a different perspective on directly experiential sources of change, rooted in an emphasis on procedural learning and on what they call "implicit relational knowing." Their perspective, however, is thoroughly compatible with that presented here; see P. L. Wachtel, 2008.)

One particularly important implication of the exposure perspective on what happens in psychodynamic therapy is that what we know about exposure as a general process suggests that usually it is necessary for the patient to experience *repeated* exposure for the anxiety to begin to significantly diminish. This

---

[2]Cognitive–behavioral therapists think of very closely related processes in terms of response–prevention, or what Barlow and his colleagues (e.g., Ehrenreich, Buzzella, & Barlow, 2007) referred to as disruption or prevention of *emotionally driven behaviors*.

is something that is implicitly understood by dynamic therapists as well and is embodied in the concept of working through, which similarly emphasizes the limits of a single encounter with what has previously been fearfully avoided (i.e., the limits of a single acknowledgment or experience of the previously repressed or warded-off thought or feeling). But because the concept of working through evolved out of a therapeutic conception that was so strongly rooted in the ideas of insight, interpretation, and *knowing about* what one has hidden from oneself, it is not as clearly and experientially spelled out, either conceptually or procedurally, as it might be if the element of exposure were more clearly and explicitly understood and appreciated. A variety of somewhat modified procedural guidelines follow from an understanding of the process of working through as largely one of repeated exposure (see P. L. Wachtel, 1997).

In the sessions that are presented later in this book, the reader will see examples of how this intersection of psychodynamic and cognitive–behavioral perspectives is played out in the therapeutic interaction (as she will see ways in which systemic and experiential perspectives figure in how I proceed as well). On the one hand, my understanding of the therapeutic process as very significantly a matter of exposure to what has been fearfully avoided leads me to engage in the process between myself and the patient in a somewhat different way from many other dynamically oriented therapists. In this sense, what is evident is a psychoanalytically guided process that is modified by an immersion in the alternative universe of cognitive–behavioral therapy. But from a reverse lens, what is at least as important is that I am largely applying the cognitive–behavioral conception of exposure to a set of experiences that are usually only incidentally or glancingly focused on by cognitive–behavioral therapists. My central concern in the work depicted in these transcripts— achieved to varying degrees in the different sessions, or even from moment to moment within each—is to enable the patient to *reappropriate* the thoughts, feelings, and perceptions that have come to feel forbidden in the course of growing up and of living one's life.

Although I share with behavior therapists and social learning theorists a concern with understanding people in relation to the actual events they encounter (i.e., in relation to what is often called the *stimulus* or *situation*—see Magnusson & Endler, 1977), I bring to the therapeutic process a particular concern with addressing the complexities of the patient's subjective experience and the aspects of his or her experience that have been warded off, fearfully avoided, truncated, construed in limited (and in certain respects distorting) ways, and in other respects too can be described as having been *defended against.* Put differently, I bring a psychoanalytic or psychodynamic sensibility that highlights a broader and deeper range of experiences than is typical in nonpsychodynamic therapies, but I elaborate that sensibility theoretically in a way that enables it to interface with important features of the cognitive–behavioral tradition and is compatible with many of the key observations and methods that derive from that tradition.

FROM SELF-UNDERSTANDING TO SELF-ACCEPTANCE

In addition to highlighting the therapeutic value of thinking explicitly in terms of exposure, a second important consequence for therapeutic technique follows as well from a clearer understanding of the central role of anxiety (along with guilt and shame) in the dynamics that bring people to therapy. As I shall now elaborate, it can point us toward an approach to the work that is less adversarial and more affirmative and supportive of the patient's self-esteem without compromising the commitment to understanding the patient (and helping him to understand himself) in depth. In older psychodynamic models, in which the primary focus was on "uncovering" and "interpreting," there was often an unwittingly adversarial and accusatory tone to the therapeutic dialogue. Much of my book on therapeutic communication (P. L. Wachtel, 1993, in press) was devoted to explicating this adversarial and accusatory dimension (which can be quite subtle, if nonetheless potent) and to spelling out alternative ways of approaching the work (see also Havens, 1986; Renik, 1993; Shawver, 1983; P. L. Wachtel, 2008; Weiss & Sampson, 1986; Wile, 1984). The discussion in this book of my sessions with Louise and Melissa aims to further this exploration of pitfalls and alternatives.

Leston Havens (1986) has put the matter especially pithily: "In the current interpretive climate of much psychotherapeutic work, patients sit waiting for the next insight with their fists clenched. Small wonder, for it is rarely good news." (p. 78) Where does this unfortunate state of affairs come from? It derives in good part, I suggest, from a failure of many psychodynamic therapists to sufficiently appreciate the implications of the revised theory of anxiety discussed above. Prior to the introduction of this revised understanding—and, for much of mainstream psychoanalytic practice, even many years after its introduction—the main issue that was seen as essential to address was that the patient was *hiding* something, denying something, evading reality. The therapist's job was to challenge and confront this deceit, in essence to force the truth on an unwilling opponent of it. Hence such concepts as resistance. The patient inevitably resisted the analyst's efforts to get at the truth, and much work needed to be done to overcome this resistance.

Of course, this was not necessarily done inhumanely or without appreciation that the patient was avoiding out of terror, that what was being hidden felt to the patient dangerous and unacceptable. In some sense the understanding that behind repression was anxiety, articulated explicitly by Freud in 1926 as a revision of his prior views, was always there in psychoanalytic thought in some form. At the very dawn of psychoanalysis, it was at the heart of Freud's differences with Breuer and with Janet—Freud saw defenses as *motivated* whereas they saw the inaccessibility of certain experiences as largely the consequence of an altered state of consciousness. Part of why we chuckle at Havens's characterization is that it (knowingly) highlights only a part of the therapeutic process. The patient is not just the target of an aggressive attacker; the history of psychoanalysis is replete with comments about the importance of kindness, caring, and the offering of the analyst's more benign vision of what is possible for the patient as a substitute for the patient's harsh superego (e.g., Ferenczi, 1926; Loewald, 1960; McWilliams, 2004; Schafer, 1983; Stone, 1961, Strachey, 1934).

But also part of what makes Havens's comment funny is that he does capture what is often a significant part of the psychoanalytic relationship, a part that has not been acknowledged in most discourse on psychoanalytic practice but that is so embarrassingly obvious nonetheless that Havens's pointing to it resonates easily with any open-minded practitioner (or patient) who reads it. In an authoritative philosophical inquiry into psychoanalysis, Ricoeur (1970) has described psychoanalysis as part of a larger "school of suspicion" in which the individual's "false consciousness" is stripped away to reveal the hidden truth behind the mask. Other later authors have similarly depicted "suspicion" of the patient's account of his life and his motives as a central feature of the psychoanalytic approach (e.g., Messer, 2000; Schafer, 1997; Wolff, 2001)

To be sure, none of these authors intended the word *suspicion* to imply anything malign about the analyst's intent; they were all *advocates* of psychoanalysis, describing what they viewed as an essential feature of any therapy that was to achieve real depth. As I elaborated on the topic elsewhere (P. L. Wachtel, 2008), attempting to capture both the positive intent and the potential problems that are unwittingly revealed in this terminology,

> the "suspicion" which the psychoanalytic way of looking or listening implies could be seen as simply another way of referring to the unconscious, to the idea that what we *say* we are feeling or *think* we are doing is far from the whole story and must be carefully probed if both patient and therapist are not to collude in an illusion that is ultimately the source of the patient's suffering. The problem arises in the implicitly adversarial cast that this "suspicion" may give to the therapeutic work, in the potential for invalidating of the patient's conscious experience as a "false" or "distorted" consciousness, in the readiness to see "resistance" when the patient views things differently from the therapist, and in the temptation to view the patient as benighted and needing the therapist to disabuse him of the distortions that constitute his conscious experience. (p. 178)

With full consideration of the implications of the "shifting of the cornerstone" of psychoanalysis, in contrast, one may approach the patient in a way that aims to go just as "deep" but that does so in a way that is more fully on the patient's side and less hampered by an unwittingly adversarial attitude. The patient, from this vantage point, is not "resisting," he is not holding out on the therapist in order to secretly gain infantile gratifications; he is *terrified*. He has learned in the course of his development that some of his deepest and most fundamental needs are unacceptable, that they threaten his attachment figures to the degree that his attachment to them and his very survival feel threatened (Wallin, 2007). And hence he has rejected vital and important parts of himself in the service of safety. The aim of the therapy, from this vantage point, is not to confront the patient with his deceptions but to create a sense of safety sufficient to enable him once again to reappropriate the parts of his own experience that have, out of terror, been cast out of his awareness and his sense of self. The differences between the therapeutic interventions that derive from these two contrasting visions of the therapeutic enterprise were a central focus of my book on therapeutic communication (P. L. Wachtel, 1993, in press). In discussing the sessions that are the focus of the present book, I will have further occasion to elaborate on these differences.

SELF-UNDERSTANDING: RATIONALIST AND CONSTRUCTIVIST APPROACHES

The shift in emphasis from undoing repression to diminishing anxiety, guilt, and shame does not mean that attaining greater self-understanding is no longer relevant or important. The goal of greater self-understanding is valued across virtually the entire spectrum of therapeutic approaches, if in different ways in different orientations. Cognitive therapists, for example, focus primarily on the assumptions that lead the patient to draw conclusions that generate problematic feelings and experiences of the self. Those assumptions are generally not in the patient's awareness in any focal way at the beginning of the therapy, and much of the process of cognitive therapy entails enabling the patient to become clearer about what they are.

It is important to note, however, that cognitive therapists differ substantially among themselves in how they address these premises once brought to light, and in certain respects those differences parallel the differences between psychoanalytic work undertaken from the vantage point of the school of suspicion and the less critical version of psychoanalytic work with which I have contrasted it. In particular, those cognitive and cognitive–behavioral therapists who emphasize disputation of the patient's premises and demonstration of their "irrationality" (generally followers of the ideas of Aaron Beck and Albert Ellis) differ quite significantly in their clinical approach from more *constructivist* cognitive therapists (e.g., Mahoney, 1995, 2003; Neimeyer & Mahoney, 1995).

In contrast to rationalist cognitive therapists, constructivist advocates of the cognitive paradigm attempt to articulate the patient's assumptions in a fashion that, to a surprising degree, resembles the work of relational psychoanalysts, who also operate from a constructivist framework (e.g., Aron, 1996; Hoffman, 1998; D. B. Stern, 1997; P. L. Wachtel, 2008). Both, moreover, resemble Rogerian and other humanistic therapists in their emphasis not on *critiquing* the patient's assumptions or pointing out their "erroneous" or "irrational" nature but simply on articulating them, bringing them closer to the forefront of the patient's awareness so that the patient himself can examine them and draw his own conclusions. In contrast, the *rationalist* cognitive therapy approach, with its emphasis on demonstrating the *faulty* or *unrealistic* nature of the patient's core assumptions about life and the world, actually bears considerable resemblance to the problematic emphasis in some psychoanalytic work on finding the "primitive," "archaic," or "infantile" foundations of the patient's psychological organization. (For an interesting critical examination of the latter and its implications, see Aron, 1991.)

Needless to say, despite this important and insufficiently appreciated convergence between the rationalist cognitive approach and the traditional psychoanalytic approach, there are also many significant differences between the two, both in theory and in specific procedural features. Clearly, both Beck and Ellis introduced their approaches as *alternatives* to the psychoanalytic approaches of the time, in which both men were originally trained. But a consequential similarity between rationalist cognitive therapy and classical Freudian therapy in *critiquing* or *unmasking* the way the patient sees the world has been insufficiently appreciated by therapists of both orientations. Similarly unappreciated on both sides of the divide are the parallels in the development of an alternative to this pathologizing vision in both the cognitive–behavioral and the psychoanalytic traditions. Here again, there are clearly important differences in the ways that cognitive–behavioral and psychoanalytic thinkers have developed their constructivist, nonpathologizing visions, but there exists as well a good deal of overlap. Both aim to *enter into* the patient's experience rather than critiquing it, and both root the therapeutic effort in the dialectic between *accepting* the patient's experience of the world and helping him to *change* those features of his assumptive world that are contributing to his pain (e.g., Bromberg, 1998b; Hayes, Follette, & Linehan, 2004; Hayes, Strosahl, & Wilson, 1999; Hoffman, 1998; Linehan, 1993; Linehan & Dexter-Mazza, 2008; P. L. Wachtel, 1993, 2008).

EMBRACING AFFECT

Further understanding of the "cross-orientation" convergence I am highlighting here leads us to consideration of the role of *affect*. In the rationalist version of cognitive and cognitive–behavioral therapy, the patient's affective experience is largely treated as both an epiphenomenon (you are only feeling the way you do because you are thinking the way you do) and as something that should be gotten rid of (if you only can learn to think rationally, there will be no need to feel angry, or hurt, or depressed).

When I first began my efforts to integrate psychodynamic and behavioral therapeutic approaches (P. L. Wachtel, 1977b) I had already completed my psychoanalytic training but needed to complement that with an immersion in the practice of behavior therapy. I found some formal training opportunities, but I also benefitted from the enormous generosity of some of the leading figures in behavior therapy at the time, who granted me first-hand access to their work in a variety of ways. I was struck by the clinical adeptness of these behavior therapists, who provided me with just what I was looking for—a set of skills and perspectives that both complemented what I already knew and *added to* my clinical repertoire in important ways. Their clinical sensitivity and humane attentiveness to the patient was a far cry from the caricatured vision of behavior therapists I had picked up by being immersed in a psychoanalytic community.[3]

Troublingly, a number of years later, as the *cognitive* influence in behavior therapy began to increase, and most behavior therapists began to think of themselves as cognitive–behavioral therapists, the clinical sensitivity and nuance I had been struck by a few years before appeared to be far less evident. Influenced by the rationalistic trend that was dominant in the early years of cognitive–behavioral therapy, some of these same therapists I had once admired began to resort to the unfortunate trend I alluded to at the beginning of this section—attempting to talk the patient out of his feelings, to "demonstrate" to him why it was "irrational" for him to feel angry or sad or disappointed. I could see these changes in their clinical practice both in observations through one-way mirrors and through watching tapes of their work. These retreats from affect and turns toward critique rather than exploration of experience seemed to me a great loss (both for patients and for the field). I was therefore heartened, after a time, to see emerging a newer thrust in cognitive and cognitive–behavioral therapy, the constructivist, dialectical, and acceptance-oriented approaches I mentioned earlier.

This alternative cognitive and cognitive–behavioral paradigm exhibits much the same attitude toward the patient's affect that is evident among many contemporary psychoanalytic thinkers. It is an attitude of acceptance of the patient's experience, including even his "irrational" affective experiences. The

---

[3]I hope it is not necessary to point out here that the caricaturing went in both directions. Behavior therapists' vision of psychoanalytic thought and practice was often equally biased and inaccurate.

aim is not to "talk the patient out of" his anger or hurt or sadness. Rather, it is to *understand* it, to accept it, and—through that very process of acceptance—to enable the patient to go *through* it and come out the other end with, potentially, a different experience of where he is in his life and what his options are. This new trend in the cognitive and cognitive–behavioral tradition, which encompasses the range of constructivist cognitive therapies (e.g., Neimeyer, 2009; Neimeyer & Mahoney, 1995), the dialectical behavior therapy originated by Linehan (e.g., Linehan, 1993; Linehan & Dexter-Mazza, 2008; Swales & Heard, 2009), and the "acceptance and commitment" therapy of Hayes and his colleagues (e.g., Hayes, Luoma, Bond, Masuda, & Lillis, 2006; Hayes, Strosahl, & Wilson, 1999), has been called a "third wave" in the cognitive–behavioral therapies, following the first wave of stimulus–response behavior therapy and the second of rationalist cognitive therapy.[4]

This new wave in the cognitive–behavioral realm converges in important ways with a related new wave in psychoanalytic thought that similarly bears labels such as *constructivist* and *dialectical* (e.g., Hoffman, 1998) but is most often referred to as *relational* or *intersubjective*. It is this version of psychoanalytic thought that is at the core of my own clinical work, interacting synergistically with related evolving ideas from the cognitive–behavioral, family systems, and experiential traditions. The reader will be able to see this approach to the patient's affective life in the sessions with Louise and Melissa that are presented in their entirety in Part II of this book. There are many things that I am trying to help Louise and Melissa to change, but my approach is not to try to persuade them that they are being irrational or that their behavior or experience is the thinly disguised product of infantile roots or of primitive and archaic mental representations.

My aim, rather, is to *enter into* their experience with them, to join them, validate them, help them to understand *what makes sense* in their experience, what it is in response to. I do hope that in helping them to see more clearly what they are feeling, in making room for feelings that they themselves may have attempted to short-circuit or run from, a process of "feeling through" the feeling and reaching a different point can be achieved. This is the paradoxical or dialectical element that is shared by a range of cognitive–behavioral (e.g., Linehan, 1993, Swales & Heard, 2009) and psychoanalytic (e.g., Hoffman, 1998) thinkers. In good part, change is reached by *not trying* to change the patient, or, more accurately I think, by *both* trying *and* not trying at the same

---

[4]In addition to this "third wave" approach, some "mainstream" cognitive–behavioral approaches similarly point to the limitations in what can be accomplished when strong affect is avoided rather than addressed (e.g., Allen, McHugh, & Barlow, 2008; Barlow, 2002; Ehrenreich, Buzzella, & Barlow, 2007; Moses & Barlow, 2006).

time (cf. Bromberg, 1998b; P. L. Wachtel, 2008). It is when the patient feels understood and accompanied in the difficult feeling (cf. Stolorow, Brandschaft, & Atwood, 2000) that he begins to be more able to reexamine and reexperience the feeling and to come out the other end feeling and seeing things differently

A SUPPORTIVE EXPLORATORY THERAPY

To offer a different, but closely related, perspective on what I have been discussing up till now, the emphasis on the centrality of anxiety in the casual nexus at the heart of the patient's difficulties and the emphasis on constructivism and on acceptance of the very experiences that the therapy is also aiming to change converge in creating a therapeutic approach that is less critical and more supportive. The central focus is not on the patient's distortions, irrationalities, or self-deceptions—though they are attended to, and the clarification is helpful and usually needed—but on the anxiety, guilt, and shame that keep the patient from experiencing it as safe to feel what he is feeling. The aim certainly includes promoting greater *understanding* of the aspects of the patient's experience and underlying psychological structure that have been hidden from view; but it is even more to create the circumstances whereby he can *feel* the forbidden feeling without the anticipated catastrophic consequences

For many years, the central tenet of psychotherapy that aimed at deep and comprehensive personal change was, as Wallerstein (1989) put it, "Be as expressive as you can be and as supportive as you *have to* [italics added] be." This way of thinking was closely associated with an emphasis on such ideas as anonymity, neutrality, avoidance of "gratifying" the patient's wishes, and avoidance of self-disclosure on the therapist's part whenever possible. In contrast, the approach that is illustrated in this book views these attitudes as anachronistic and therapeutically limiting. I titled one chapter of an earlier book (P. L. Wachtel, 1987), for example, "You Can't Go Far in Neutral," and have written pointed critiques of the traditional psychoanalytic attitudes toward self-disclosure and support (P. L. Wachtel, 1993, 2008). In contrast to the rubric described by Wallerstein, I have suggested that a more useful principle to ground the therapeutic work might be, "Be as *supportive* as you can be, *so that you can be* as expressive or as exploratory as you will need to be" (P. L. Wachtel, 1993, p. 155). The assumption in my work, in other words, is that not only are support and deep exploration not as antithetical as has often been assumed but indeed, a warmly supportive stance toward the patient is the best facilitator of his capacity to explore previously warded-off thoughts, feelings, and wishes.

ATTENTION TO THE PATIENT'S ACTUAL BEHAVIOR
AND THE GENERATION OF VICIOUS CIRCLES

Another central characteristic of the integrative approach that guides the work presented in this book is its strong focus on the patient's actual behavior in his daily life and on the ways that behavior tends to become organized into feedback loops that perpetuate both the behavior pattern itself and the intrapsychic and relational configurations that are at once a cause of the behavior pattern and its consequence. It is this repetitive playing out of vicious circles, virtuous circles, and self-fulfilling prophecies that is at the heart of the theoretical perspective I call "cyclical psychodynamics" (e.g., P. L. Wachtel, 1987, 1993, 1997, 2008), a point of view in which neither "internal" nor "external" influences are primary but rather their repetitive recreation of each other.

For many years, psychoanalytic thinkers regarded overt behavior as but a surface expression of deeper currents that were the true source of the patient's difficulties and the necessary target of therapeutic focus and therapeutic work. Daily interactions were certainly not ignored by analysts (and, even in that earlier era, *good* analysts, one suspects, spent a good deal more time immersing themselves in the details of the patient's daily life than their writings might suggest). But there was (and often continues to be) a theoretical bias that gave relatively short shrift to these "surface" details. As a consequence, the degree of attention I give in my work to the patient's actual behavior and its consequences is rather atypical of psychodynamic approaches. (In contrast, it scarcely needs to be said, behavior therapists have always been interested in the patient's behavior—although their interest was most often on the particular individual behaviors that were direct targets for change, not on how complex *patterns* of behavior and the feedback they generate contribute to cyclical processes in which intrapsychic and behavioral–interactive elements perpetuate and reproduce each other.)

In my own efforts to draw on the strengths of both the psychoanalytic *and* the behavioral traditions,[5] a key element in reconciling the two paradigms was attention to the vicious circles that provide the link between manifest behavior and more "internal" psychological phenomena such as thoughts, feelings, and motives. These feedback loops characterize both the basic structure of personality (P. L. Wachtel, 1977a, 1994) and the processes at the heart of the difficulties that bring the patient to therapy (P. L. Wachtel, 1987, 1993, 1997, 2008). If one observes closely and pays attention to a broad sample of the

---

[5] As will be apparent shortly, as my work evolved I aimed to include as well methods and perspectives from family systems and experiential therapies. This broader emphasis will be apparent in the sessions presented later in this book.

patient's behavior and experience, with remarkable frequency one comes upon a tendency for internal and external processes to reproduce each other in recursive fashion. The characteristics of each person's inner state and psychological organization lead her to behave in the world in ways that evoke a particular subset of responses from others, and those responses in turn feed back to affect the first individual, more often than not recreating the same or a very similar mental state or organization. As a result, the conditions are in place for the same sequence to be repeated yet again. The process—on the part of all who interact to create the repetitive pattern—includes not just the "behavior" per se but the affective tone, which is often the crucial element in keeping the pattern going.

Consider, for example, someone who learns early in life that expressions of anger or disagreement are met with a chilling withdrawal or laceratingly demeaning reaction from key attachment figures. As he attempts to gain a measure of safety or security in such circumstances, he is likely to begin to suppress awareness or expression of such feelings, even where appropriate. He may begin to exhibit a notably unassertive way of interacting with other people or to manifest what psychoanalytic writers describe as a reaction-formation against anger or expressions of disappointment in others, creating a gap in his capacity to deal effectively with some of life's common challenges and demands. He may become *excessively* nice, cooperative, helpful to others[6] and as a consequence may give short shrift to his own needs. He may so dedicate himself to avoiding ruffling anyone's feathers that the harmony he achieves is at the expense of being consistently overlooked or given the short end of the stick.

The irony is that living in such a way almost inevitably stirs feelings of envy and resentment, whether consciously acknowledged or not. In turn, the stirring of such feelings once again evokes anxiety, and so once again, even more urgently, the individual entrapped in such a pattern *suppresses* these resentful feelings, acting in such a way as to hide them, both from others and from himself. But the result is that the circumstances are thereby created for still more experiences of being overlooked and short-changed, hence still more evoking of unacceptable resentment, still more automatic exaggerations of more "acceptable" emotions and behavior, and so on and so forth. The pattern may have *started* early in life, as psychoanalysts often highlight, but it continues not just because of its early origins but because *every day* it is being

---

[6] I emphasize the excess here because obviously being kind or cooperative or helpful to others is not a bad thing in itself, nor is it even a trait that leads the kind or cooperative person to lose out on his fair share. Cooperativeness and consideration for others—when not driven to excess by fear of *ever* expressing disagreement or asking for more—can often result in obtaining the rich share of life's rewards that comes to people who are liked and respected.

refueled anew by the consequences it evokes. The other people in his life, who may not intend to treat him dismissively, are almost inevitably drawn into such behavior by the way the patient's real wishes are disguised, and hence they become "accomplices" (P. L. Wachtel, 1991) in the pattern whether intending to or aware of it or not.

In similar fashion, someone who has learned early in life that expressions of need or dependency are likely to be ignored or treated dismissively may develop a tough skin and a seeming independent streak that leads to asking little of others and, often as a corollary, taking on too burdensome a share of responsibilities on one's own. Living this way often creates a sense of isolation and of deprivation of the support and sympathetic understanding that most people need to sustain a sense of comfort in the world. Consequently, such a life pattern is likely to stir forbidden wishes for the nurturance or reassurance that has not been forthcoming. But given the patient's anxieties and conflicts in this realm, and the need to protect himself against painful and humiliating disappointment, whatever expressions of these wishes the patient allows himself are likely to be so hedged and ambiguous that they are easily ignored or not noticed by the other person. This then "confirms" the feeling that one cannot rely on others or dare not ask others for help because others continue to appear to be unhelpful and unresponsive. As a consequence, the sense of vulnerability associated with the awareness and expression of such feelings is sustained, as is the tendency to submerge them or to express them in the most hedged and indirect way. Thus, here too the pattern is repeated and perpetuated by its own consequences, and others are recruited into the pattern as accomplices, perpetuating the problematic state of affairs as their response to the highly ambivalent and overly subtle signals for help—or to the implicit and anticipatory resentment that comes with expecting not to get that help—ends up confirming the first person's deepest fears.

In thinking about such patterns and their implications for psychotherapy, it is important to understand that one implication of the circularity of the patterns I have been describing is that the starting point for the description is arbitrary. Who is the "first" person and who is the "responder" is a matter of where one begins the narrative, as family therapists have frequently discussed under the rubric of "punctuation" of systemic patterns. Similarly, one could as readily begin the account not with the inner state but with the behavior, or with the situational context. The point is that (especially once the pattern is well established) each element brings forth the next in predictable fashion, thereby creating the circumstances for the other elements in the pattern to call forth the first yet again. Much of the debate between different theoretical models largely comes down to different theories focusing on different parts of the sequence or on different starting points in describing it (E. F. Wachtel & P. L. Wachtel, 1986; P. L. Wachtel, 1973b, 1977a, 1994).

VARIATIONS IN THE PATTERN AND THEIR THERAPEUTIC IMPLICATIONS

It is also important to be clear that none of these patterns are inexorable. If they were, there would be little point to attempting psychotherapy. To begin with, the patterns are both probabilistic and never exactly the same each time. Heraclitus's point that we never step into the same river twice holds even more fully for the flow of behavior and experience. The interactive sequences I am discussing here are, to use Sullivan's (1953) apt phrase, "envelopes of insignificant differences" (p. 104). That is, there is enough similarity in form and outcome that a meaningful pattern can be discerned by a good observer and that, often without awareness, the perceptual processes that lead each party to react to the other's behavior are likely to register what is happening as "more of the same." But the pattern *is* different each time, and thus there is always a possibility for a slightly different outcome that can become the beginning of a new direction instead of the perpetuation of the old.

Further contributing to the possibility of change in these patterns is that they are contextually responsive and dynamically interactive. The power of the patterns that bring people to therapy lies in the pervasiveness of their perpetuation—that is, in the way that the patient seems to evoke a similar (and problematic) response from *a wide range* of people, leading once again to a similar response on his part that evokes still again a similar response from others, ad infinitum. But even the most general and pervasive patterns in people's lives are rarely if ever manifested with everyone. The same behavior or affective cue may evoke one response from one interactive partner and a different response from another. (For example, a style of interaction that many people find hostile and difficult may feel like amusing and enlivening banter to at least a few.) The range of people, roles, and relationships that we encounter in the course of a day or week or month is such that, almost inevitably, some people will respond quite differently to the very behavior that has evoked pattern-confirming responses from most people.

When such atypical responses occur—as they almost always do at least occasionally—several things can happen. Perhaps the most common is that the pattern becomes more differentiated. It is manifested in certain contexts and not others. One implication of this, often given minimal attention in discussions of psychopathology, is that even the "sickest" patient is likely to look "normal" or "healthy" some of the time. Few, if any, people are miserable (or angry, or demoralized, or deluded) *all* of the time.[7] People come to us, rather, because they feel bad more than most people, or more than they wish they did, not because they feel bad *all* the time (and this is so even if the patient himself does not frame it this way). Moreover, it is important to be clear that the times and circumstances in which the patient feels better are not theoretical chaff or error variance. Rather, they are a crucial part of the overall clinical picture that provides an essential foundation for therapeutic change. Without these alternative kernels of healthier or more adaptive behavior, successful psychotherapy is extremely difficult (see P. L. Wachtel, 1993, especially Chapter 7).

A second important implication of the variability in the way that different people respond to the same behavior by the patient is that when the anticipated response does not occur, it can, over time, contribute to weakening the pattern as a whole. This is the logic behind such therapeutic concepts and strategies as the corrective emotional experience (Alexander & French, 1946), new relational experience (Frank, 1999), new object experience (Loewald, 1960), moments of meeting, (D. N. Stern et al., 1998), passing the patient's tests (Weiss & Sampson, 1986), repairing ruptures in the therapeutic relationship (Safran & Muran, 2000), and "an actual relationship with a reliable and beneficent parental figure" (Fairbairn, 1958, p. 377). When the patient has repeated experiences with the therapist that disconfirm his problematic beliefs or expectations, the strength of those expectations and the likelihood of the behaviors and affective experiences associated with them gradually diminish.

These considerations do not, of course, imply that all of the variance lies in how other people respond to us. To be sure, I have been highlighting here the responsiveness of our behavior and experience to the actual occurrences in our lives. But it is important to be clear that I have done so in the context of a theoretical outlook in which the traditional concerns of dynamic therapists regarding the patient's subjective experience and psychological organization also have a central role. The point has been that "internal dynamics" and "external events" are not really separate domains but aspects of a larger recursive pattern in which each facet is both crucial and dependent on the other. In attending to and attempting to intervene in that pattern, it is essential not to give short shrift to the dynamic organizing processes that *give meaning* to the events encountered (P. L. Wachtel, 1980, 2008). We do not respond to events in some "objective" fashion that is unmediated by our proclivities, anticipations, perceptual biases, and so on. Much of the process of psychotherapy, after all, entails enabling the patient to see alternative ways of understanding, experiencing, and responding to what goes on in his life.

---

[7]When this variability is not evident, or is evident only very minimally, it is likely that we are dealing with a disorder that has a strong biological component, and the use of adjunctive medication is something that the therapist should be especially open to considering.

THE IMPORTANCE OF THE PATIENT'S LIFE
OUTSIDE THE CONSULTING ROOM

From a different vantage point, it is also essential to be clear that new experiences with the therapist are likely to have limited impact if not accompanied by efforts to address the patient's experience with people *outside* the consulting room (see P. L. Wachtel, 2008, especially Chapters 4 and 12). As I noted above, the patterns in the patient's life, rather than being completely general and pervasive, are likely to become differentiated, evident in certain contexts and relationships and not in others or manifested to different degrees in different contexts. Therapists who pay too much attention to the therapeutic relationship, apart from its relation to the *other* important relationships and experiences in the patient's life, may be misled into thinking the patient is getting better because his relationship with *them* is getting better. But the patient may, in essence, learn that *in this room* it is safe to express his true self and true feelings but may still find that difficult in the rest of his life (perhaps even without noticing that this differentiation is taking place).

It is not that the therapist is necessarily a more empathic person per se; in their own personal lives, therapists probably vary in this quality as much as the general population does. But the therapist does have two important qualities that enable her to respond to the patient differently in certain ways from most other people in his life. First, she has a set of skills that derive from her training—skills both in observation and in knowing how to respond facilitatively to the patient's struggles. Second, she has the luxury of being both in *and* not in the patient's life; that is, we care about the patient and have an emotional stake in his welfare, but we do not expect the same reciprocal gratifying of other needs that we do in the rest of our lives or that others in the patient's life reasonably expect.

We do, of course, get caught at times in what has come to be called *enactments*, and, indeed, the working through of those mutual enactments is a central feature of the therapeutic process (see, e.g., Bass, 2003; Frank, 2002; Safran & Muran, 2000; D. B. Stern, 2003; P. L. Wachtel, 2008). But the degree of our dogged persistence in the role of accomplice is, one hopes, considerably less than it is with those who are not in a *therapeutic* relationship with the patient. In other relationships, even with close friends and loved ones who have the patient's interests very much at heart, the degree of reflective distance from the pattern in which they are entrapped is likely to be considerably less, and hence the unwitting perpetuation of the pattern is likely to be considerably more.[8] As a

---

[8]This holds, of course, even if these personal relationship partners are psychotherapists in their professional life.

consequence, it is crucially important that even therapists who center much of their therapeutic efforts on the immediate relationship in the room *also* attend—and attend closely and continuously—to the patient's life outside the therapy room. Helping the patient extend whatever changes are achieved in the consulting room into his daily interactions with other people, working on the ways that his behavior with others may evoke different responses from them than from his therapist, helping him to break those cycles and to see how the way he feels about himself has been affected by them—these are essential features of an effective and comprehensive therapeutic approach.

It is important to be clear as well that the cyclical patterns that characterize the patient's life are not limited to patterns with negative consequences. Facilitating change as effectively as possible requires as well that we understand and work with the *positive* cycles in the patient's life. The patterns in people's lives that yield satisfaction, intimacy, and harmonious relationships are *also* characterized by feedback loops in which the internal state of each individual brings about consequences that help to maintain that state and thus to bring about a similar consequence still again. As I have emphasized strongly elsewhere (see especially P. L. Wachtel, 1993, 2008), and as will be evident in the sessions presented in this book, attention to and building on the patient's strengths, rather than attending to pathology alone, is a central key to good therapeutic practice. Good relationships don't just maintain themselves automatically. They remain good when—and because—they continue to elicit the responses from others that are needed to maintain them. This is not a tautology but a statement about their dynamics.

SYSTEMS, NARRATIVES, AND UNDERSTANDING PEOPLE IN CONTEXT

Not long after I completed my first major integrative effort, focused specifically on psychoanalysis and behavior therapy (P. L. Wachtel, 1977b), I became aware that much of the way I was conceptualizing the development and dynamics of personality dovetailed with the theoretical perspectives of family therapists and other systems thinkers (E. F. Wachtel & P. L. Wachtel, 1986). Much of the convergence relates to the shared emphasis on vicious circles and recursive feedback loops that is characteristic both of the cyclical psychodynamic model and of most systems models (see E. F. Wachtel & P. L. Wachtel, 1986; P. L. Wachtel, 1997). It will be evident particularly in the sessions with Louise presented in Chapters 3 and 4 that the work is very much rooted in attention to how the interactions between Louise on the one hand and her husband and his family on the other create such feedback loops in ways that perpetuate the problem she wishes to address. In considering those sessions, it will be apparent that they reflect simultaneously attention to her individual dynamics (including the persisting legacy of some central experiences and themes from her childhood) and to the systemic dynamics in her marriage and between her and her in-laws. In certain ways, the session works on the couples and family issues through the medium of the individual session and works on the individual issues through examination of the couple dynamics and their larger systemic context.

An additional point of convergence between the cyclical psychodynamic perspective that underlies much of the therapeutic work presented in this book and the methods and viewpoints of therapists guided by a family systems perspective lies in the ways that forward-pointing alternative narratives[9] are used both by a range of family therapists and other systems thinkers (e.g., Angus & McLeod, 2003; Molnar & de Shazer, 1987; E. F. Wachtel, 2001; Watzlawick, Weakland, & Fisch, 1974; White & Epston, 1990) and by the cyclical psychodynamic approach. In a related vein, at workshops over the years in which I have presented the approach described in this book, quite a few attendees have pointed out similarities to the set of approaches deriving from the work of Milton Erickson (e.g., Erickson, 1982; Erickson & Lankton, 1987), which also is strongly rooted in narrative redescription or what has been called a *solution-focused* approach (e.g., McNeilly, 2000; Miller, Hubble, & Duncan, 1996; O'Hanlon & Weiner-Davis, 1989; Zeig, 1985).

This interest in narrative redescription points to another way in which the effort to help the person understand himself differently has evolved from the early conceptions of "insight" that dominated the field for many years. Even within psychoanalysis, there has been increasing recognition that the insights achieved in analytic work are not simple "discoveries," resembling the process of digging up buried archaeological shards. Rather, they are more a matter of new constructions or new narratives, of the patient's coming to organize his understanding of himself and his life in ways that have more benign implications for how he feels and lives in the future (see, e.g., Hoffman, 1998, Schafer, 1992; Spence, 1982, 1983; P. L. Wachtel, 2008). When successful, psychotherapy helps the patient to retell his life story, to provide a different frame and give a different moral to the story. Hence, it enables him to give different *meaning* to events and experiences that had previously been a source of hopelessness and blockage and had contributed to a demeaning or depressing view of himself and of his life. In this respect, the approach described in this book converges with those aspects of cognitive and cognitive–behavioral therapy that also aim to help the patient see himself and the prospects in his life differently. But it does so in a less didactic and objectivist manner than in the rationalist tradition of

---

[9]Elsewhere (P. L. Wachtel, 2008) I have discussed such alternative narratives for the patient's life as narratives of possibility, in contrast to the narratives of *explanation* that are more typical of "interpretations."

cognitive therapy and more in the spirit of the constructivist and acceptance-oriented approaches discussed above.

THE EXPERIENTIAL DIMENSION

From another vantage point, the approach depicted here overlaps considerably with a variety of approaches that have come to be described as *experiential* (e.g., Fosha, 2000; Fosha & Yeung, 2006; Greenberg, 2002; Johnson, 2004; McCullough, 2003; Pos, Greenberg, & Elliott, 2008). From the very beginning, of course, insight-oriented approaches have aimed to promote "emotional insight," not just "intellectual insight." But that idea has often been honored more in the breach than in practice. The emphasis on "discovery" of the hidden sources of the patient's difficulties (see P. L. Wachtel, 2008, especially Chapters 2 and 6, for a discussion of the origins and consequences of this tendency) led to an overvaluation of words and an inclination to "explain" to the patient why he is experiencing what he does (see Aron, 1996) and to insufficient appreciation of the need to *experience* the forbidden, to *go through* it in order to move beyond it. (See in this connection the earlier discussions regarding the role of exposure in overcoming anxiety, as well as the importance of *acceptance* of the patient's experience as part of the very process of promoting change in that experience.) The importance of "embracing affect," discussed earlier, implies that the patient must fully *experience* the forbidden. Here again, the idea that the forbidden must be experienced with full affect represents in one sense a return to a fundamental early tenet of psychoanalysis; but it also again represents an ideal that has often been honored more in the breach. The contemporary approaches that cluster under the label of experiential psychotherapies do take this idea seriously, and it is no coincidence that they have often also described themselves as affect-centered or emotion-focused.

THE IMPORTANCE OF CULTURE

In addition to approaching the therapeutic task in ways that are informed by psychoanalytic, cognitive–behavioral, experiential, and systemic perspectives, the approach described in this book places a strong emphasis on attending to the impact of the historical, cultural, and economic dimensions of people's lives (see, in this connection, P. L. Wachtel, 1983, 1999, 2003). These latter influences on our experience of ourselves and our lives are recognized as crucial by almost every therapist in the course of her everyday life. We all "know" this, and our daily conversations with friends, colleagues, acquaintances, and loved ones attest to and reflect this. But in clinical practice, these crucial dimensions of living are often bracketed, kept separate from the focus of the therapeutic work, as if they were "something else." But they are *not* "something else"; they are an integral part of the way the patient experiences and constructs his life and of the stresses or opportunities to which he responds. Even the very role of the therapist, or the very idea of psychotherapy as a profession, are historically contingent reflections of a particular cultural context. As Frank (1973) has ably demonstrated, for most of human history the functions we serve were the reserve of priests and shamans, and the particular practices in which psychotherapists engage today are infused with the sanctions and meanings that our particular society attributes to them.

In my own thinking about personality and the therapeutic process, sociocultural and sociohistorical dynamics are not something external to or separate from psychological dynamics and experience but are part and parcel of them. I have used the same vicious circle analysis that guides my thinking about my patients as individuals in addressing the broad cultural and historical dynamics that have underlain modern societies' emphasis on economic growth, an emphasis that is associated with multiple ironies and contradictions from the vantage point of individual human experience (P. L. Wachtel, 1983, 2003), and I have similarly used the analysis of vicious circles to address equally significant ironies in the realm of race relations (P. L. Wachtel, 1999).

The impact of cultural values and assumptions in shaping the context of patients' choices and in framing their experiences will be evident throughout the sessions that form the core of this book. For Melissa, they are strongly evident in her initial framing of her dilemma as a conflict about choice of jobs. In a society in which health care and resources for retirement were organized differently than in the United States, Melissa's conflicts about her work and career would necessarily take a different form. Indeed, whatever deeper uncertainties might be feeding this conflict would very possibly be expressed in a realm other than work altogether. In the case of Louise, the issues she is addressing are strongly reflective of her struggle to reconcile the experience of growing up in Sweden and now living in the United States. She wrestles both with the stereotypic conceptions that place boxes around the idea of Swedishness or Americanness for her and with the very real differences that characterize life in the two societies. In turn, these cultural differences are both expressed in and contradicted by the similarities and differences between the family she grew up in and the family into which she married. In these sessions, as in the lives of all of us, the closer we look, the more arbitrary appears the difference between "internal" and "external" or "individual" and "social." Like a path along a Moebius strip, we cannot proceed in exploring the "inside" without finding ourselves encountering the "outside," nor can we then move very far along the "outside" without finding ourselves back "inside" again. "Inside" and "outside" are distinctions we are virtually forced to make by the nature of language, but it is their intertwinedness and mutual cocreation that must be at the heart of our understanding.

THE CULTURE OF PSYCHOTHERAPY

No discussion of culture in the practice of psychotherapy would be complete without attention to the culture of psychotherapy itself. Our field is presently marked by deep divides that separate the proponents of the different orientations to theory and clinical practice. We are accustomed to thinking of these differences in terms of deep seriousness: They are *philosophical, theoretical, empirical*. On closer examination, however, they often appear to be akin more to the divisions between ethnic groups. In many respects they are less matters of rationally evaluated judgments than they are matters of identity and identification, of which group I *belong* to. Stereotyping, "us–them" thinking, and a strong emotional preference for one's own group's linguistic forms—these are the characteristics of ethnic identity and ethnic rivalry or mistrust. They are also, to a striking degree, the lens through which therapists of one theoretical orientation view therapists of another. As an integrative therapist, it is in part my aim to break down these stereotypes through pointing to convergences in conceptions or in practice that are missed by those immersed in the particular style and the particular theoretical language of their own orientation. But my experience as an integrationist, which has brought me into close contact and exchanges with therapists of each of the key orientations in our field, has also brought home to me how hard these stereotypes are to overcome.

In this chapter, I have attempted to show in various ways some of the overlaps that exist between orientations if one goes beyond the different language used to express closely related ideas. In the next chapter, I discuss in more detail the aspects of my thinking and my clinical work that derive from what has come to be called the *relational* point of view in order to help the reader understand as fully as possible what I was up to in the sessions that follow. In good measure, my aim is to alert the reader to some significant changes in psychoanalytic thought in recent years, changes of which many from outside the psychoanalytic world are unaware. As Westen (1998) has noted, to many nonanalysts (and, to be sure, to a subset of analysts as well), psychoanalysis is about egos and ids, Oedipus complexes and phallic symbols, life instincts and death instincts. These concepts, which are close to or more than a hundred years old, fit comfortably into the stereotypes held by therapists of other orientations and serve for some to bolster their image of psychoanalysis as the product of fevered minds with little interest in or connection to either science or common sense. Today, however, as Westen pointed out, "most psychodynamic theorists and therapists spend much of their time helping people with problematic interpersonal patterns, such as difficulty getting emotionally intimate or repeatedly getting intimate with the wrong kind of person" (p. 333). Moreover, as Westen also demonstrated, many of the key concepts in contemporary psychoanalytic thought have received significant empirical support from a range of studies conducted from the vantage point of cognitive psychology, social psychology, experimental personality research, and cognitive and affective neuroscience.

For readers whose "ethnicity" is other than psychoanalytic, I wish to alert you to the unfamiliar territory you are about to enter in the next chapter. My aim is both to clarify how psychoanalytic thought and practice contribute to the overall integrative approach represented in the sessions and to explicate some of the newer modes of thought in psychoanalysis with which many readers may not be familiar. I ask the nonpsychoanalytic reader to attempt to enter this unfamiliar territory with the same open-minded curiosity with which I would hope she approaches her encounters with the experiential world of her patients. Elsewhere (e.g., P. L. Wachtel, 2010a), I have addressed in some detail the nature of the evidence for the ideas that guide the range of contemporary therapeutic approaches and the complexities and confusions that have characterized discussions of "evidence-based" or "empirically supported" treatments. But my aim at this point is to invite the reader to entertain a more subjective mode of inquiry, rooted in the experience of both parties in the therapy room and the effort to achieve some sense of order and understanding in the complex back and forth that constitutes the therapeutic interaction.

2

INSIDE TWO HEADS:
THE TWO-PERSON PERSPECTIVE
AND ITS IMPLICATIONS
FOR THEORY AND PRACTICE

Two heads, we are frequently told, are better than one. A key premise of this book is that for the purpose of practicing and understanding psychotherapy, being *inside* two heads is better than being inside just one. My aim in presenting and discussing the sessions that are the heart of this book is to enable the reader to know not only what I think was going on for *the patient*—both from moment to moment and with regard to longstanding psychological configurations and inclinations—but also what was going on in my own head. This latter perspective includes not just my thinking about interventions and therapeutic strategies but my *emotional* state as I sit with the patient and am (inevitably) affected by her. Thus, as I attempt to get "inside the head" of the patient and to share with the reader my perception of her experience and dynamics, I also present to the reader, to the extent that I myself have access to it, *my own* experience as the session proceeds.

In part, obviously, including what is going on inside my own head is a way of informing the reader about my "approach" or "orientation" to psychotherapy, the ways I am thinking about what happens as the session proceeds and how it affects my evolving understanding of the patient, my decisions about what to say (or whether to say nothing), and so on. This much conforms to the agenda of virtually any book on psychotherapy, a depiction, in essence, of what the therapist is "up to" (though in this case it includes an account of such thinking from moment to moment throughout the session, something that is *not* so typically presented). But my aim in emphasizing being "inside two heads" goes beyond that. It also reflects my conviction that one of the most valuable ways to understand the patient is to attend to *one's own* experience in interacting with him or her. What it feels like to *be with* a person is one of the most powerful tools we have in understanding what it feels like to *be* that person. It is one of the most powerful tools as well as for understanding the dynamics that are shaping his behavior and experience outside of his awareness.

Of course, the therapist's subjectivity is by no means flawless as a guide to understanding the patient. Therapists, although better trained and better positioned (see Chapter 1 in this volume) to observe perceptively, are by no means immune to the danger of confusing a possibly rather idiosyncratic experience of the other person with a valid insight into what the other person is like. At the same time, however, it is also essential to appreciate that we would all be far less able to negotiate the subtleties and challenges of human relationships if we *could not* make use of our own subjective experience in doing so. Subjectivity is both deeply flawed *and* indispensable in understanding another.

THE TWO-PERSON VIEWPOINT: ADVANCES AND LIMITATIONS

What the discussion thus far largely amounts to is that this book is written from the vantage point of what has come to be called the *two-person* point of view (e.g., Aron, 1990; Ghent, 1989; P. L. Wachtel, 2008). The contemporary usage of that term is rooted in a distinction between the one-person perspective (which characterized psychoanalytic thought for most of its history) and a newer way of thinking that has evolved mostly in the past 2 decades, though with important earlier antecedents (e.g., Balint, 1950; Rickman, 1957; Sullivan, 1953). The *one-person* viewpoint refers to the clinical and epistemological stance in which the therapist's field of study is the other person sitting in the room with her and in which her own role in generating the phenomena she observes is minimized. The two-person perspective, in contrast, views the events occurring in the therapy room as inevitably a product of the interaction between the *two* people in the room, with the therapist participating not only by dint of the inevitable bias and selectivity in what she sees or attends to and how she interprets it but also as a function of her active engagement in an interpersonal or relational field that shapes the behavior and experience of both parties. From a two-person perspective, experience is always *co-constructed* (a term that is a central one in the literature of the two-person point of view). One can never observe "the patient" or "the client" as an autonomous phenomenon of nature free from the setting in which the person is being observed. The therapist necessarily observes the patient *in relation to her* and in the context of that relationship. This, it is important to understand, does not mean that we cannot gain useful knowledge and understanding of another person (see P. L. Wachtel, 2008, for a discussion of this issue and how it is often misunderstood), but it does refine our conception the nature of that understanding and of its limits.

The two-person critique is, in my view, a very important advance; I write as a strong proponent of its essential premises. But several clarifications are important to introduce at this point. First, as I shall elaborate later in this chapter, the two-person perspective is part of a larger paradigm shift in psychoanalytic thought that underlies in important ways the clinical work presented in this book. This larger paradigm shift generally goes by the label of *relational* theory, and although the two-person point of view is a central part of it, it includes considerably more (for a fuller review of the relational point of view and its many features and implications, see P. L. Wachtel, 2008). At this point, the relational point of view may well be the dominant version of psychoanalysis in the United States and is rapidly growing in influence in a number of other parts of the world, but it remains relatively unfamiliar to many therapists outside the psychoanalytic community. Later in this chapter I address a number of features of this new mode of psychoanalytic thought as they bear on the clinical work presented in this book and on the integration of psychoanalytic thought with methods and perspectives deriving from the cognitive–behavioral, systemic, and experiential points of view. (Readers who wish to examine the relational viewpoint in more detail may wish to consult such works as Aron, 1996; Bromberg, 1998a; Hoffman, 1998; Mitchell, 1988, 1993, 1997; D. B. Stern, 1997; Stolorow, 1997a, 1997b; and P. L. Wachtel, 2008.)

I will proceed for now, however, with further consideration of the narrower concept of the two-person point of view, both because it is perhaps the most essential component or defining feature of the larger relational paradigm[1] and because it is especially germane to a book such as this, whose purview includes the way that my own thinking and experience in the sessions that constitute the heart of this book contributed to shaping what transpired between the patient and me. In the literature of relational psychoanalysis there have been at least three different meanings to two-person thinking, or three different realms in which it has been applied.[2] The first, and perhaps most widely used meaning in the relational literature, is an *epistemological* meaning. It is this dimension that is the focus when relational writers emphasize the problems in

---

[1] As I discuss later in this chapter, *relational* is in certain respects an umbrella term that includes a range of concepts and viewpoints that not all relational thinkers share.
[2] Spezzano (1996), in a slightly different way, also distinguished between three meanings of the concepts of one-person and two-person theorizing.

reporting or conceptualizing "the patient's" characteristics without taking into account that the observations are always observations from within a relational matrix in which both parties are embedded. The second dimension in which one may distinguish between one-person and two-person thinking as representing significantly different premises and modes of thought has to do with the dynamics and development of personality. As I discuss later in this chapter, it is entirely possible (and even common) to advocate for a two-person epistemological position and nonetheless evidence what are essentially one-person premises in one's substantive formulations about the nature of personality dynamics. Finally, one may distinguish between one- and two-person approaches to therapeutic technique. This dimension includes assumptions about therapeutic intervention; thinking about the roles of insight, autonomy, neutrality, anonymity, and self-disclosure; and conceptualizations regarding the therapeutic relationship and its potential impact on the patient's difficulties. In all three of these dimensions, I argue, it is actually more useful and accurate to refer to a *contextual* point of view than a two-person point of view; but because the terms *two-person theory* and *two-person perspective* are widely used in the literature of relational psychoanalysis, I discuss the issues from this vantage point as well as that of contextuality.

Still another necessary clarification about the distinction between one-person and two-person theory is that it is only from the vantage point of the *two*-person perspective that the older mode of thought is described as a *one*-person point of view. That is, few, if any "one-person" thinkers describe themselves that way. The depiction of a one-person perspective is a depiction viewed through the lens of the two-person perspective, and it is offered, almost without exception, as a *critique* of the former (P. L. Wachtel, 2008). This does not necessarily mean that the critique is invalid. It does, however, suggest that because it is a characterization of a group of thinkers that is not endorsed by the members of the group being characterized, at least some further reflection is required.

ONE-PERSON AND TWO-PERSON THINKING IN COGNITIVE–BEHAVIORAL, HUMANISTIC, AND SYSTEMIC APPROACHES

The final clarification of the meaning and implications of the two-person point of view that I wish to introduce is less a caveat than an expansion: Although the initial discussions of one-person and two-person perspectives arose primarily in the psychoanalytic literature, the distinction to which they refer is not really at its core a psychoanalytic distinction but one that is applicable to proponents of *all* of the major traditions in the field of psychotherapy.

As implicit in the discussion of rationalism and constructivism in cognitive therapy in Chapter 1, for example, there are one-person and two-person versions of cognitive and cognitive–behavioral therapy as much as there are of psychoanalysis. That is, in this realm too, there are therapists who view themselves as objective observers, standing outside the phenomena they are observing and participating only in the sense that they "point out" what is going on; and there are others, also identifying themselves as cognitive–behavioral, who view themselves as genuine participants in a co-constructed experience.

The same holds for humanistic therapists, such as Rogerians, whose observations too may be made from a stance either of observing "the client" or of full recognition of the interconnectedness between oneself and the client and of the degree to which the observations are observations-of-the-client-within-this-relationship, rather than observations of the client per se. It may be easier to overlook these differences in this realm because the basic premises of most Rogerian and other humanistic therapists include the therapist's *empathy* as the key observational tool and because their approach is usually strongly affirmative of the client's experience rather than a critique of its irrationality. But a closer look suggests that empathy is sometimes viewed as a quasi-objective tool ("accurate" empathy) that directly grasps the client's experience rather than as the means by which (and the lens through which) this *particular* therapist arrives at her particular take on the client's experience.

Similarly, the notion of unconditional positive regard can reflect, in some hands, an unspoken assumption that one is not really part of the interactive field being observed but rather a benignly neutral observer who does not judge (and hence, implicitly, does not manifest the range of *complex and conflicted* emotions one inevitably brings to interactions outside the therapeutic field). At the same time, many other Rogerian therapists approach the work with a significantly different set of assumptions, rooted in an understanding of the inherently *participatory* stance emphasized by two-person thinkers of all orientations. From this vantage point, for example, although one also strives to be affirmative of the client's experience rather than to offer critiques from an outside or "rational" perspective, there is an appreciation of, and even emphasis on, the therapist's emotional response to the client, whether "pretty" or not, as providing important clues to the client's experience. There is as well a recognition that the experiences the therapist is empathically responding to are experiences that are not just the client's "organismic" response, but the client's response *to the experience of the two of them being together* in the particular way that this particular pair interacts; that is, that the experience is co-constructed.[3]

---

[3]Again, referring to co-construction does not mean that the patient or client does not enter the interaction with already formed characteristics and inclinations. It means, to anticipate a point I emphasize throughout this book, that those characteristics and inclinations are contextual in nature.

Indeed, even group therapists or family therapists—who clearly interact with *more* than just one other person, and who refer frequently to systems—may, from an epistemological vantage point, approach the session and the observations that derive from it from a perspective that differs little from the "one-person" point of view if they do not take into account the impact of their own presence and their own particular style of interacting on what they "observe" in the family or group. I have, for example, been a participant on several occasions in group relations workshops that were conducted from the vantage point of Bion (e.g., 1961), a thinker often cited by two-person theorists. Rarely have I encountered a more "one-person" approach to group process, in which the inscrutable and omniscient observer informs the group about its primitive and even "psychotic" assumptions. At the same time, many other group and family therapists view what is transpiring in the room, even when it seems to be strictly between the other members of the group or family, from an understanding that they are a part of the particular system or relational field that has been created in the room and hence that they are an important part of the very phenomena they are observing. In that sense, although they are working with *multiple* individuals, they are, from the vantage point of the one-person/two-person distinction, "two-person" thinkers. It is not really the number of people who are being taken into account that is at issue; it is the claim to have strictly observer status.

THE LIMITS OF THE ONE-PERSON/TWO-PERSON DISTINCTION: TOWARD A CONTEXTUAL POINT OF VIEW

What emerges from these considerations is that on the one hand, the two-person point of view represents an important advance in our understanding of the epistemological status of our formulations and, on the other, that the *term* "two-person" is not really the best one for expressing this advance. It is potentially confusing as well as potentially limiting. Its essential insight, I believe, is better expressed by referring to the newer perspective as representing a *contextual* point of view, a point of view in which we regard our understanding of a person as an understanding of how she is in any particular context, attending both to how she may manifest similar inclinations across a variety of contexts and how she may vary from one context to another. This viewpoint has been increasingly evident both in the psychoanalytic literature and in the literature of experimental social psychology and personality research (e.g., Andersen & Chen, 2002; Andersen, Saribay, & Kooij, 2008; Andersen, Thorpe, & Kooij, 2007; Mischel & Shoda, 1998; Orange, Atwood, & Stolorow, 1997; Rhodewalt, 2008; Shoda, Cervone, & Downey, 2007; Stolorow & Atwood,

1992; Stolorow, Atwood, & Orange, 1999; E. F. Wachtel & P. L. Wachtel, 1986; P. L. Wachtel, 1995).

As I elaborate later in this chapter, such an understanding does not imply that there is no core or coherence to the individual personality but rather that even in the ways we remain very much "ourselves" as we move from situation to situation or relational context to relational context, we are never *just* ourselves but always "ourselves in relation to what is going on about us." The invoking of a *two*-person point of view to express this understanding is an artifact of the origins of this shift in perspective—at least in the clinical realm—in the rethinking of what transpires in the therapy session and of the nature of the understanding achieved in that setting. In *that* context, what goes on appears to be mostly about two people, and the advance that the two-person perspective represents is in its emphasis on the relevance of "the other person in the room" to what transpires and what is observed.

It is in this sense that I describe the discussions of the sessions that constitute the heart of this book as reflecting a two-person perspective. My aim is not just to convey to the reader what I think are the patients' enduring personality characteristics or the nature of the dynamics or causal networks that contribute to their problems or complaints. Nor is my aim solely to indicate what I believe the patients are thinking or feeling at various points in the session; it is as well to place those experiences and dynamics in the context of what is going on for me at the same time and how we are interacting. But the term *two-person* to refer to this idea does not sufficiently capture the larger point of view that guides my thinking, and in some ways it misrepresents it. That it works at all is due to the fact that *in these sessions* there are, indeed, two people in the room. But it will be very evident, even in these sessions, that my concerns very much include, for example, Louise's transactions with her husband, with his family, and with the cultural differences between Sweden, where she grew up, and the United States, where she now lives, as well as Melissa's encounters with the larger context of the U.S. health care system. There are two people in the room in the sessions, but even in that setting, many other people and contexts are a part of what we are discussing and trying to understand.

ONE-PERSON, TWO-PERSON, AND CONTEXTUAL PERSPECTIVES ON PERSONALITY DYNAMICS: OBJECT RELATIONS AND ATTACHMENT PERSPECTIVES

The advantages of thinking of the shift in perspective I am discussing as a shift toward a *contextual* point of view, and the limitations of the distinction between one-person and two-person thinking, are even more apparent in the second realm in which the one-person two-person distinction has been invoked, the realm of personality dynamics and development. Here too, however, it is useful not to simply consign to the rubbish heap the concepts of one-person and two-person theory, which by now have generated a rich and valuable literature, but rather to use this older distinction as both a link to previous theorizing and a way station toward a more fully contextual understanding. Indeed, one advantage of retaining the terminology of one-person and two-person theorizing is that this terminology, for all its limitations—and *as a result of* its limitations—helps to illuminate a central point I wish to make: the ways in which writers who are in certain respects two-person theorists may continue to engage in "old paradigm" thinking when they move from the realm of epistemology to that of substantive personality theory. As I have discussed in some detail elsewhere (P. L. Wachtel, 2008), many "two-person" theorists—in the sense that they critique the way earlier analysts assumed they could observe the patient and his dynamics apart from the relational context from within which the observation was made—nonetheless manifest, in their accounts of personality dynamics, an essentially "one-person" way of thinking. That is, instead of depicting the person's motives, thoughts, and representations of self and other as always in some way in relation to the emotional and relational context in which the person is operating at the moment, they depict an "inner world" of "internalized" objects, a *fantasy* world that has an impact on but is scarcely touched by the ongoing experiences of daily life.

Such a mode of thought is especially evident in the writings of thinkers in the object relations tradition, who, following the lead of Melanie Klein in particular (e.g., Klein, 1952, 1957, 1961, 1984), have conceptualized "internalized objects" as psychological configurations that are split off from the evolving personality, frozen in time and remaining "infantile, "primitive," or "archaic." The one-person nature of these formulations is often obscured by the fact that the *content* of the fantasies of central concern to object relations thinkers is about relationships. Less readily noticed is the degree to which the focus is on *imagined* relationships, "fantasy" relationships, and, indeed imaginal or fantasy relationships *from infancy*, rather than *actual* and *ongoing* relationships with real people (see Modell, 1984). From Fairbairn (1952), to Winnicott (1965, 1971, 1975), to Kernberg (1976), to a host of others, object relations thinking is an intriguing and confusing mélange of, on the one hand, the older one-person or "monadic" (Mitchell, 1988) mode of thought and, on the other, the newer understanding of the ways that personality is shaped by actual experiences with others.

The degree to which object relations thinking retains significant elements of one-person thinking may perhaps be better grasped by contrasting it with Bowlby's attachment theory (e.g., Bowlby, 1969, 1973, 1980), which emerged from the same matrix of British psychoanalytic thought at about the same time.

In certain respects, one can view Bowlby's concept of internalized working models as the equivalent, in his theory, of the object relations concept of "internalized objects." But in contrast to the thinking of most of his contemporaries in the British psychoanalytic world, Bowlby conceived of internalized working models not as fixed infantile or primitive structures split off from development and from access to influence by new experiences, but as cognitive–affective schemas evolving in relation to continuing experiences with successive attachment figures throughout life. He did view internal working models as persistent and difficult to change, but not because they were based on fantasy and inaccessible to actual experience; rather, they were persistent for two key reasons, which have critically important implications for our understanding of psychopathology and for the practice of psychotherapy.

First, internal working models were rooted in the developing person's efforts to *feel safe* and in the perceived *danger* that various kinds of caretaking experiences could create. As a consequence, they reflected the same potential rigidity and resistance to change as in any other aspect of psychological functioning that is driven by anxiety. There is much less risk in seeking out new opportunities for pleasure or stimulation or the satisfaction of appetitive needs than in altering a pattern of behavior one has experienced as keeping one safe.[4] Second, internal working models had *consequences*. They led the child to behave in ways that were likely to evoke in the original caretaker (and later in others) the same kind of behavior that had generated the internalized expectation in the first place. In this, they were one more instance of the vicious and virtuous circles discussed in Chapter 1. Children who developed secure attachment patterns were likely to evoke in others the very responses necessary to keep them feeling secure. Children who developed one of the varieties of insecure attachment were, as a consequence of the very expectations insecure attachment embodied and of the behavior such expectations lead to, likely to encounter behavior and affective cues from others that maintain the pattern of insecurity. (For a further elucidation of the dynamics of attachment as reflecting repetitive, cyclical processes of mutual dyadic regulation, see P. L. Wachtel, 2008, 2010b.)

Thus, Bowlby's conceptualization, although also attentive to the ways that early experiences can leave a lasting mark and to the critical role of the individual's psychological organization in interpreting and giving meaning to experiences, casts his understanding of this phenomenon in terms of the developing individual's response to actual relational events. Indeed, so different was

---

[4]For further elucidation of the ways in which psychological tendencies that are driven by anxiety can become uniquely peremptory, see the much underappreciated—and still very valuable—contribution of Horney (e.g., 1939).

Bowlby's "two-person" emphasis on the impact of what *really* goes on between mother and infant from the emphasis of Kleinian and object relations theorists on the individual's "phantasies" as the source of his perceptions and expectations that Bowlby was rather thoroughly rejected and shunned by the British psychoanalytic Establishment. It is perhaps the most potent sign of *changes* in psychoanalysis, not only in Britain but throughout the world, that Bowlby and attachment theory are now not only respectable but in many ways at the very center of psychoanalytic interest (e.g., Cortina & Marrone, 2001; Fonagy, 2001; A. N. Schore, 2003; Wallin, 2007). But the degree to which the conceptual bias that led to the original rejection of Bowlby's ideas still remains in the foundations of object relations thinking has been insufficiently examined. In certain respects, it might be said, Bowlby's ideas have been accepted in a "sloppy" fashion that places them alongside other ideas that are actually incompatible with them. Much work remains to be done to probe the compatibility or incompatibility of ideas that are currently viewed as cohering because they all share a concern with "relationships" but that at times view relationships in such a different fashion that the seeming convergence in thinking masks a deeper, and in many ways more significant, difference in fundamental outlook (P. L. Wachtel, 2008, 2010b).

THE NURSERY AND THE CONSULTING ROOM: THE RESTRICTED CONTEXTS OF TWO-PERSON THEORY

In order to further clarify the important clinical implications of a thoroughgoing two-person or contextual perspective, it is useful to clarify further the ways in which "one-person" thinking persists, in unexamined and often unwitting fashion, among many influential writers who, in the epistemological realm, are strong critics of the one-person point of view. In pursuing this topic, it is illuminating to ask where two-person or contextual thinking is usually applied—*and where it is not*. As I elaborate in this section, the answer to this question is that two-person thinking has been strongly evident in two contexts—in the relation between patient and therapist and in the interaction between mothers and infants—and has been surprisingly absent in the relational literature in discussions of the many other aspects of people's lives as the individual continues to evolve and to respond to new events throughout the life cycle (cf. Eccles, 2004; Erikson, 1950, 1980; Mancini, 2009). But this absence has been largely obscured by the fact that with the increasing influence of two-person thinking with regard to the mother–infant interaction, it *appears* that such thinking has been extended beyond the therapy room to a much greater extent than it actually has. In this sense, the presence of two-person thinking in this one extratherapeutic context has subtly created a misleading impression that two-person thinking has become the general framework for thinking about personality dynamics for object relations and, more generally, relational thinkers.

Maroda (1999), for example, sets the stage for her valuable discussion of clinical work from a relational standpoint by stating that "as the two-person psychologies take hold, *with their emphasis on early mother–child formative interaction* [italics added], analysis struggles to redefine itself" (p. 2). Note here the almost casual equating of two-person psychology and early mother–child interaction.[5] Similarly, Mitchell (1995) comments that the most significant feature of post-Kleinian British object relations theorizing is "the importance it places on the environment—on the crucial significance of the interactions between the infant and caretakers and the crucial significance of the interactions . . . between the analysand and the analyst" (p. 78). These are two realms in which, indeed, many object relations theorists apply an interactive, two-person perspective. But notice that Mitchell's comment, like Maroda's, *does not* refer to the other realms of the person's life, to the thousands upon thousands of interactions that occur *outside* of the mother–infant or patient–therapist relationships. In the interactions of older children with peers or teachers, or of adults with everyone from bosses, subordinates, and coworkers to friends, neighbors, parking attendants, or their children's teachers, life is *filled* with two-person, mutually constructed experiences (or, again, to formulate things in a more fully satisfactory way, with contextually responsive, mutually constructed experiences); yet the object relations literature has little to say about these experiences and often views them as mere *reflections* of already existing "internal" object relations rather than as the product of the kinds of bidirectional cyclical processes discussed in Chapter 1.

As I have put it elsewhere in discussing this omission,

> The expanse between infancy and analysis becomes a kind of "excluded middle," *seemingly* addressed by a theory that stresses relationships and "the environment," but in fact largely neglected. That is, while the experiences of everyday life are, of course, discussed and attended to by relational theorists, they are often viewed primarily as the context for *revealing* or *expressing* what is already "inside," rather than as a realm in which— just as in analysis or infancy—mutuality, co-construction, and reciprocal causation is the focus of concern. . . . Although the mother–infant relationship and the relationship between patient and analyst are thoroughly probed in relational theorizing for bi-directional processes of mutual influence and mutual construction of experience, the ways in which such processes characterize *all* of life tend to be far less thoroughly explored.

---

[5]Like many relational writers, Maroda (1999) also emphasized, elsewhere in her book, the two-person nature of the patient–therapist relationship as well.

Concepts such as internalization, developmental level, and developmental arrest direct attention inward, to tendencies that are implicitly treated as more or less context-free properties of the single individual. (P. L. Wachtel, 2008, pp. 56–57)

In citing quotations from Maroda and from Mitchell, I have taken pains not to be dealing with straw men or women. Both are prominent relational thinkers (Mitchell, indeed, could be viewed as the single most important originator of the relational point of view), and both are writers whose overall contributions and perspectives I greatly admire and whose clinical and theoretical positions actually overlap with my own in many respects. The intent of both Maroda and Mitchell was certainly not in any explicit fashion to exclude consideration of the role of two-person thinking in the rest of life. Indeed, Mitchell's (1988) critical discussions of the "metaphor of the baby" and the "developmental tilt" in psychoanalytic writings overlap substantially with the points I have been making in this and the preceding chapter. Rather, my intention in citing these two quotations (there are many others which I could also have included) is to show how readily, and without real reflection, the two-person focus that is indeed widely evident in the object relations and relational literatures in discussing *the therapy interaction* or the interaction *between mother and infant* can be confused with a more thoroughgoing two-person point of view that encompasses the rest of life as well.

From One-Person to Two-Person Thinking in the Consulting Room: The Contribution of Merton Gill

Further clarity regarding the ways in which the two-person perspective has been largely restricted to the realms of the patient–therapist and mother–infant interactions, and largely absent in discussions of the rest of the person's life, may be gained by looking more closely at the evolution and applications of two-person thinking in these two specific realms. As is implicit in what I have already discussed, the realm in which two-person thinking about the nature of personality dynamics has been most extensively applied is within the psychotherapy session. It was here that the epistemological problems with the one-person point of view were first clearly articulated; but it is important to notice that within this specific realm many relational thinkers also recognized (as they did not in other realms) that the *causal dynamics* that shape behavior and personal experience were two-person in nature as well. That is, it became clear (and was indeed almost inseparable from the epistemological point) that the patient's experience was not just a function of the "internal" dynamics that he brought to the session. His experience in the session was understood as *a response to what was actually occurring*, even while it *also* was a valuable guide to the patient's dynamics and to the unconscious dimensions of his psychological organizing processes (e.g., Aron, 1996; Gill, 1982; Hoffman, 1998; P. L. Wachtel, 2008).

The way in which this view evolved as the psychoanalytic vision began to shift from a one-person understanding of the events taking place in the session to a two-person understanding is especially clearly illustrated in the writings of Merton Gill. Gill was for many years one of the leading thinkers in the Freudian or ego psychological branch of psychoanalytic thought, but he subsequently became one of the leading figures in shifting psychoanalysis toward a two-person perspective that critiqued some of the very views he had earlier championed. The shifts in his own thinking thus capture especially well the core assumptions of both points of view and the way in which psychoanalytic thought evolved over time. In 1954, Gill offered one of the most influential and clearly stated articulations of what, in retrospect, one would call the one-person point of view.

> The clearest transference manifestations are those which recur when the analyst's behavior is constant, since under these circumstances changing manifestations in the transference *cannot be attributed to an external situation, to some changed factor in the interpersonal relationship* [italics added], but the analysand must accept responsibility himself. (Gill, 1954, p. 781)

In contrast, several decades later, Gill articulated some of the sharpest critiques of this position. In part, these critiques were from the vantage point of therapeutic technique. In this respect, one of Gill's main points in his later work is that acknowledging that the patient's experience does have something to do with what is actually going on *does not* preclude the patient's understanding his own role in how things have proceeded or in how he has experienced what has proceeded. Indeed, Gill argued, such acknowledgment, which is both more respectful toward the patient *and* a more accurate statement of the complex intersubjective processes going on in the room, *makes it easier* to promote the patient's engagement in exploring the contribution of his own unconscious assumptions and organizing processes in generating his experience of the transaction. This is the case because instead of utterly denying the patient's experience and treating it as a distortion deriving solely from the past, the two-person perspective regards the patient's experience as *both* a response to what is actually transpiring in the room *and* reflective of his deeply held assumptions, whose developmental roots and potentially problematic implications remain important to explore.

Thus Gill states that

> because analysis takes place in an interpersonal context there is no such thing as non-interaction. Silence is of course a behaviour too. . . . It may be intended to be neutral but silence too can be plausibly experienced as anything ranging from cruel inhumanity to tender concern. It is not

possible to say that any of these attitudes is necessarily a distortion. (Gill, 1984, p. 168)

Then, explicitly addressing the issue of whether the therapist's acknowledging her own role in what transpired aids or impedes the process of exploration, and the change in atmosphere when the patient's experience is not dismissed or reduced solely to a transferential response deriving solely from the past, he goes on to say,

> The change in atmosphere is one from the patient being wrong and misguided to one in which his point of view is given initial consideration. In other words his rational capacity is respected rather than belittled. It is in such an atmosphere, after his point of view has been acknowledged, that he is more likely to be willing to look for his own contribution to his experience. The position is of course contrary to the one which argues that to acknowledge the rationality of the patient's point of view is to confirm his belief that his experience is fully accounted for by the current behaviour of the analyst. (Gill, 1984, p. 173)

Here, in this explicit challenge to the argument that he himself put forth in his 1954 article, quoted earlier, we may see that the move toward a two-person perspective regarding the epistemological status of the knowledge achieved in the session was accompanied by related shifts in the understanding both of therapeutic technique and of personality dynamics. Gill, first as a prominent exponent of the one-person view and then as a leading figure in challenging that view, illustrated and articulated the broader implications of this new point of view. The individual was no longer seen as a system unto himself, with the causes of his behavior and experience strictly internal, but as a person living in the world and responsive to events as they occur—responding to their actuality, as Gill (1979) put it in another influential article. But at the same time, because we always respond to events *as we experience them*, rather than via some godlike "objective" understanding of what has "really" transpired, the patient's experience reflects as well the affective, motivational, and perceptual schemas through which he makes sense of the world.

Moreover, the relation between the events occurring and the schemas via which we grasp them and respond to them is bidirectional. For each individual, those schemas reflect his or her unique developmental history; each of us has somewhat different experiences growing up, and hence our psychological structures and the contents of our inner world have their own unique nature. But at the same time, although the succession of experiences shapes our personal and interpersonal schemas, the evolving schemas also shape the succession of experiences. That is, it is through the schemas that the events take on psychological meaning, and it is through the schemas that behaviors are generated that evoke particular responses from others. With different life experiences, our affective, behavioral, and motivational schemas would be different. But with different affective, behavioral, and motivational schemas, our life experiences would be different. We would behave differently, perceive differently, and evoke different behaviors from others. The two sources of our behavior and experience are thoroughly intertwined. As Gill has put it, in a formulation that very much parallels the cyclical psychodynamic point of view described in Chapter 1,[6]

> The individual sees the world not only as his intrapsychic patterns dictate, but also as he veridically assesses it. Furthermore, the two kinds of determinants mutually influence each other. The intrapsychic patterns not only determine selective attention to those aspects of the external world which conform to them, but the individual behaves in such a way as to enhance the likelihood that the responses he meets will indeed confirm the views with which he sets out. This external validation in turn is necessary for the maintenance of those patterns. *It is this last insight that psychoanalytic theory often ignores, postulating instead an internal pressure to maintain the intrapsychic patterns without significant reference to the external world* [italics added]. (Gill, 1982, p. 92)

Gill's observations and reformulations have been very largely incorporated into the relational view of what transpires in the psychoanalytic session. But it is important to note that their applicability is by no means limited to that setting. In principle, they point to a more adequate and comprehensive account of how people function in every sector of their lives. As I noted earlier, however, in much of the relational literature this perspective is not very evident in discussions of the patient's day to day experience outside the consulting room. The dynamics that *first* shaped the person's schemas, as they evolved in the earliest years of life, are frequently depicted as bidirectional and reciprocal in nature; but once the person grows beyond infancy, he is primarily discussed (again with the one exception of behavior and experience inside the psychotherapy session) as "expressing" his "internal" structures rather than as continuing to be part of a causal nexus in which the *mutual* impact of people on each other creates cyclical feedback loops that are an essential contributor to any consistencies in personality that are observed (cf. P. L. Wachtel, 1994, 2008).

The Nursery as the Second Isolated Realm of Two-Person Theorizing

As I have noted earlier, the presence of a second realm, in addition to the consulting room, in which two-person thinking is also widely evident in the

---

[6]In personal conversations, Gill commented to me that reading my first book, *Psychoanalysis and Behavior Therapy* (P. L. Wachtel, 1977b), and particularly its discussion of the light shed on the concept of transference by Piaget's concepts of schemas, assimilation, and accommodation (see also P. L. Wachtel, 1980), contributed to his shift toward a two-person perspective. In turn, his reformulations helped to further shape my own thinking on these issues.

relational literature, has contributed to obscuring the ways that two-person thinking has been *absent* in discussions of the rest of the person's life. The way that personality is shaped in the earliest years of life by the bidirectional transactions between mother and infant has been a prominent interest of relational theorists for some time; to many it is one of the defining features of relational theorizing (see, e.g., the quotation from Maroda. 1999, cited earlier in this chapter). The scope of this interest includes research on the process of attachment, the mutual cuing that creates the rhythms of interaction between mother and infant,[7] and a range of other aspects of the bidirectional co-construction of experience between infant and caregiver (e.g., Beebe & Lachmann, 2002, 2003; Cohen & Tronick, 1988; Jaffe, Beebe, Feldstein, Crown, & Jasnow, 2001; D. N. Stern, 1985; Tronick, 1989). In this arena, there is a strong prevailing emphasis on the way that the two parties to the interaction shape each other's behavior and experience and on the responsiveness of each to the other and, more broadly, to the ever-changing context within which experience unfolds. The enduring and often highly structured characteristics of both parties are taken into account in this work—even babies come quickly to have very identifiable personalities and individual proclivities—but the understanding is that what transpires is not sufficiently explainable by the "internal" or "internalized" characteristics of either party alone. Rather, the model is a fairly thoroughgoing two-person model, and as with the model of the therapeutic interaction, it readily resolves the only apparent tension between, on the one hand, an emphasis on personal qualities and enduring characteristics and inclinations and, on the other, the continuing influence of the contexts in which those characteristics are manifested, shaped, maintained, or changed.[8]

In contrast to discussions of the two realms of infancy and therapy, however, many discussions in the relational literature of that vast area of living between the nursery and the consulting room reflect much less of a two-person point of view. Here the more traditional psychoanalytic vocabulary and conceptual repertoire of internal states and forces "playing themselves out" is much more common. The patient's difficulties later in life are seen as *reflecting* the already internalized psychological structures that evolved in infancy or in rather early childhood. That is, in addressing the day-to-day experiences that have brought the patient to therapy or the nature of the enduring characteristics that constitute his unique personality, there is much less attention to co-construction or to the ways in which, as discussed in Chapter 1, people

---

[7]Obviously this work on infancy and early childhood has relevance for interactions with caretakers other than the mother, but the preponderance of the research has focused on the mother.
[8]See, regarding the evidence for and the broader implications of these reciprocal processes, P. L. Wachtel (1973, 1977a, 1980, 1994) and Wachtel, Kruk, and McKinney (2005).

are drawn in as accomplices to the person's dominant patterns of behavior, experience, and interaction.

Between the two "anchor points" of two-person theorizing—the nursery and the consulting room—lies the "excluded middle" I referred to earlier, a realm in which essentially one-person thinking still reigns. When it comes to descriptions of the patient's personality patterns in daily life or of the causes of the difficulties they bring to therapy to work on, there often remains an insufficiently examined assumption that the problem lies "within," deep down and buried. As Mitchell (1988) has described it in critiquing the developmental arrest model that is widespread in object relations thinking, it is true that frequently the *early* experience of the child is treated as dyadic and interactive, but at a certain point, emotional growth is seen as "arrested," and once that happens an understanding that had been dyadic regarding the earliest stages of life becomes "largely monadic" thenceforth. In this monadic conception, which Mitchell notes is shared by a wide range of psychoanalytic thinkers, "Infantile needs become frozen and static; the deepest, most significant psychological recesses of the personality become isolated, buffered from new elements in the interpersonal field. . . . Relational configurations established through interaction become invariant, with inherent forces shaping all subsequent experience." (p. 131)

In elaborating on an alternative to this conceptualization, Mitchell (1988) provides an excellent illustration of what a more thoroughgoing two-person—or, better, contextual—conception of personality dynamics looks like. In an account that has much in common with the cyclical psychodynamic view guiding the clinical work presented in this book, Mitchell offers an implicit critique of some of the key assumptions that often underlie relational theorizing:

> I do not believe that interpersonal interactions are merely an "enactment" of a more psychologically fundamental world of internal object relations or "representations," nor do I believe that subjective experience is merely a recording of actual interpersonal transactions. *The most useful way to view psychological reality is as operating within a relational matrix which encompasses both intrapsychic and interpersonal realms.* (p. 9)

BEHAVIOR AND EXPERIENCE IN CONTEXT: TOWARD A CONVERGENCE OF PSYCHOANALYTIC AND BEHAVIORAL PERSPECTIVES

I wish now to consider how the two-person (or, as I have suggested is preferable, contextual) perspective creates a more differentiated understanding of personality and its dynamics and, in the process, contributes to the project of reconciling the observations deriving from psychoanalytic work and those that have been the focus of cognitive–behavioral and systemic observers.[9] Central to enabling the virtues of each of these approaches to be brought together in a coherent fashion is recognizing that the attention given in the psychoanalytic tradition to the complexities of the patient's inner world need not entail ignoring the powerful influence of the situational or systemic context, an influence that has been amply demonstrated by therapists and researchers from both the cognitive–behavioral and systemic traditions. The inner world is best understood as a *contextual* inner world. That is, the configuration of perceptual, motivational, and affective inclinations that gives shape and direction to our experience and behavior is, by its very nature, responsive to the events around us rather than hermetically sealed off from those events, as it sometimes appears to be through a psychoanalytic lens. This alternative perspective on the observations that have accrued from psychoanalytic observation has been gaining strength rapidly in recent years, as psychoanalytic writers who, to varying degrees, view the inner world as contextual and responsive rather than sealed off have presented important challenges to older forms of psychoanalytic theory and practice. These new versions of psychoanalytic thought point, potentially, both to the integration of psychoanalytic ideas with the broader stream of thinking and research on the therapeutic process and to a conception of personality that transcends the pathocentric and overly internal vision that dominated psychoanalytic thinking for so long and was often confused with its essence (see P. L. Wachtel, 1997, 2008).

Forebears of this newer psychoanalytic approach had already articulated many decades ago a version of psychoanalytic thought in which the person's responsiveness to the events around him (and the consequent variability in his behavior and experience from context to context) was integrated into the psychoanalytic perspective itself. Sullivan's interpersonal theory (e.g., Sullivan, 1947, 1953) is perhaps the most thoroughgoing example of a psychoanalytic perspective that is rooted in our responsiveness to the interpersonal or relational field in which we are embedded. Interpersonal analysts did not ignore unconscious motivation, conflicts, or fantasies (though they were often misunderstood as doing so), but they placed these intrapsychic phenomena in a context and emphasized the way that the person could only be properly understood by understanding him in relation to those with whom he was interacting. These interactions were simultaneously shaped by the joint participation of each person concretely behaving in relation to the other and by the "personifications," based on past experiences and idiosyncratic constructions of their meaning, that colored each party's perception of the other—and of himself (Sullivan, 1953).

---

[9]In the next section, I also consider how this more differentiated understanding enables us to avoid pathologizing and to ground the therapeutic work in the patient's strengths as well as his difficulties.

Unfortunately, Sullivan was given to rhetorical excesses in the battle to introduce an interpersonal or contextual emphasis in a psychoanalytic world that viewed the intrapsychic as a kind of lost continent quite apart from the world of everyday transactions with others. As part of this rhetorical disposition, he referred to "the illusion of unique individuality" (Sullivan, 1950), a phrasing that made the caricaturing of interpersonal views as easy as shooting fish in a barrel. Thus, although the interpersonal perspective highlighted how a consistent patterning could be seen even while *also* attending to the significant variability in behavior and experience from one interpersonal context to another, the interpersonal perspective was viewed by the psychoanalytic mainstream as alternative to, and even opposed to, the study of the intrapsychic, to which most analysts were strongly committed. As a consequence, for many years the interpersonal perspective was very largely marginalized in the psychoanalytic world.

This marginalization of the interpersonal point of view, reflecting biases and misconceptions that were broadly shared by psychoanalytic thinkers, contributed to maintaining a number of problematic features of mainstream psychoanalytic thought as it was understood at the time. In particular, the failure to incorporate the interpersonalists' important observations of our responsiveness to the varying relational contexts of our lives perpetuated the conception of an inner world that was very largely sealed off from the world of everyday experience. This contributed to viewing the examination of the patient's daily interactions with other people—apart from the analyst—as a relatively "superficial" activity (see Boston Change Process Study Group, 2007; P. L. Wachtel, 2003), which in turn impeded access to the very observations that would have demonstrated just how consequential the interactions of daily living actually are.

More recently, the interpersonal perspective has gained greater influence, as an important component of the broader *relational* point of view. A number of the leading figures in the relational movement, starting with Mitchell (1988; Greenberg and Mitchell, 1983), and including other major contributors to the relational literature such as D. B. Stern (1997) and Bromberg (1998a), have begun their explorations from an interpersonal base and, no longer writing in isolation from the psychoanalytic mainstream, have extended the interpersonal perspective through dialogue with and assimilation of other points of view in the psychoanalytic spectrum. The cyclical psychodynamic perspective that guides the work presented in this book also is an expansion of a point of view that had its original foundation largely in interpersonal theory and later became a part of the broader relational synthesis (cf. P. L. Wachtel, 1977b, 2008). Cyclical psychodynamic theory, however, further extends the process of theoretical assimilation and accommodation by integrating the interpersonal perspective not only with other theoretical perspectives within the psychoanalytic spectrum but also with ideas and modes of practice deriving from cognitive–behavioral, systemic, and experiential approaches.

A different early source of contextual thinking in psychoanalysis was offered by Erikson (e.g., 1950), whose political identifications in the psychoanalytic world were quite different from Sullivan's but whose ideas were in many respects equally marginalized. The marginalization of Erikson, however, was "polite" and almost invisible. Whereas interpersonal theory was largely treated as "other" by mainstream analysts, and fairly explicitly refuted and rejected, Erikson's theoretical perspective was treated with great respect but largely ignored in the actual evolution of psychoanalytic thought and practice over the decades following its introduction to the literature. Associated with the then prevailing ego psychological version of psychoanalytic thought, someone who had known Freud personally and was analyzed by his daughter Anna, Erikson would seem to have been a figure well situated to introduce contextual thinking into the psychoanalytic mainstream. Although Erikson was as attentive as Sullivan, Horney (e.g., 1937, 1939, 1945, 1950), or Fromm (e.g., 1941, 1956) to the powerful role of culture in shaping the evolving personality, he was not labeled a "culturalist" as they were and was not dismissed by mainstream analysts as ignoring Freud's "hard-won" insights regarding the powerful role of unconscious instinctual drives. Erikson, rather, approached the contextualization of psychoanalytic insights by offering a reconfigured vision of the drives themselves, presenting his revised theory as but a minor renovation of the fundamental Freudian structure and organizing his account of personality around the standard Freudian stages (Erikson, 1950). What this mode of presentation effectively concealed was the genuinely radical nature of Erikson's revision. No less than Sullivan, Erikson presented a *contextualized* psychoanalysis, in which the individual's character, behavior, or experience could not adequately be described without reference to the context—both personal and cultural—in which it was manifested and in which, therefore, the *variability* of behavior and experience in relation to varying contexts was clearly highlighted.

Indeed, the concept for which Erikson is most often cited—identity—highlights that very variability. To many readers, identity was a concept that stressed the *coherence* of the personality, the ways in which we felt *the same* from situation to situation, in which we managed to infuse a sense of "I-ness," of our particular vision of ourselves, into every facet of our experience. And in one sense this is true. The concept of identity *is* about coherence. But it is a *constructed* coherence, a sense of coherence *in the face of great variability*. Identity is important not because we are always the same—if we were, we would scarcely think about our identities, nor would Erikson have concerned himself with the concept. It is precisely because we can be so different in different contexts that we need to ask ourselves "who am I?"[10]

A similar attention to the variability of behavior and experience from context to context—as well as to the tendency to construct a subjective sense of sameness out of what is in fact very considerable variability—was emphasized by Mischel (1968) in a work that in most other respects could not have differed more from Erikson's outlook and sensibility. Writing from the standpoint of social learning theory and advocating the therapeutic methods of behavior therapy as an alternative to psychoanalysis, Mischel rooted his arguments not, as Erikson did, in observations of people engaged in the most meaningful activities and struggles of their lives and in the social and cultural settings that were of the very greatest importance to them but in observations that derived primarily from laboratory research and that focused primarily on behavior that is an *analog* of the most important experiences of our lives rather than behavior representative of those experiences themselves (see P. L. Wachtel, 1973b, 1977a).

Mischel's (1968) book was highly influential, and he made a strong empirical case for personality being characterized by much greater variability from situation to situation than had been commonly assumed both by psychoanalytic thinkers and by trait theorists whose work derived from measures such as the California Psychological Inventory (CPI) and the Minnesota Multiphasic Personality Inventory (MMPI). I experienced his arguments as important and was indeed intrigued by them, but I also approached them with a good deal of skepticism. The skepticism derived from what I viewed as a biased and misleading depiction of the essentials of psychoanalytic thought and its evidential foundations (P. L. Wachtel, 1973b). But as I further immersed myself in Mischel's arguments, I began to be struck both by the weight of the evidence he presented and—to my surprise—by the ways in which Mischel's *critique* of psychoanalysis converged with the *version* of psychoanalysis that had increasingly begun to characterize my own thought. Although I continued to view Mischel's presentation of the psychodynamic point of view as problematically tendentious and his account of the role of situations, at least in that initial presentation, exaggeratedly one-sided (see Bowers, 1973; Magnusson & Endler, 1977; P. L. Wachtel, 1973a, 1973b), I nonetheless found much in his book that was trenchant and stimulating. In particular, in his emphasis on attending to the ways our behavior and experience *varied* from context to context, he had called my attention more focally to phenomena and experiences that had been

---

[10]I do not intend to imply here that the question "who am I?"—or its answer—is necessarily conscious. Erikson, a psychoanalyst after all, was largely concerned with processes that go on out of awareness, though they ultimately powerfully shape the individual's subjective experience.

silently shaping my own evolving theoretical perspective—including my preferences for certain versions of psychoanalytic thought over others—for a number of years. In important respects, the confrontation with Mischel's social learning approach ended up clarifying to me the nature of my own *psychoanalytic* thinking and sparked an interest in thinking about how to reconcile my evolving psychoanalytic views and the challenging alternative point of view that Mischel's book brought so forcefully to my attention. In both respects, what emerged was the cyclical psychodynamic perspective that underlies the clinical work presented in this book.

At first, my integrative efforts built primarily on the interpersonal tradition and on the contextualized version of ego psychology represented by Erikson's work. In attempting to further expand my theoretical perspective so that it could incorporate at the same time the observations at the heart of the psychoanalytic perspective and those that were central to behavioral and systemic approaches, I found, as noted in Chapter 1, that an understanding in terms of vicious circles was a key to the integrative effort. In this, I drew inspiration from the ideas of Karen Horney (e.g., 1939, 1945), whose much underappreciated work powerfully illuminates how people get trapped in self-perpetuating cycles that form the real bridge between past and present. I did not yet think of my evolving integrative theory as an instance of the *relational* point of view because at the time I began my integrative reformulations, an explicitly labeled relational psychoanalytic perspective did not yet exist. The two books that were probably most influential in initiating the conceptualization of a distinctly relational point of view in psychoanalysis, Greenberg and Mitchell's (1983), *Object Relations in Psychoanalytic Theory* and Mitchell's (1988) *Relational Concepts in Psychoanalysis*, appeared only some time *after* my first critique of Mischel's characterization of psychoanalysis (P. L. Wachtel, 1973a) and my first full-scale effort at integrating psychoanalytic and behavioral viewpoints (P. L. Wachtel, 1977b), which, in essence, marked the beginning of the cyclical psychodynamic point of view.

Initially, even after the emergence of a relational movement in psychoanalytic thought, the development of my own approach to psychoanalytic theorizing and its integration with other theoretical perspectives in our field proceeded largely separate from, and in parallel to, the evolution of the relational movement. But as the relational viewpoint came increasingly to my attention, I was struck by the ways in which I and the writers in the relational tradition had built our theoretical formulations on similar foundations in a number of respects. As I immersed myself in the literature of relational psychoanalysis, it became clearer that in fact "relational theory" was best understood as an umbrella term, encompassing a *range* of theories that overlapped in important ways but also differed in ways that were important and interesting. From this vantage point, and with an interest in the fertile new ideas emerging out of this complex set of interacting perspectives, I began increasingly to view my own cyclical psychodynamic theory from the perspective of the relational point of view and to become interested in both the ways in which cyclical psychodynamic theory shared key assumptions with other relational theories and the ways in which it diverged from them (P. L. Wachtel, 2008). Out of the complex experience of being part of *both* the relational movement, with its focus on integrating a spectrum of *psychoanalytic* viewpoints, and the psychotherapy integration movement, with its attention to the full range of contemporary perspectives on the therapeutic process, emerged the theoretical perspective that guides the work presented in this book. At this point it is appropriate to call this perspective either *cyclical psychodynamic therapy* or *integrative relational psychotherapy;* they essentially come down to the same thing.

MULTIPLE SELF-STATES AND THE CONVERGING EMPHASIS ON ACCEPTANCE IN PSYCHOANALYTIC, COGNITIVE–BEHAVIORAL, SYSTEMIC, AND EXPERIENTIAL THERAPIES

I wish now to discuss a second, and equally important, way in which the more differentiated understanding of personality dynamics afforded by the two-person or contextual perspective contributes to our understanding of the therapeutic process and to its effectiveness. In addition to providing a path toward facilitating the integration of the major theoretical approaches in our field, the understanding that derives from a contextual perspective also enables the therapist to see more clearly the patient's sometimes hidden or overlooked strengths and to build on those strengths in promoting therapeutic change.

In exploring this implication of the contextual point of view, it is again useful to recognize that similar understandings have emerged in different theoretical orientations but have been obscured by different theoretical terminologies and by the differing phenomena and methodological preferences emphasized by each. In my immersion in the relational literature and in the writing of my book on relational theory (P. L. Wachtel, 2008), I was struck by the tendency on the part of many relational writers to emphasize the concept of dissociation (e.g., Bromberg, 1996, 2003; Davies, 1996; Howell, 2006; D. B. Stern, 2003, 2004), a concept that, except for the Sullivanian branch of psychoanalytic thought, had been largely cast aside by psychoanalytic writers for many years (Berman, 1981; Dimen, 2004; Loewenstein & Ross, 1992). In emphasizing dissociation (usually in a fashion that did not completely reject the concept of repression, but which definitely removed it from its role at the center of the psychoanalytic point of view—see Chapter 1, this volume), these writers also reconfigured the psychoanalytic conceptualization of the structure of personality. Whereas the psychoanalytic model had previously been characterized by a largely vertical image of the structure of personality, with some phenomena at "the surface" and others "deeper" (Boston Change Process Study Group, 2007; P. L. Wachtel, 2003, 2008), the model that emerges from giving a greater role to dissociation both evokes and derives from a rather different set of images and assumptions. Rather than the vertically organized "archaeological" model of surface and depths, the dissociation model points to multiple modes and organizations of experience, each of which, at different times, can be dominant, generative of interpersonal behavior, experienced as genuine expressions of the self, and describable as on the "surface"—and each of which can, at other times and in other contexts, be dissociated, *out-of-awareness*, and hidden by the very appearance of what was previously submerged or latent.[11]

In more extreme forms (even short of a full-blown dissociative identity disorder), the dissociation may be such that the person very largely disavows as "not-me," or becomes very largely unaware of, the aspect of himself that was manifest just a short while before. But more often, the shift amounts to the changes in mood, focus, sense of self, and sense of what is appropriate with which we are all familiar. The processes and phenomena of dissociation, whereby some aspect of our experience or way of being in the world becomes at least temporarily inaccessible, overlap in important ways with processes and phenomena more familiar to and emphasized by social psychologists and social learning theorists. Research deriving from these latter perspectives highlights the ways in which our behavior and experience change from one context to another as the cues and demands of different social and interpersonal contexts are registered through our individual proclivities, rooted both in genetic/temperamental variables and in prior experiences and the interpretations and meanings we have given to them. Much as Erikson has discussed in relation to identity, sometimes these shifts can all be incorporated within a flexible and expansive (yet simultaneously relatively stable) sense of self, and at other times the contradictions and incompatibilities between these different ways of being, feeling, and acting become painful to bear, and the appearance of one state of mind renders the other almost impossible to consciously access.

The conceptualization in terms of dissociation—in contrast to the repression model, in which some aspects of self-experience and self-organization are permanently rendered subjectively unacceptable and inaccessible to

---

[11] See also Apfelbaum (2005), writing on the fluidity of defending and defended-against inclinations and psychological organizations from a somewhat different vantage point.

consciousness[12] (even while they may continue, without awareness, to affect our responses to the life circumstances we encounter)—is more compatible with the premises of social learning theory and the findings of social psychological research and contemporary cognitive–affective science (Bargh, 2006; Cacioppo & Berntson, 1992; Cacioppo, Berntson, Sheridan, & McClintock, 2000; Hassin, Uleman, & Bargh, 2005), as well as closer to the facts of clinical observation. Even Freud, the great champion of the concept of repression (recall his statement that repression was the very "cornerstone" of psychoanalysis) and of the archaeological model, with its vision of material that is permanently buried beneath layers of defenses, noted that

> forgetting impressions, scenes or experiences nearly always reduces itself to shutting them off [translated in the Basic Books edition of his Collected Papers, where I first read the passage, as "dissociation" of them]. When the patient talks about these "forgotten" things he seldom fails to add: "As a matter of fact I've always known it; only I've never thought of it." He often expresses disappointment at the fact that not enough things come into his head that he can call "forgotten"—that he has never thought of since they happened. (Freud, 1914/1957, p. 148)

In the relational psychoanalytic literature, the phenomena of dissociation are very frequently discussed in relation to the depiction of multiple self-states, different states of mind and organizations of experience that appear more or less alternatively and in dissociation from each other (e.g., Bromberg, 1998a; Burton, 2005; Davies, 1996, 1998; Harris, 1996; Pizer, 1996; Slavin, 1996; D. B. Stern, 2003). Although this theoretical language may appear radically different from the language of social learning theories or family systems theories, in fact there are important convergences among the phenomena these differing conceptualizations are designed to address. In order for these potential convergences to be realized, however (and in order for the multiple self-states conceptualization to fully realize its potential), the shift from one self-state to another must be understood contextually. That is, it must be understood not just as a "spontaneous" shift from "within" but as a response to changed circumstances.

It is important to be clear, however, that those circumstances are by no means limited to what are usually described as "external" events or variables. In referring to "circumstances," I include the person's current affective state and

---

[12] It must be noted that the concept of repression does include the observation that repression can be variable, with particular experiences being accessible at one moment and inaccessible the next (Freud, 1915/1959). But the *direction* or *structure* is seen as more or less stable. That is, although the degree or intensity of defensive efforts may vary, the "vertical" or archaeological structure remains. What is on the surface and what is buried, what is the repressing agency and what is the repressed, is not viewed as readily reversing in the way that it is in conceptualizations of dissociation.

conscious and unconscious thoughts and perceptions, all of which are part of the context that contributes to a shift to a different psychological configuration, which in turn affects what thoughts, perceptions, and affects then come to the fore. Moreover, apropos the cyclical and recursive causal structure I have been emphasizing throughout, the "circumstances" must also be understood very centrally in terms of the overall relational and personal context—the product of the continual back and forth between the individual's actions and subjective experience and the responses those actions and the accompanying affect evoke in others.

With this expanded meaning of "circumstances" in mind, we may say that in understanding changes in self-state as a response to *what is going on*, one both gains a more refined and differentiated understanding of those alternating self-states and approaches them as meaningful rather than arbitrary. That is, the person is not just manifesting *shifting* or *multiple* self-states but *meaningful* self-states, states of psychological organization that are in response to events and experiences in the person's life, and that therefore are not just indicators of psychopathology but manifestations of his way of adapting to the continually varying experiences of daily life. This emphasis on the meaningfulness and responsiveness of the person's varied states of psychological organization, it should be clear, facilitates the attitude of acceptance that I discussed as a crucial element of effective psychotherapy in Chapter 1.

Viewed in this fashion, the concept of multiple self-states introduces a point of view with quite different implications for clinical practice from those of the archaeologically organized conceptions of repression and "depth." In place of the idea of a deep and hidden core that represents the more fundamental or "real" aspects of the personality, and a view of conscious experience and manifest behavior as superficial or as hiding or defending against the person's more genuine inclinations, the concept of multiple self-states suggests a rather different structure. It is certainly true that some of our experiences and our motivational and affective inclinations are more persistently treated as unacceptable and denied access to conscious elaboration. We do have faces we present to the world (and to ourselves) quite regularly and other aspects of ourselves that we consistently hide and need to be helped to reappropriate. But it is also important not to be so taken by this dimension that one overlooks (as psychoanalytic writers did for many years) that it is also the case that what is acceptable and accessible to consciousness and what is not may vary considerably depending on mood, social context, and what has more recently been referred to as *self-state*. The personality consists of many facets, many potential ways of experiencing self and other and of acting in the world, and even aspects of the self that most of the time are inaccessible and treated as "not-me" may at times be expressed and experienced quite directly, even if temporarily. When we enable the person to acknowledge and give voice to an aspect of himself that had previously been very largely kept out of his experience of self, we are not unearthing the "real" self that had been hidden by a false facade; we are making room for *another dimension* of the person, an aspect of his experience that is no less, but also no more important than those aspects with which he has long been familiar and which have formed the core of his sense of who he is.

To be sure, when conflict or dissociation is particularly intense, the appearance of any one facet may actively serve to obscure or mute or prevent awareness of others. Put differently, *at any given moment,* there may well be a "surface" and "depth" to experience, in the sense that certain features of the affective–cognitive–motivational processes shaping the person's behavior and experience are readily accessible to awareness and other features that are also operating at the same moment (recall the contemporary understanding of the brain as an organ characterized by parallel processing) may be only marginally accessible to consciousness or not accessible at all. Moreover, although some of this differentiation of conscious articulation is a result of "structural" features of brain functioning, some of it is a product of what are usually referred to as *defensive processes;* anxiety evoked by the arousal of certain inclinations or by awareness of that arousal initiates inhibitory processes that at times impede the further elaboration of an impending chain of behaviors and affective responses and at times merely impede conscious awareness of some of the *sources* of behavior that is nonetheless expressed (as when we behave aggressively toward someone we love without conscious acknowledgment that we are doing so). In the process of therapy, helping the person to make room for, to notice, and to integrate the marginalized aspects of experience—whether they are experiences that are marginalized only at the moment, as part of the organization of a particular self-state, or whether they are aspects of the personality that have been chronically and pervasively regarded as unacceptable and repeatedly rendered inaccessible to consciousness or to the evolving sense of self—is a central feature of good therapeutic work. But each of the variant manifestations of the personality that may appear—whether easily and regularly accessible to consciousness or whether requiring a good deal of therapeutic work to make accessible—is "real;" and each is important. Within the perspective I am elaborating here, one part of the person is not anointed as the "true self" with another denigrated as the "false self."

Among relational writers, Mitchell (1993) has been especially clear on this point. As he has put it, "deciding what is true and what is false when it comes to self is a tricky business" (p. 133). Mitchell does not reject the observations on which concepts such as false self and true self are based. Rather, he attempts to transcend the reified way in which this manner of conceptualizing the observations is often used and to shift the focus to the phenomenological experience of authenticity or inauthenticity. In referring to authenticity, however, he cautions that we are not "measuring our experience against some implicit standard, some preconceived idea of what is 'me'." Rather, he argues,

> The sense of authenticity is always a construction, and as a construction, it is always relative to other possible self-constructions at any particular time. . . . What may seem authentic in the context of one version of self may be quite inauthentic with respect to other versions. (p. 131)

Moreover, he notes, "There are . . . times that an action that seems inauthentic with respect to preceding experience becomes more authentic over time, as one grows into and fully identifies with a new possibility" (p. 131). I have noticed in my own work that patients not infrequently will experience the emergence of some new aspect of themselves—often a healthier, and even *wished-for* way of behaving or thinking—as "that's not really me" or as "not really being myself." In such instances, I sometimes find myself saying things like, "So it seems that sometimes you have to be a little more 'not like myself' in order to be more fully yourself."

What all of these considerations point to is a way of approaching people that is characterized by an emphasis on *acceptance*—on regarding all aspects of the person as in some way genuine and deserving to be understood. In this respect, the development I have been describing from within the theoretical framework of relational psychoanalysis converges with an evolving emphasis in the realm of cognitive–behavioral therapy, represented particularly by such writers as Linehan and Hayes (e.g., Hayes, Luoma, Bond, Masuda, & Lillis, 2006; Hayes, Strosahl, & Wilson, 1999; Linehan, 1993; Linehan & Dexter-Mazza, 2008; Swales & Heard, 2009). It converges as well with the work of systemic therapists who emphasize narrative redescription of problems and "solution-focused" approaches to therapeutic work (e.g.., de Shazer et al., 2007; Molnar & de Shazer, 1987; White & Epston, 1990). In my own clinical work, I often find it useful to say to the person some variant of "There is *another side* to you which is not being honored or acknowledged [or "which you have learned to view with fear or disdain" or "which you have felt you needed to reject and cast out"], but it is as important a part of you as the parts you are more comfortable allowing yourself to see."

This way of approaching the clinical work will be particularly evident in the first session with Louise, presented in Chapter 3 of this volume. It relates especially to the distinction that I have highlighted elsewhere (P. L. Wachtel, 1993, 2008) between the implications of the words *really* and *also* in the clinical dialogue. When the implicit (and indeed, sometimes even explicit) message to patients is that we are pointing to what they are "really" feeling, the implication is one of invalidating what they are feeling or experiencing at the moment or even the way they have long thought about themselves. When, in contrast, our comments are directed to what they may "also" be feeling—for example, "Perhaps you are *also* feeling that toward me" rather than suggesting that although the patient may be talking about some external figure, he is "really" referring to the transference—we are *adding* something to the picture. We are not invalidating the ways that the patient has already experienced or understood himself. We are conveying that there is *even more* to him than he has appreciated and that the new aspects of himself, which may have been frightening in the past, can be safely—and enrichingly—assimilated. The same holds when we say something like, "I hear that you feel a lot of love and gratitude toward your mother, but I also sense that you are angry at her as well for some of the things she has done," instead of some version that conveys that the loving feelings are a defense and that the patient "really" feels angry at his mother.

Thus we may see that attention to the variability in behavior and experience from context to context is not only a link between psychoanalytic conceptualizations and observations, especially as recently formulated in terms of multiple self-states, and the observations and emphases of cognitive–behavioral and systemic thinkers (including the early challenging analyses of Mischel, 1968, which first sparked my interest in developing a broader integrative model of psychotherapy). It is also an important foundation for finding and focusing on the patient's strengths and enabling him to feel more fully and comprehensively understood. A two-person or contextual point of view calls to our attention that any experience or psychological inclination is likely to be manifested in some contexts and not in others and to be manifested *in different ways* in different contexts. It highlights as well that other characteristics and inclinations—no less real or genuine expressions of who the person is—are likely to come to the fore in other contexts. From this vantage point, the patient's strengths are brought to our attention as readily as his difficulties and are enabled to be as central a foundation of the therapeutic effort. Put differently, the patient's strengths are very largely *manifested in* the variability of behavior and experience from one context to another. That is, what serves as a counterweight to the presenting problems and characterological difficulties that are likely to be what first attract the therapist's attention is the fact that those problems are not evident *all the time*. Even in so-called Axis II disorders, the traits and patterns that warrant an Axis II diagnosis are in fact not evident at every moment of the person's life. Much of the time, he or she may behave or may experience the world quite differently from what the diagnosis might suggest, and if these variations are viewed as important data in their own right rather than as a distraction from the "real" (that is, pathological) nature of the patient's personality organization, one is much more able to create a balanced picture of the personality and, as discussed in Chapter 1, to build on the kernels of strength that are always a part of the picture as well.

Consistent with the emphasis on the dialectic between acceptance and change that I have highlighted as a cutting edge development in both psycho-analytic and cognitive–behavioral approaches (e.g., Bromberg, 1998b; Hayes, Follette, & Linehan, 2004), a central feature of the theoretical and therapeutic approach illustrated in this book is the confrontation with the patient's difficulties in a way that is consistently respectful of her experience and personality and that sees in an empathic and clear-eyed way her pain and dysfunction without losing sight of her strengths. The discussion throughout will illustrate how the kinds of issues that therapists are often tempted to discuss in terms that emphasize "disorders" and "diagnoses" can be addressed fully and in depth while viewing and presenting the patient as the author of her own life—that is, as making meaningful and understandable choices in light of her prior experience, even when those choices are a source of the very difficulties she comes to therapy to resolve. The transcripts presented next provide an opportunity to illustrate this patient-affirming point of view as they also (alas and inevitably) illustrate the ways in which the therapist can at times slip from and fail to meet this ideal.

II

THE SESSIONS

3

LOUISE: SESSION 1

As I mentioned in the Preface, the sessions presented in this volume were conducted in a somewhat unusual setting. I had been invited to come to Chicago to tape a video of a session for the American Psychological Association psychotherapy video series, "Systems of Psychotherapy." The sessions were thus held not in my office but in a television studio on the campus of Governors State University. I had done a demonstration session in a television studio once before (Psychological & Educational Films, 1989), and I was aware that at least some anxiety would be an inevitable part of the experience. In taping a session intended to be sold to the public for training and research purposes, there was always, somewhere in the background, the knowledge that "anonymous" viewers would be making their own judgments about what I was doing and how well I did it.

In one sense, of course, one faces something similar every time one writes a book or article. Books are judged by readers and reviewers, and the author is vulnerable to the reviewer's take on what is written, whether positive or negative, insightful or reflective of misunderstanding or ideological bias. But at least with a book or article, one can go over multiple drafts until it feels—to the author, at least—like this version "gets it right." One can't control the judgment, but at least one can control the product being judged.

With a video of a session, in contrast, one loses control the moment either party says something and the unique cocreated, and ultimately unpredictable experience begins. The tape is rolling, and, unlike a Hollywood production, one cannot yell "cut" and stop the action and begin again. One is stuck with what is spontaneously happening in real time.

Even in a "good" session, this spontaneous evolution of the way that the patient and therapist interact with each other includes difficult moments, impasses, misunderstandings, "errors." An error-free therapy is not only an unrealizable fantasy but probably not even a therapeutically valuable process even if it were to occur. As a number of theorists and researchers have pointed out (e.g., Kohut, 1984; Ruiz-Cordell, & Safran, 2007; Safran & Muran, 2000; Safran, Muran, & Proskurov, 2009), much of what is growth enhancing in the process of psychotherapy is the occurrence of impasses, breaks in empathy, or "ruptures" in the therapeutic alliance and their repair through the therapist's sensitivity to these ruptures and the dialogue that ensues. The first part of the process, of course, requires no special skill on the therapist's part. Impasses, breaks in empathy, or ruptures occur naturally; they come unbidden and counter to the therapist's intention. But the second part of the process, the repair and working through, does indeed require both expertise and the kind of personality and sensitivity that distinguishes the good therapist from the poor or mediocre one. Our task is not to avoid mistakes, which we cannot do in any event, but to respond in a therapeutically facilitative way when we do, inevitably, make them. Notwithstanding this by now widely understood process of ruptures and repairs, videotaping a session that can be viewed by colleagues all around the country nonetheless puts one in a situation of vulnerability. The ruptures don't always get repaired in the same session that they occur, and so there is the prospect that the viewer will see the therapist's error without seeing his or her resolution of it. Consequently, there may be an almost inevitable inclination, in such a context, for the therapist (even if unconsciously) to work harder than she usually does to *avoid* making errors, an avoidance that can create a conservatism of technique that is not necessarily optimal. It is important for the reader to be alert to this possibility in reading the transcript, since the session did occur in this unusual context.

Another potential artifact of the particular circumstances under which this session was conducted is that it is possible that I moved *faster* than I usually do in a first session because the session was an opportunity to demonstrate "what I do." This was not something I did consciously during the session; my conscious experience was of following the patient's lead in the sense of not going any faster than she was comfortable with. But in discussing the session with my graduate students, to whom I showed the video in a class on therapeutic technique, they, at least, were struck by how much intervention there was in the course of just one (and, indeed, one *initial*) session. And in watching the session afterward on tape, although I did not see myself as going too fast or inter-vening too much (I operate from an integrative framework in which psycho-dynamic understanding and active intervention go hand in hand), I *was* struck by the degree to which this single session had a narrative arc that resembled in certain ways the narrative arc of an entire therapy. A *lot happened* in the session. I wondered if, without being aware of it, the fact that it was a teaching video led me to "show my wares," to try to demonstrate the range of ways I work and thus to pack more into the session than would ordinarily be typical for me in an initial session. I am not able to evaluate this myself; my subjective experience was of its being an organic response to the interactive dynamics between me and the patient. But I do want to mention this as a possibility in preparing the reader for the sessions that will appear in their entirety in this and the follow-ing chapters.

In some respects, these speculations also raise an interesting question about whether in a session whose pace and style were more typical of how I work, there is actually a tendency to do *too little*. That is, to the degree that valuable things happened in the session, perhaps for the very reason that I was (unconsciously) a bit more active in order to demonstrate the full range of ways I work, then perhaps in a more typical session I (and other therapists, too) am too inclined to "listen" rather than intervene, a bit too laid back and inclined to let the patient take the lead. On the other hand, there are also potential drawbacks in working this way. On the very day I was writing this introduc-tion to the chapter, one of my patients told me that I was working too hard to fix things and that I needed just to stay with her in the dark for a while before she could feel safe to move ahead. I did not "stay in the dark" very long with Louise or Melissa, the patients whose sessions I present here. Probably, under these specific circumstances, that was just as well—both for the purpose of cre-ating an interesting session for observers to view or read about *and* for these two patients, since they had come for a different kind of experience than some-one who comes for a long-term therapy.

In any event, it is important to bear in mind that whatever the specific characteristics of these sessions that make them in some ways distinctive, they are nonetheless "real" sessions, not staged representations. There have been demonstration sessions available for training in which professional actors improvised on a basic script, "creating" a patient for the therapist to interact with. Although there is value in such training materials as well, I think it is important to distinguish between them and the sessions presented in this book. In every sense, these were real patients. Louise and Melissa were not *playing* characters, they were *being* themselves. Their responses were not just genuine and spontaneous; they were *theirs*. Moreover, both Louise and Melissa were there seeking help. They were not "representing" a process; they were engaging in the process to get something for themselves. Each was struggling with a dilemma in her life, and each was having enough difficulty in resolving that dilemma that she thought that speaking to a therapist might be helpful.

To be sure, the "rules of engagement" were different than they are for most therapy. To begin with, there was a camera in the room. That "therapeutic third"[1] no doubt changes in certain ways both the experience of each party and the dynamics of what proceeds, and the ways in which it does change things cannot be readily evaluated. As I noted earlier, there no doubt *were* ways in which the presence of the camera and the knowledge that the videos would be available to students and colleagues influenced how I proceeded. This influence was not so much a conscious one in the sessions as an influence I became aware of in watching the videos later. In the actual experience of conducting the session, the presence of the cameras seemed to recede from consciousness remarkably rapidly. I was self-consciously aware of it as the session began, but—as happens in my own consulting room—my attention shifted rapidly and rather thoroughly to the person sitting opposite me. It was Louise and Melissa who were the focus of my attention, not the camera. How much something similar happened for Louise and Melissa is a matter that the reader will probably wish to evaluate for herself.[2] My own impression was that (again to a surprising degree) it seemed that they largely ignored the presence of the camera and proceeded as they might have without it being there. Perhaps this was added to by the fact that they wanted something from the sessions, that they were there to get something for themselves and were focused on that goal.

The other major departure from "typical" psychotherapy, of course, was that these were intended as single-session therapeutic encounters. There was no expectation of follow-up.[3] The intention was to accomplish whatever therapeutic goals we could within the constraints of this single session. Single-session encounters between patients and therapists are not that unusual, but they are most often construed as consultations rather than as psychotherapy per se. Their aim is usually either to assess the patient and her difficulties and make an appropriate referral or to help the patient gain some perspective on an ongoing therapy with someone else that has felt at an impasse. I am experienced in doing

---

[1] I am using here more loosely and metaphorically a term that has been used increasingly and influentially in recent years in the literature of relational psychoanalysis (e.g., Aron, 2006; Benjamin, 2004; Ogden, 1994, 2004). Although I intentionally use a term here that alludes to their conceptualization, I do not necessarily intend to bring into play the full theoretical apparatus implicit in these more elaborated discussions of the therapeutic third.

[2] Here those readers who have also seen the video will be in a better position to make their own judgment about this.

[3] As I discuss in Chapter 4, there was in fact an unanticipated second session with Louise, which is included in its entirety in that chapter.

both, and I can attest that these sessions felt different.[4] My aim in these sessions was not primarily one of evaluation per se (though, of course, careful evaluation is an ongoing part of *all* psychotherapy, especially at the beginning but in fact at all stages). Rather, my aim was, within the constraints created by the particular circumstances, to do as much *psychotherapy* as I possibly could. That is, my aim was, to the degree possible, to actually help the patient resolve some of her dilemmas and to engage in the process much as I would with the people I work with on a longer term basis.

In this and the following chapters, my comments are interwoven with the transcript, providing a running commentary on what is happening at various points in the session. I offer both my own experiences and thoughts about why I did or did not intervene in any particular way, as well as my impressions and evolving understanding of the patient. These are offered in the context of particular moments in the session, so that the reader can see how I am thinking at various points and how my understanding evolves and changes in the course of the session. This is in contrast with the more typical presentational style of offering a retrospective understanding at the end, derived from reflecting on the entire session. There are advantages to each mode of presentation. The latter way of presenting offers a more "polished" and comprehensive account based on all the data available to the therapist. What I am offering here is different, reflecting the particular aims of this book. My aim is to enable the reader to see what I was thinking and feeling at any given moment and how my perceptions changed over time—in part as new perspectives or new ideas occurred to me, in part as a consequence of the experience of *being with* the patient for a period of time, in part as a response to particular new events and revelations in the sessions, and in part as a result of what I said or did as a consequence of my *prior* perceptions. That is, I aim to enable the reader to see how the session as a whole evolves over time and how both my own perceptions and experiences and the patient's evolve in relation to the experience of the other and to what proceeds between us.

Some readers, however, may prefer to get their own sense of the session before considering what I have to say. To facilitate this alternative mode of reading, each of my interpolated comments is set in regular text and preceded

---

[4]The reader will notice, in reading through Session 1 with Louise, that she refers to currently being in therapy and to increasing the dosage of her antidepressant. She has thus been troubled enough about the issues she is dealing with both to seek therapy and to take medication. In one sense, that makes the session with me more like a "consultation" in the sense that I have just described. But I did not know that she was currently in therapy until she mentioned it. The ground rules for the filming of the video were that I walked into the room knowing nothing about her, just as would be the case when anyone first walks into my office. And I approached the entire session not as a consultation in the sense I referred to above, but as an attempt to offer *psychotherapy* (again, to the degree I could within the limits of a single-session encounter).

by a row of asterisks. If one reads down the page, attending only to paragraphs that are set in the indented dialogue style, it should be easy to just read the transcript alone and to return to my comments after you have formed your own impressions of the session.

THE SESSION

Louise: Hi.

Paul: Hi, Louise.

Louise: Hi.

Paul: So tell me a little bit about what brings you here today.

Louise: Basically I'm having, I'm struggling with my husband's family. And my dad passed away from cancer, he had term, he was diagnosed with terminal cancer last summer. And he passed away 6 months ago on May 7th. And I guess the problems I had with my husband's family prior to that came to a head. So that's basically why I'm here today.

* * * * *

Louise's opening statement is interesting in a number of respects. First of all, it alerts me to a potential feeling on Louise's part of being overwhelmed. In just two sentences, she mentions not just her struggle with her husband's family (which will be the central theme of the session) but also her father's death. There is thus a sense of a "double whammy" hitting her. It will be clear as the session proceeds that events surrounding her father's death played a role in heightening her concerns about her husband's family but that the difficulties predated the death and were already significant. It was thus a *second* issue for her to deal with, *alongside* that of losing her father.

This is thus an alert to the therapist to be gentle with Louise, to treat her supportively and with respect rather than "interpreting her defenses" or being the voice of the "hard truth" or the "*deep, dark* truth". Such considerations, which I introduced in Part I, are especially relevant here, because we encounter here at least two potential "temptations" to be the kind of clinician I earlier cautioned about. First, just hinted at in her opening statement, but more evident shortly, Louise could be seen as "externalizing"—as making the issue her husband's family, not her. Here this is less clearly evident because she does say "*I'm*" struggling and "the problems *I* had with my husband's family." Later, it will be clearer that part of what keeps Louise unable to resolve her difficulties with his family is that these difficulties feel to her like something *happening to* her, something over which she has little control. One aim of the therapy—a thought probably already going through my head at this moment in very provisional and not yet articulated form—will be to help Louise feel more empowered vis-à-vis her husband's family, to enable her to experience more degrees of freedom in interacting with them and expressing her feelings and point of view to them. And this will include and entail Louise's being able to see her own role in the pattern that has evolved with them and to examine more closely what she feels toward them, where it comes from in her own history and her own makeup, and what alternatives are available to her. These alternatives, of course, must be consistent with her own integrity, personality style, values, and sense of self.

Put differently, what will be called for is keen attention to what is usually called *externalizing* but in a fashion that is not accusatory, critical, or pathologizing. Louise "externalizes," if you will, for good reason: She has felt helpless and unable to address the conflicts between them in any other way. She has construed the experience with her husband's family as she does because she has not seen a way of bringing herself into the picture that is not at the expense of her deeply felt grievances just melting away. The aim of the therapy, then, is to enable Louise to experience alternatives, to see possibilities, to feel empowered and legitimated. She will not be able *usefully* to bring herself into the picture through being accused of leaving herself out. The therapist needs to find a way to *invite* her into the picture and to enable her to experience that when she accepts this invitation, she has a greater sense of power and of options.

A related consideration is evident in thinking about how to address a second feature of how Louise copes that is hinted at in this opening statement and becomes clearer shortly: what is traditionally depicted as "obsessional defenses." Here, Louise's telling us the exact date of her father's death may not seem especially noteworthy, or may simply signal (as indeed, as one part of the causal nexus, it almost surely does) how raw the pain of his death is. It is as if the date is imprinted on her memory, a dark anniversary that will not go away. But before long it will become evident that Louise spends *a lot* of time focusing on details like the exact dates, enough indeed to confuse herself at times.[5] The concept of obsessional defenses points to the ways in which such a focus on detail can serve to distract the individual from more pressing and emotionally relevant experiences that bear on, and could illuminate, her conflicted feelings and inclinations.[6]

---

[5]It is this further elaboration of and focus on the dates (which will be evident to the reader shortly) that creates the confusion for her and gives a somewhat different shading to the first instance in retrospect. Louise's mentioning the date of her father's death does not in itself imply very much. The anniversaries of significant deaths are noted and remembered by many people, and this alone would give little justification for thinking of an obsessional defensive style.

[6]See Shapiro (1965) for a more complex and extremely valuable additional take on obsessional style, less rooted in a linear impulse-defense model and more attentive to the consequences of the individual's style of experiencing and attending to the world—both the external world and the world of subjective experience.

But here again, although the clinician must be alert to the kinds of observations such a concept points to, I believe it is best to address the patient's experience in ways that are less diagnostic or pathocentric. Louise is clearly stressed, hurt, and confused. Understanding how some of the ways that she copes with that stress, hurt, and confusion unwittingly contribute to perpetuating the very experiences they are designed to keep at bay is of the essence of good clinical work. But the core of that understanding needs to be *through the patient's eyes*, in a way that attends not just to the ironies but to the ways in which, in the short run, these efforts *make sense* to the patient. Invalidation is not therapeutic.

Thus, there is a very important difference in tone between the formulation that Louise uses obsessional defenses (a rather objectivist and potentially critical formulation) and saying/thinking that in the face of painful stress that may seem unresolvable to her, she tries to make the best of it by maintaining a precise hold on "the facts of the matter," and that sometimes this effort can have ironic and unanticipated consequences. This distinction holds not only for what one overtly says to the patient but also for how one *thinks* about the clinical phenomena because one's thoughts have consequences for how one proceeds and for the subtle affective tone of the patient–therapist interaction.

> Paul: Uh huh. Uh huh. Can you tell me a little bit about what the troubles are like?
>
> Louise: It's a very long story, so I'm gonna try and just give you the most important things. I felt that, my dad passed away right before Thanksgiving, and then I had to go to, I live at, my parents live in Sweden 'cause that's where I'm born and raised. And so I had to go to Sweden over Thanksgiving, 'cause I went there for my dad's memorial service. But prior to that, when my husband called his mom—my husband's name is Ken—so Ken called his mom and he told her, you know, Louise's dad passed away. And they'd all known he'd been sick, but I didn't, you know, I hadn't felt really any support from them then either. And then he called her and said, you know, he passed away, and she was kind of the one who was gonna call the family and let them all know. And his, he has two sisters and a brother. The one sister called me the day after she found out right away and said, you know, "If there's anything I can do for you, I apologize, you know, I'm sorry about what happened."
>
> Paul: Uh huh.
>
> Louise: The other sister, the one I have the biggest problem with, she called on—my dad died on the Monday, and she called on Wednesday—and basically said well, you know, "Sorry I haven't called you, I haven't had time to call you."

Paul:	Uh huh.
Louise:	And when she . . .
Paul:	As if it was a trivial event, rather than something so centrally important.

* * * * *

Here it seemed important to me, even at the risk of interrupting Louise's narrative, to interject a note of sympathy and solidarity. She is describing how something crucially important to her had been minimized. I didn't want to repeat the trauma, as it were, by another act of omission. In phrasing it as I did, I was not necessarily making a judgment that Ken's family had viewed her father's death as trivial or treated it that way. The details of what actually goes on among them remained to be explored. But I did want to underline my appreciation of how it was experienced *by Louise*. In doing so, I was not only validating her experience and signaling that I was interested in seeing things through her eyes but also working to create the circumstances in which she would be able to *further articulate* that experience.

Some therapists would hesitate to offer a comment such as this, believing that to express sympathy and support in this fashion interferes with the possibility of the patient gaining access to angry, hurt, or other negative feelings toward the therapist—in other words, that I was short-circuiting a part of the patient's potential experience by protecting myself as a "good object." (cf. Brenner, 1979, P. L. Wachtel, 2008). It is true that here, and elsewhere in these sessions, I am going out of my way to be on the patient's side. But I *do not* believe that such actions necessarily prevent the patient from becoming angry at the therapist. (At times I have wished that they did!) Over time, whatever the patient is inclined to feel toward us will be felt. It is not necessary to create artificial deprivations or failures of empathy or sensitivity to bring those feelings about. It is not our job to act in ways that will leave the patient feeling hurt or angry or unsupported so that we may explore that hurt or anger or feeling unsupported. Rather, it is to be continuously alert to when the patient does feel hurt or angry in response to something we have done (or not done) and create a safe space to explore those experiences. We will have plenty of opportunity to lapse, given our inevitable human failings. We do not need to lapse *intentionally* in order to enable the patient to complain about it. To do so seems to me rather manipulative.

Louise:	Exactly, and that's how I felt. 'Cause you know, she started out saying "and we're very sorry to hear about your dad," and then, you know, "I should have called you sooner." And this was like 3 o'clock in the afternoon and she says, "I should have called you sooner, but I was too busy to call you." And that, you know,

I didn't know if it was just me, but I was really hurt, you know. And his brother, my husband's brother and his wife, I didn't hear from them at all.

Paul: Uh huh.

* * * * *

Here, and in many places further on, the printed words "uh huh" don't quite capture the interactive feel of the session. In most of these instances, I wasn't really "saying" anything to Louise. She was basically just continuing with her narrative, and I was signaling, as much with a nod of the head or via eye contact as with my almost sotto voce "uh huh," that I was listening and interested in her continuing. In that sense, the transcript looks more like a sequence of alternating turns than it actually was. In many instances throughout the transcript, what looks like two separate statements by the patient, with my turn intervening, was in fact one continuous statement by her with my merely indicating continuing interest.

Louise: And it turns out later that they didn't find out right away. They found out about a week later. But even when they found out, I still didn't receive a card or phone call or anything. And I was trying to think, okay, well you know, I didn't want to be childish about it, but at the same time I felt like my dad just died, and they're not acknowledging it. And that really hurt me. But then I thought, you know, I'm just gonna let it go, I'm just gonna go to Sweden, deal with my mom and whatever. Then I come back from Sweden, and I brought my mom with me. I talked her into coming with me. And she stayed from, she came with me, she came back with me on November 30th, she stayed until December 25th. We actually celebrate Christmas on the 24th, which is why she left on the 25th, or 26th, it doesn't matter.[7] Then on December 23rd, this is 6 weeks after my dad died, Ken's older sister—her name's Denise—comes over to the house with Ken's mom and basically decides to stage an intervention, telling me what a horrible person I am, and telling me all the, you know, everything that I've done wrong basically, and just letting me have it. And I mean I haven't seen, I haven't talked to his mom, I haven't seen any of them in 5 and a half months now. And it just, I don't know how to, I don't know how to build that bridge again.

---

[7]Here is another, and clearer, example of the style I referred to earlier as obsessional. Louise gets caught up in details to a degree that it throws off her story; diverts her from her main point; and leaves her with the feeling, from her own vantage point, that "it doesn't matter."

*****

We have an important indication here of one of Louise's goals. Although it will be amply evident to the reader as the session proceeds that Louise is rather ambivalent about reconnecting with Ken's family, it should also be clear that she does wish to do so, although to do so on terms that feel to her more just and more validating of her own experience than those she feels they demand. Much of the reason she wishes to build that bridge have to do with concern that if she does not it will harm her relationship with Ken. But it will also become clear later that there are ways in which she (ambivalently) longs for something from them as a conflicted desire in its own right.

The importance of this observation and perspective is that what is required to "be on Louise's side" is not a *simple* support or affirmation of her position or a simple effort to help her be more assertive with them. Rather, what is required is a more *systemic* understanding, in which it is essential—even for Louise's interests per se—to also understand the point of view of Ken and his family, to see things through *their* eyes too, and by doing so to see Louise's own experience and Louise's desires and interests in an expanded context. All too often, behavioral emphasis on training the patient to be more assertive or psychodynamic and humanistic/experiential emphasis on entering into the patient's world and seeing things through her eyes can lead to a one-sided focus that, in essence, makes the patient the hero of the story and the others the villains. Entering into the patient's world and seeing things through her eyes, as well as enabling her to be more assertive and to permit her own interests and point of view to have their due, are clearly valuable and important parts of the therapeutic process. But if not tempered with a more systemic understanding of the experiences of other people in her relational world and of the ways that those experiences are intertwined with hers in bidirectional feedback loops, these efforts can create puzzlingly counterproductive consequences.

> *Paul:* Uh huh.
>
> *Louise:* Because I just feel so violated and so hurt and just so, I was telling, I'm in therapy and I was telling my therapist, I said, "I just feel like running through the streets screaming, 'My dad died, and nobody cares.'" So it's very difficult for me.
>
> *Paul:* Right, right. Help me to understand a little bit about the history of your relationship with his family. How long have you been married?

*****

As I read this as a bit of written transcript, it seems to me easily misunderstood as dismissive of Louise's pain and outrage. The words "right, right," for example, are without tone in written prose. They can easily seem like a very minimalist or dismissive acknowledgment of Louise's experience, a mere stepping-stone to my changing the subject to gathering some historical information. As is more evident in the video of the session, the words were actually said in a tone that clearly was one of sympathetic acknowledgment and affirmation, an equivalent of "I see" or "I understand." Recall, moreover, that I had earlier made a point of saying, in response to Louise's telling me about Ken's sister saying she just hadn't had time to call, "as if it was a trivial event, rather than something so centrally important." I am feeling here, from the nonverbal affective cues that are always an unspoken part of the interaction and that are not as readily evident in a written transcript, that Louise has registered that I am sympathetic and on her side. I will continue throughout the session to convey my understanding of her pain and her perceptions, but in order to help her I also need to have access to the additional perspectives she is not able yet to generate or experience, and so I am introducing here a line of inquiry that may help lead me to such additional perspective and understanding.

> *Louise:* We've been married for 4 years in July, I believe. Yeah. And it's been strained from the beginning, because the family I come from, I'm an only child. We didn't really celebrate holidays together. We didn't really spend a lot of time together period, but we always, we were always there for each other. We knew that if we needed each other, we were there for each other. While his family is very much the family that, you know, they get together on holidays no matter what, and birthdays, and they've very, they're the collectivistic family, while I'm the individualist family, come from an individualist family. And that's a huge clash, because I feel like they don't respect that sometimes I can't, I mean I, it was brought up that I didn't come to Easter 2 years ago.

* * * * *

Although I did not comment on it right here, Louise's reference to collectivist and individualist families immediately caught my attention and informed in an important way my understanding of Louise's struggle and of how I might best help her. In the technical language of some theoretical orientations, one could call Louise's statement an instance or reflection of splitting. Whatever one's theoretical language, it represents a sharply dichotomous way of seeing things that defines, articulates, and exaggerates in such a way that reconciliation becomes much more difficult.

It will become apparent as the session proceeds that in fact there are ways in which Louise's own family was rather problematically "collectivist," in the sense of creating demands and "shoulds" that conflicted with Louise's needs as an evolving, separate individual. It will also become apparent that the "individualist" side of Louise's family atmosphere was a rather mixed blessing, in the sense that it could be isolating and lacking in empathy or room for mutual needs and neediness.[8] Partly as a consequence of this, what will emerge as the session proceeds is a *longing* on Louise's part for certain features of Ken's family, a longing Louise finds threatening and therefore rejects and denies. This threatening dimension to her positive feelings toward them, and the rejection and denial of those feelings that result, I come to believe in the course of the session, is one of the factors contributing to her difficulty in connecting with them. When this is addressed toward the end of the session, one vector that is introduced is that as Louise becomes more able to acknowledge and accept that longing, she evidences an enhanced ability to view Ken's family in a more three-dimensional manner (and she does so without it entailing any diminished attention to her own needs and perceptions).[9]

Paul: Uh huh.

Louise: I mean this was 2 years ago. And even though I'd explained that I couldn't go because I had a take-home exam I had to do. And my husband, you know, they were telling my husband, "Well, she could have come for just an hour." So it's always these little trivial things blown out of proportion because they, they don't take my schooling seriously. They feel like, they compare it to their nieces who are in seventh grade. So they, they don't understand what I do, and they're not trying to understand what I do.

* * * * *

Here once again, Louise is conveying a profound sense of not being understood or acknowledged, an experience of the world that we will see later in the session parallels some rather striking features of her experiences in her own family growing up. Here, however, I do not attend to this dimension but, in my next comment, inquire about Ken's role in the picture. At this point in

---

[8]It will be apparent as the reader proceeds through the session that the statement that "if we needed each other, we were there for each other" could at times be countervailed in distressing—and even shocking—ways.

[9]It is also worth noting that the terms *individualist* and *collectivist* are a rather intellectualized way of describing an emotionally powerful state of affairs and hence are consistent with the utilization of obsessional defenses discussed earlier. The terms almost certainly derive from her college courses, not from immediate experience. In noting this, however, it is important once again to remind ourselves that our clinical language is often unacknowledgedly disparaging (see, e.g., P. L. Wachtel, 1993, 2008; Wile, 1984). Using her intellect, including what she has learned in college, to address and better understand her life experiences is, after all, not simply "obsessional." The reader would not be sitting reading this book instead of watching television or playing a video game if she did not believe that there is something valuably adaptive about applying ideas and categories from one's studies to addressing the challenges—even the interpersonal or emotional challenges—of daily life. It is also interesting to note that Louise's depictions of collectivism and individualism are counterstereotypic. That is, Scandinavian societies are usually thought of as more collectivist than American society.

the session, I am still trying to sort out the systemic picture. I am wanting to assess to what degree she can count on Ken as a sympathetic ally, whether *he,* in her experience, is an exception to the general rule of feeling dismissed and misunderstood. I am hoping that this is so, because, as in every case, the patient—and the work we are doing—needs all the allies that can be found. But I am also wanting to assess just what the situation is, because how to proceed will in part depend on whether Ken does or does not show a capacity to see things through Louise's eyes.

Paul: Uh huh. Uh huh. And where is your husband in this? What's, what's his position about it all?

Louise: Well, I feel sorry for him because he's, he's very hurt by the whole thing, and he's trying to do his best, he's trying to be on, be on my side, and is trying to, he's, you know, he still doesn't want to let go of his mom.

Paul: Uh huh.

Louise: But I'm trying to tell him your mom isn't innocent in all, in all this. And he's, how I feel, he's gone behind my back a lot of times to talk to his mom when I've said, you know, that's not okay for you. That's your mom, I know, but when it affects me, you can't just go and talk to her and tell her things that I've told you that are private between us.

* * * * *

I am curious at this point what she means when she says he went behind her back. I don't ask about this right away, however, but just keep listening. As I have noted at several points, the evolution of a session is a continually branching process with many branches ignored for the moment even if noticed. Every statement (and posture and tone of voice) is pregnant with multiple meanings, and the process of the dialogue is shaped by which one the therapist—and the patient as well—picks up on. No matter what one responds to, that very response means that some other meaning, potentially equally important, lies fallow for the moment. One must store much of what one hears in one's head for later.

Shortly after this exchange, what Louise meant does become clearer. It will also be clear that Ken's behavior could also be seen quite differently—as standing up for Louise, taking her side, intervening on her behalf. But it also needs to be understood as *she* experiences it, which becomes clear as well as we proceed.

Paul: Uh huh. Uh huh.

Louise: And so our relationship has suffered. And we've been fighting a lot. And when I try to talk to my husband now about his family, he says, "Well, what's the point of talking about it? They don't want to do anything about it anyway." And I say, "It doesn't matter, because somebody has to do something." I say, you know, "If we're gonna have kids" (we plan on having kids, you know), "what's gonna, what is gonna, what's it gonna be like then, you know?" And I just, the only one who can change anything is me and Ken. We have to reach out to them, but I've been so hurt by them that I don't know even where to begin. And usually I'm the kind of person who if I have a problem with somebody I run, I don't stay and deal with it.

* * * * *

Here I am registering as important in thinking about Louise her self-description as "I'm the kind of person who . . . " When I come across a self-description such as this, it alerts me to a potentially restrictive self-definition that I will want to work on with the patient at some point. The challenge is to convey that one understands—and can value—the trait she is describing but is also interested in finding the *other* sides of the person that almost always exist. She may *frequently* run from conflict, and clearly that is important and should not be denied or brushed over; but one must also be interested in when she *doesn't* run, when she does stand up and express what she is feeling. As previously noted in Part I, these alternative ways of being are important building blocks in the therapeutic effort, and often a significant part of the patient's difficulties derive from her inability to notice that she is sometimes different.

In this particular instance, were I to have picked up on this theme (which for the moment I just registered in my consciousness), I might have said something like, "You said *usually* you're the kind of person who runs. When are the times when you do stay and deal with it?" I might also inquire into just how she does deal with it, including examining whether, when she does stand up for herself, she does so in ways that exacerbate rather than resolve the tensions and helping her find the voice within her that "works"—works, that is, not from an external perspective, or from the therapist's, but from her own frame of reference. I also might inquire with her about what *makes it hard* for her to stay and deal with the situation. That is, she is not just someone who "runs" but, at the very least, someone who runs *for a reason*. An important part of the therapist's job is to understand that reason, to help *make sense* of her running rather than leave her to interpret it simply as a failing on her part. To some degree, that making sense of her experience is implicitly what I am doing in the comment that follows next. I am following up on her description of herself as someone who "runs" and depicting her (not as a contrast, but in an additional—and partly explanatory—perspective) as someone who has *been hurt* and feels that the burden of righting the relationship has been unfairly placed solely on her, even though she feels like the aggrieved party.

Paul:	Uh huh. Uh huh. So they, they hurt you . . . and it then becomes hard for you to have the burden of reestablishing the relationship. Especially since you feel like the aggrieved party, right?
Louise:	Uh huh.
Paul:	So when you and Ken talk about it, I mean do you, are you able to talk about it much? Or is it a topic that sort of has become a taboo between you?
Louise:	It's a hot button definitely. It usually ends up with screaming. With me screaming at him, or him screaming at me or something.
Paul:	Uh huh. Uh huh.
Louise:	So it's, which is very frustrating 'cause I keep telling him, I'm like I'm just, I'm trying to make, I mean I've called his mom to try and, I called his mom a week ago today. And after a day I, you know, she hadn't called me back and I said to Ken, "Your mom hasn't called me back. Why isn't she calling me back?" 'Cause she's saying, you know, they're all telling me I need to reach out and I need to fix this and I need to apologize. For what I don't know. So I called her a week ago, she still hasn't called back. Ken, and then Ken called her the day after and said, "Why haven't you called my wife?" And I said to Ken, "Why did you do that? You know, I wanted to give her the chance to call me." 'Cause she's saying that she wants me to talk to her. And then she, because she called me at 7 o'clock in the morning, and I'm not a morning person, I'm usually not up at 7 o'clock. But I was up for a reason.

* * * * *

"For what I don't know" is clearly intended by Louise as a rhetorical statement, as equivalent to, "They want me to apologize, and I have nothing to apologize about." But it can be useful for the therapist to also register it and address it as a real question. That is, to a considerable degree Louise really *doesn't* know what she has done that has offended them, and in order for her to be successful in healing the breach between them, she will *have to* know. This is clearly not the same as simply acceding, simply agreeing that they are right and she is in the wrong. But she has to *understand* what has offended them, because without understanding, she is unable to repair the breach. That repair might include apologizing—if, after reflection, it *feels to her* like an apology is in order in some respects—but it includes as well the ability to properly and effectively to defend herself. Just as in our legal system we require that the accused be completely and clearly informed as to what the charges are against him, so that he may be able to mount an effective defense, so too in everyday interpersonal relationships, it is difficult to stand up for oneself, to represent one's own point of view, if one does not know what one has been accused of.

Thus, here is another instance in which effectively helping the patient requires understanding not just the patient's "inner" experience but what has actually transpired between her and another person, and in which it requires as well that one understand *the other's* point of view. Therapists all too often define their task as understanding "the patient" essentially *in opposition* to others' point of view. There is obviously an important value in understanding the patient's point of view, and I have emphasized this in numerous places in this book. One of the experiences that most of our patients are seeking and have usually felt deprived of in at least certain circumstances or relationships is the experience of having *their* point of view understood and affirmed. Being able to do this is perhaps the most crucial task of the psychotherapist. But at the same time, the tangles and difficulties that people get into in their lives and that are at the heart of what brings them to therapy are rooted as well in their misunderstanding of *others*. We all (therapists included, of course) manifest such misunderstanding a fair amount in our lives. It is part of being a "mere" human being.

I do not actually go into the "for what I don't know" with Louise at this point. As I have already noted, there are always so many choice points that we can never pick up on all of them. But I do want to call *the reader's* attention to it as part of my interpolated comments. In the session itself, it will be apparent as we proceed that I do give considerable attention—indeed, as one of the central themes of the session as it evolves—to the ways in which Louise's actions create more hurt and angry feelings in Ken's family than she realizes. Part of the art of therapy, which I hope is illustrated in this session, is to call the patient's attention to such occurrences in a way that does not feel to the patient that one is placing the "blame" for the problematic pattern on her. Here holding to a vicious circle perspective, as I described in Chapter 1, is very helpful. Such a perspective enables the therapist to see *both* parties as caught in a pattern that neither of them necessarily intends. This does not mean, of course, that one automatically absolves the other person of any harmful intent or bad behavior; at times what the patient needs is our acknowledgment and affirmation of her having been mistreated, and a falsely "fair and balanced" approach is unhelpful. But often, especially in cases like this where the patient is seeking a reconciliation that seems elusive and obdurate, an understanding that encompasses the viewpoints of *all* the parties is the best expression of the therapist's skills.

An additional noteworthy point that is important to mention at this juncture concerns Louise's annoyance at Ken for calling his mother. I will comment on this shortly, after my exchange with Louise about her experience that he was undermining her and going behind her back.

Paul: Uh huh.

Louise: And she said, "Well I don't want to talk to you on the phone." She left a message. She said, "I don't want to talk to you on the phone, so I'm just gonna stop by." And I was livid. And I thought, you know, why is she just gonna stop by, you know? I don't want to see her in person, I just want to talk to her on the phone. And that's when I found out Ken had called her. And it's just so frustrating for me because I feel like he's undermining everything I'm trying to do.

* * * * *

Louise wanted to talk with Ken's mother on the phone because that felt more controllable and limited. In Ken's mother's insistence on talking in person and on coming by, Louise feels *invaded,* which is what she feels so much of the time. (See the discussion at the beginning of the session regarding Louise's feeling overwhelmed.) There will be further rather startling material later in the session that further amplifies the ways in which Louise has felt overwhelmed at various times in her life.

Paul: Uh huh. Now what was it that made Ken talking to his mother about it feel like he was undermining it rather than sort of representing you or standing up for you? I'm not saying it should have felt that way, I'm just . . .

* * * * *

I am addressing here Louise's unhappiness at Ken's comment to his mother, which one might think would be experienced as his coming to her support and defense. One might easily see a contradiction between, on the one hand, Louise's understandable anger and bewilderment at being told the family wanted her to reach out to them and then receiving no response to her phone call for a week and, on the other hand, her upset with Ken for what seems like coming to her defense around just this issue. It is important to find the right way to address this issue because one of the biggest mistakes therapists make, I believe, is to point out "contradictions" to patients, to try to show them how they are being illogical, inconsistent, defensive, what have you. This may be very effective in an argument or in a game of "gotcha," but it is positively harmful in the context of therapy.

I perhaps tried a little too hard to make sure that Louise didn't think I was criticizing her. She seems to have granted me more good will than I automatically assumed she would, interrupting my explanation of why I was asking with, "Oh no, I understand what you're saying."

Louise: Oh no, I understand what, I understand what you're saying. The only reason it feels that way is because previously when

I've said things to him that I've said out of hurt or anger, he's passed that along to his mom. And then she has passed it along to other people, and then it's been completely misunderstood, and it's gone, and it's just taken to something I didn't mean.

Paul: Uh huh.

Louise: And they don't ever blame Ken for anything, they blame me for everything. And they've basically, I've heard from my sister-in-law, Ken's brother's wife, she's basically come out and said to me that Ken has changed for the worse since he met you. And everything that Ken says is, because he has changed, they see this change in him as being my fault.

Paul: Uh huh. And it sounds from what you've described so far about the family, like mostly I'm, I would guess what they mean by change for the worse is that he's less immersed in the family, that he's more with you and less with them. Is that, is that, is that what . . . ?

* * * * *

I am trying here to reframe or restate the issue, putting it in a way that goes beyond the simple good–bad frame of reference that it was initially placed in and helping her to see what they are upset about in a more specific way. In this, I am in a sense trying to help her to see that they are responding to a *loss*, to Ken's having become closer to her than to them. This both opens a path toward some sympathy and reconciliation with regard to them (one of the aims of the therapeutic work as Louise has stated it) and frames the issue as one in which Louise has "*won*"; that is, as a reflection of Ken's being strongly committed to her.

Louise: Absolutely. 'Cause his family, they have no boundaries. They don't respect each other, they don't, if, you know, like his sister always, his sister Denise always says, you know, "I have two kids and you don't have any kids, and you have nothing to do, and who do you think you are" kind of thing. And when I tell her, you know, "I have school, I have homework, I have things to do," that's just like "whatever," you know? And she thinks that, you know, she kind of, she's the puppeteer, you know? And everybody else just follows her lead. [*The affective tone in Louise's voice at this point is one of feeling beset*] And I'm the first, for the first time Ken is standing up for himself. 'Cause she feels more like a mom to Ken, 'cause their dad passed away when he, when Ken was 20. So that was a while ago, and ever since then she's kind of taken over the role as dual mom. And she completely controls her own mother, and she's very resentful of the fact that, you know, I've, I'm starting to stand up for myself and say, "Me and Ken are a family, we have our own boundaries, you know. If I say I can't come it's not, don't take it so personal, just respect me."

* * * * *

Louise is clearly more agitated here than she has been up till this point. Her voice has a tone of being beset, and there are more "you knows" here than in much of the session. She is talking about something that touches close to where she hurts in this tangle with Ken's family.

Note here also, apropos my earlier comment about collectivist and individualist families, the global comment by Louise, "They have no boundaries." My point here is not that Louise is "wrong"; when Louise says, at the end of this long passage, "Just respect me," she is pointing not just to something she wants from Ken's family but something that is a key requirement for the effective therapist as well. But I do wish to note that by perceiving them so globally, she contributes to making it feel impossible to her to find any path at all toward the goal of reconciliation or connection that she mentions early in the session is important to her. It will also be apparent, later in the session, that in fact the absence of appropriate boundaries was a serious issue in her own family of origin, an issue to which she was sensitized in her own upbringing but which she now perceives only in Ken's family. Helping Louise get past that split is one of the aims of the work.

> Paul: Uh huh. Uh huh. So it sounds like one of the issues that needs to be worked out, the Easter invitation for example . . .

> Louise: Uh huh.

> Paul: There it sort of happened that you had something else that prevented you from coming, and you wanted that respected.

> Louise: Uh huh.

> Paul: But that you also want, and what you, what is really a source of conflict between let's call them the two families—meaning you and Ken and this other grouping of people . . .

> Louise: Yeah. That's a good way of putting it.

> Paul: . . . is that you have a different vision of what family is than they do.

> Louise: Uh huh.

> Paul: And what would ideally occur is some way of the two of you actually being able to talk about that, and finding some way to sort of live together rather than you . . . it sounds like the experience right now is that you are, or were before the breach, sort of periodically bombarded with demands as you experienced it . . .

Louise:	Uh huh.
Paul:	And you could either accede to them, or wriggle out of them, but there was never an opportunity to say, "I'd like to talk with you about who I am and what I'm like."
Louise:	Exactly, exactly.

* * * * *

In the foregoing exchange, I have been trying to articulate some of the ways that Louise experiences Ken's family as problematic for her and also to implicitly model some of how she might address it. I offer this from a vantage point that on the one hand is rooted in Louise's own direct experience and on the other is aimed at reaching out to them in a way that, although maintaining her own integrity and the legitimacy of her perceptions, also takes into account that they too may have a legitimate point of view.

In a related vein, the earlier comment that "you have a *different* vision" is an attempt to move the discourse from the realm of right and wrong, good and bad, to one of *difference*. She won't be able to accomplish *her own* aim of reconnecting with them unless in *some* way she can see their views as also having a certain validity, as different rather than just wrong.

Paul:	It's not, it's not something inherently easy to do, I know that. But nonetheless, if we think about what particularly might make that hard for you to do with them, are there any things that come up?

* * * * *

My aim here is to pursue the questions and new perspectives I am introducing here in a nonaccusatory fashion (see Chapter 1). It is important that Louise not feel that there is *something wrong with her* for not approaching Ken's family in the way I am implicitly suggesting. It *is* difficult. But it is useful to ask what makes it *especially* hard for *her* and what are the issues and conflicts she will need to deal with in order to be more effective in dealing with them.

Put differently, the aim is to address the externalization or splitting mentioned earlier in my comments on the session, to interest Louise in examining her own role in what has transpired between her and Ken's family, without leaving her feeling accused that it is her fault. I believe that the tone of the session as a whole makes it clear that Louise does experience me as being on her side.

Louise:	I'm very stubborn. And I don't like conflict. I don't know how to deal with conflict.

Paul: Uh huh.

Louise: I'm trying to learn to deal with conflict. I'm trying to learn to stand up for myself. I think what makes it the most difficult is that after my dad died I was having some problems with my mom, and she was grieving obviously, and I was grieving, and you know, we were having issues together. And when they came over to the house, they just surprised us basically. And they didn't know my mom was there, so my mom was in another room. And she just basically, I feel pathetic saying it, but she just ran into my house and scared me to death basically [*said with much affect, and in a childlike voice*]. And I was just so shocked after that whole experience that, I mean I was looking for a car, and I was being paranoid, and I mean my state of mind was so fragile when she came over that I think that that contributed to, I mean I had to, I'm on antidepressants—I had to raise the milligram on my antidepressants. And I think that's, she, I feel so incredibly hurt by her that I just want nothing to do with her, and she scares me. Not physically scares me, but she's just such a bully, she just reminds me of these people when I was little that hurt me. And she just stirs up all these childhood things within me.

* * * * *

Several things are worth noting here. To begin with, it would probably have been good to address Louise's comment, "I feel pathetic saying it." This was said in a plaintive tone, and it expresses a feeling of considerable vulnerability centered around the very process of opening up in the session about what happened. Some encouragement or feedback conveying that in fact she was being honest and courageous, not pathetic, might have been useful here.

In some way, my next comment, asking her about the bullying in her childhood, addresses the same affective state in a different fashion. The "pathetic" feeling she is having in the session is probably very similar to the feeling of being a victim of bullies—especially of verbal bullies, as she clarifies they were—who leave one with precisely the feeling of being "pathetic" in not having an effective retort.

We might note, incidentally, that the fact that Louise spontaneously recalls and associates to the bullies and to "all these childhood things within me" may well be a product of my earlier query about what might make it *particularly hard for her* to deal with the things Ken's family does. Shortly after my raising this question, Louise for the first time refers to having had some problems with her mom. Then, just a bit later, she recalls these childhood experiences with the bullies and notes that childhood things are being stirred up in her. Often, the therapeutic fruits of what we say to the patient are evident only indirectly. Louise was not directly "answering" the question of what makes it especially hard *for her* to deal with Ken's family, and she probably was not consciously aware that that comment had anything to do either with her mentioning, for the first time here, her present-day issues with her mother (who had been steadfastly kept on the "good" side of the ledger up till then) or with her recalling the experience of being bullied and having her childhood "stirred up." But it seems to me quite likely that my comment was a part of what was reverberating in her neural networks as these new associations were stirred. Much of what is most effective in our work as psychotherapists consists of dropping seeds into the ground in this fashion and then in being attentive to what emerges from the soil. I did not know what my query would open up for Louise, but it was indeed intended to turn our attention to her specific life experience and the psychological inclinations that have thus far been its consequence. Like so much of what we do as therapists, it may have looked somewhat casual or incidental, but it was in fact a product of both thought and clinical experience. We may not know exactly what our comments or queries will open up, but we learn from years of clinical work that certain kinds of comments or questions and certain ways of speaking (P. L. Wachtel, 1993) can be more powerful and effective than might be anticipated by someone who has not long been immersed in the process of trying to facilitate people's reappropriation of their submerged experiences.

There is some ambiguity regarding just whom she is referring to when she says "she scares me." At some points in this passage, Louise says "they" came into her house; later she says "she" scares me and "she" is such a bully. "She" in this regard could refer to either her mother-in-law or Denise. Denise seems in some ways the more aggressive and frightening member of Ken's family for Louise, but in other respects, it is her relationship with her mother-in-law that most concerns her. To the degree that it is to her mother-in-law that she is referring, we may note that by the end of the session a more complex picture of the mother-in-law, and of Louise's feelings about her, emerges. This more complex vision is one of the accomplishments of the session. At this point, what is evoked in Louise's experience is not only a very simplified, one-dimensional view of her mother-in-law but a very *childlike* experience, something that she actually acknowledges spontaneously and explicitly.

Finally, it is also worth noting that the fairly dramatic account of her in-laws bursting in and terrifying her relegates to the role of an incidental background item another element that will in fact turn out to be rather important in a number of respects. Louise mentions that she was "having some problems" with her mom and that they "were having issues together." As will become apparent as the session proceeds, there is good reason to think that part of the difficulty Louise is having with Ken's family has to do with painfully conflicted feelings toward her own mother, which she often seems to protect herself from by focusing on what is wrong with *Ken's* family. This splitting into a black-and-white dichotomy between her good, nondemanding, but there-for-each-other family and Ken's "collectivistic," intrusive, unempathetic family is one source of her difficulty in connecting with Ken's family. Even in this one session, it will become apparent, some progress is made in helping Louise make contact both with her more troubled feelings about her own mother and her warded-off warmer feelings toward Ken's mother and longings for some things that were more evident and available in Ken's family than in her own. The emotional cubbyholing has been necessary to protect her from feelings toward her mother that she is not yet ready to face fully, but the price has been to exacerbate the problems she is having with Ken's family, potentially threatening her relationship with her husband and preventing her from satisfying longings that were not very well met in her own family of origin.

> *Paul:* Tell me a little bit about these experiences as a child when you were bullied.
>
> *Louise:* It was more emotional bullying. They made it, the girls particularly made it clear they didn't like me, and made fun of me, and took advantage of me 'cause I was very naive and very trusting. So I didn't have, didn't have many friends. I, I believe part of it was jealousy, 'cause I, I was very close to my mom and they didn't have a good relationship with their mom. And my dad . . . we traveled a lot . . . and it was just very, very hard for me growing up because I felt I never knew who was gonna stab me in the back.

* * * * *

The reader might want to mark this particular description of her family to go back to after reading the entire session. Note here Louise's description of her relationship with her mom as being so good and so close that, as she depicts it, the other kids were jealous. Note also the reference to her dad here, just a sentence fragment ("and my dad"), stated but not followed up, and left ambiguously hanging. In retrospect, it might be viewed, in its fragmented structure, as a possible indicator of stress or conflict. But as one hears it in the context of what Louise has said so far, the phrase seems at first to be part of her elaboration of what the other kids were jealous of her about. One hears it at first as the beginning of a sentence one expects to proceed as something like "and they were jealous of my relationship with my dad too." But as only a fragment, it can also seem like it was possibly the beginning of a different sentence, maybe related to the next phrase, "We traveled a lot." The incomplete sentence fragment regarding her father then seems associatively linked to the family's travels—a link that will take on much meaning later in the session but which is difficult to really appreciate or understand the implications of at this point.[10]

All in all, in this context, the uncompleted and unelaborated references to her father and to travel seem to be part of the impression Louise is conveying of her family as a "normal" one that other kids would be jealous of. What is implied is an image of an intact family, a present dad, and a family that travels together. We will see that, sadly, the fuller picture was rather different.

Note also that the sentence beginning with "and my dad" and "we traveled a lot" ends with " it was just very, very hard for me growing up because I felt I never knew who was gonna stab me in the back." Hearing Louise's account the first time, in the context of what she is presenting to me, the stab in the back seems to refer to the bullying kids, not to her parents. As the session proceeds, and the associative links of this phrase to "and my dad" and "we traveled a lot" take on different meanings, the implications of the rest of the sentence may seem much less clearly directed toward the bullying children. (Bear in mind here as well what I noted in my previous interpolated comment about Louise's tendency to protect her precarious sense of a benign and attentive family atmosphere and the price she pays for those "purifying" efforts.)

I was not aware of any of the implications I am hinting at here at this point in the session. One of the advantages of having a video or a transcript is that one can understand what has been transpiring differently in retrospect than one did at the time it occurred.

> *Paul:* Uh huh.

> *Louise:* I always felt like I couldn't really trust anybody, and it wasn't till I was about late teens, early 20s that I finally had some really good friends that I could trust. But I still to this day expect people to turn on me.

> *Paul:* Uh huh. Uh huh. Do you have a vision of it being possible for you to have more friends and feel more comfortable? Is that something that you sort of aspire to and think of as a possibility in your life?

> *Louise:* I used to want as many friends as possible. But now I have a handful of friends that are really good friends. And I'm very happy with the friends I have.

---

[10]It will become apparent later in the session, when Louise talks about events that occurred in Paris when she was 14, that the family's traveling, being away from Sweden, was a rather loaded topic and that her father was associatively linked to this in a rather disturbing and powerful way. That is not evident at this point, where the reference to travel, like the reference to her father, seems to refer more to something to be envious of.

Paul:	Uh huh. Uh huh.
Louise:	So I feel like I'm in a place now where I don't feel like, I don't have that need to, to have more friends.
Paul:	Uh huh. Uh huh.
Louise:	And I don't feel like I would be a better person if I had more friends.
Paul:	Right. You've, you actually have achieved what you had hoped for.
Louise:	Yes, now. Yeah!

* * * * *

The video reveals that Louise broke into a glowing smile at this point. It was an important therapeutic moment in the sense that it evoked in her, and on an affective level, a sense of herself that was *different* from the way she usually sees herself and that contained a sense of possibility that also felt new. This sequence is also an example of the value of the therapist's being as attentive to positive developments and positive ways of seeing the patient and her life as to pathology.

Therapeutic moments of the sort occurring here are unlikely to be Hollywood-style moments of a single life-changing event. They are incremental and cumulative, and almost always must be multiple, not singular. Nonetheless, they each have real significance. The therapeutic experience occurring here differs in a number of important ways from the "moments of meeting" described by the Boston Change Process Study Group (Lyons-Ruth, 1998; D. N. Stern, 2004; D. N. Stern et al., 1998), but it has in common with their conception a focus on change brought about through the evocation of an affective experience that alters the patient's internal process rather than change being brought about primarily through insight.

Paul:	Yeah.

* * * * *

My own explicit (but also spontaneous) resonating in affirmation of Louise's affective state and self-affirmation.

Louise:	Yeah.
Paul:	Yeah. You seemed almost surprised when I said that, or am I misreading it?
Louise:	When you said I've achieved?
Paul:	Yeah.

Louise: Yeah. I never thought about it, so yeah, yeah, I am, I guess I am surprised that I have achieved it.

Paul: Uh huh.

Louise: 'Cause I, but I'm so afraid that it's gonna disappear that I'm not . . . I'm afraid that if I acknowledge it then it might go away.

Paul: Uh huh. Uh huh. Uh huh.

* * * * *

Louise here expresses the fear that if she acknowledges the change it will go away. Often, however, what happens is almost the opposite—it is the *failure* to acknowledge the change that prevents it from being sustained.

In this vein, I have elsewhere (P. L. Wachtel, 1993) called attention to the important and insufficiently appreciated work of Tenzer (1984), who stressed the critical importance of the patient's *noticing* changes that are taking place. Drawing on both psychoanalytic thought and Piagetian research, Tenzer argued persuasively that if this does not happen, even real and significant change can rapidly evaporate. She also illuminated how fundamental features of human cognition—especially the tendency to discount what does not fit in with prior expectations—can mitigate against that noticing. Thus, I argued, "without explicit effort on the therapist's part to *promote* the patient's awareness of change, the patient is likely to assimilate what has transpired into his old structures and schemas, and the change will be short-lived." (P. L. Wachtel, 1993, p. 257)

More recently, I have thought of this process in terms of the idea that the patient needs to have *the insight that she has had an insight*. Otherwise, the *implications for action* deriving from that insight, the ways in which it points to doing things differently, to *living* differently, become dissolved. When that happens, the insight is likely to become an isolated intellectual acknowledgment with little capacity to generate emotional or behavioral change.

In this connection, my commenting that Louise seemed almost surprised when I made my comment was intended to help Louise to *notice* that she had been pleased at the comment, that it had made her smile in joy and, relatedly, that it meant she was in a different place with regard to the capacity to make and maintain close friendships than she has long thought of herself as being.

Louise: So I cherish my friendships and I . . . but it's . . . part of me's still worried. You know?

Paul: What, what would make it fragile, and what, when you have the sort of fearful image of losing these friends, what's connected with that image?

* * * * *

I am here focusing on Louise's *anxiety*, reflecting the view, discussed in Chapter 1, that attention to the patient's anxiety is a central feature of good therapeutic work. Although I am cued in this by Louise's reference to being worried, there is a sense in which I am taking Louise's anxiety more seriously than she does, or at least addressing it in a different way. I am not merely noting that she is worried; I am inviting her to explore what that worry is really about, and I am doing so in a way that is not primarily intellectually focused, that is, asking a "question" that has a verbal "answer." Rather, I am asking Louise to attend to *images* associated with the anxiety. Such a mode of inquiry is more likely to include the affective component.

In this particular instance, the inquiry did not have particularly fruitful or profound results. But it is nonetheless a mode of exploration that I believe is all in all more likely to bring the patient into contact with the experiences and cues that she must confront if she is to overcome her anxiety.

> *Louise:* It would just trigger in me that I'm disposable. 'Cause I felt, I always felt that people were friends with me until they got a better friend.
>
> *Paul:* Uh huh. Uh huh.
>
> *Louise:* And I feel like maybe you know, it would just trigger—that's why it feels fragile. 'Cause I'm worried they're gonna find somebody else they like better. Which I know is not real.
>
> *Paul:* Uh huh. Uh huh.
>
> *Louise:* Yeah.
>
> *Paul:* 'Cause they really are good solid friends.
>
> *Louise:* Yeah they are. And I mean I know that realistically, but still somewhere my insecurity, that I'm working on, but I don't know if it's, it's, I feel like it's so deeply ingrained in me that I don't know if it's ever gonna go away.
>
> *Paul:* Uh huh. Does it ever express itself in the way you are with them? Like do you find yourself being overly sensitive to something and saying something, when they really weren't being rejecting or something like that?

* * * * *

Louise—here thinking like many therapists do—is viewing the cause of her anxiety as almost completely "internal," something that is "deeply ingrained" in her. I am raising another possibility—that at least some of her experience of others' behavior toward her is not simply "how she is," or for that matter "how *they* are," but rather is a consequence of the way that she interacts with them. That is, I am implicitly inquiring about the possibility of a *vicious circle*, in which her anxiety leads her to behave with them in ways that evoke responses from them that keep the anxiety going and make it likely that the same sequence of events and feelings will occur again. If that is the case, and if Louise can come to see this and do something about this, then the cycle can be broken.

Here, as in much of psychotherapy, one of the challenges for the therapist is to introduce the role of the patient's own behavior in a way that is not accusatory (for a more extended discussion of this topic, see P. L. Wachtel, 1993, 2008; Wile, 1984). The tone is not one of pointing out to the patient that she is leaving out her own role in the process, which can easily have the feeling and connotation that what happens is *her fault*. Rather, much of the aim is to enable her to see almost the opposite—that is, that it is *not* her "fault"—because it is a consequence of the vicious circle in which she is *trapped*, an almost inexorable consequence of the very feelings that she is aiming to overcome. At the same time, the inquiry into how she acts with them provides her with a handle that may help her in *breaking* the cycle.

It is also important to keep in mind, of course, that this inquiry *is* an inquiry; that is, that one is raising a *question*, not that one has the answer. In Louise's response to my question, for example (immediately below), there are some indications consonant with the hypothesis that her own behavior plays a role in perpetuating the cycle in that she indicates that she *was* overly sensitive, and her friends did seem to register that. But there are also indications that, perhaps in response to the medication, her *behavior* has changed, and yet the *feeling* seems, at least to some degree, to persist. On the other hand, there is also some indication that in fact her changed behavior toward her friends has helped to *break* a cycle in which both she and they were caught and that *all* of them are now more able to disembed themselves from the pattern, to reflect on it and thereby help to change it (see Wallin, 2007).

> *Louise:* Before I started taking medication—it's an antidepressant and antianxiety—before I finally reached out for help, yes. I was very, very sensitive to what everybody said. Any slightest little thing, you know, what did they mean? Or do they not want to talk to me any more? And I've worked on that a lot. And I, now I, now I have my friends actually telling me, "Oh I hope, you know, I laughed when you said something, you know, I hope that you didn't misunder, misunderstand that." And that's something I didn't even, I'm like, "Oh okay, well no, I didn't even think about it." So . . .

> *Paul:* Uh huh. So they've sort of registered that you can be hurt that way.

Louise:	Yeah, I think they know. I mean, and that's why I said it. I think they're really good friends 'cause they know I'm very sensitive. So they actually pick up on that and they come back and tell me, you know, "I hope you're okay."
Paul:	Right, right.
Louise:	So . . .
Paul:	Right.
Louise:	And that means a lot to me.
Paul:	Uh huh, right, 'cause it shows they really do care about you.
Louise:	Yeah.
Paul:	Yeah.
Louise:	'Cause even though they think I'm a little, you know, they still, you know, they're, they care about me.
Paul:	Right, I mean being sensitive isn't a war crime.
Louise:	No. But I, it does, when somebody calls me that, usually I, I tend to be like, no, I'm not sensitive. 'Cause it's used, Ken, Ken's family calls me sensitive in a, in a very negative way.
Paul:	Right, right.
Louise:	So . . .
Paul:	Right.
Louise:	. . . it's always been used as a negative connotation.
Paul:	Right, right. And how secure do you feel in your relationship with Ken?

* * * * *

Here I am now turning to another thread in the interrelated set of issues in Louise's life. In reflecting now on why I made this comment at this point, it seems to me that to some degree I am changing the subject because at the moment I'm not seeing further where or how to explore the topic we have just been addressing. I would certainly expect that further important work on it will be forthcoming over time, but as happens so often, the well has run dry for the moment.

Some therapists might say that it is only *my* well that has run dry and that if I just waited silently, Louise would likely come up with more that was at least thematically and affectively connected to the topic (even if it came as a seemingly irrelevant "association"). I think, in this particular instance, that that might well be true. To at least some degree, the tenor of the entire session was at least subtly shaped by the fact that it was a session that was being videotaped for public viewing. I probably felt more need to "do something" and to "make something interesting happen" than I would in an ordinary session. In retrospect, for example, even apart from silent waiting, the pump might well have been primed by statements such as, "Tell me more about what it means to you to be sensitive"; "Tell me some more about how people have 'accused' you of being sensitive"; "I'd like to hear more about how you worry you are too sensitive"; and so on. There are many ways to go further into the topic. Sometimes as therapists we "change the subject" too quickly. Sometimes we do not change it quickly enough, continuing doggedly well past the point at which it stops being a fruitful collaboration; wells sometimes *do* run dry, at least temporarily.

In any event, it is important to be clear that shifting the topic to inquire about Louise's relationship with Ken was by no means simply a "mistake." The topic is obviously an important one in its own right, one needing to be addressed at some point. Moreover, there is a way in which my query was in a very real way my "association," my affective resonance, rooted in not yet articulated thoughts, feelings, and ideas (what D. B. Stern, 1997, has referred to in a salutary phrase as "unformulated experiences"). Clearly, Louise's relationship with Ken, apart from being important in its own right, is another version of, and hence another route of access to, the topic we were already immersed in—Louise's experience of close relationships and when she feels valued and understood or dismissed and "disposable."

> *Louise:* I feel very secure, but I'm, I'm concerned because I know regardless of what he says about, you know, I can, you know, do without my family, his, his words and his actions are not congruent. And I know that he wouldn't be happy without having his family in his life.

* * * * *

Here, it seems to me, the "change of subject" has turned out to be a useful one. It gave both of us further perspective on why it *is* important for Louise to work on improving her relationship with Ken's family rather than just be more assertive with them—though obviously the two are not incompatible or inconsistent; part of making the relationship work includes being able to be sure that her needs too are taken into account in their exchanges. Otherwise, her resentment will always be there as at the very least an underlying factor that accounts for some of the subjectively puzzling hostility she encounters *from them*. As I discussed in Chapter 1, vicious circles are a pervasive presence in human experience and human relations, and the processes that constitute these circles are often not in one or both parties' awareness. As family therapists frequently point out, much of the seeming intractability of impasses between people is a function of the differing ways each "punctuates" the sequence. *Each* is likely to feel that he or she is just "responding" to the behavior of the other, and as a consequence the pattern repeats itself over and over. *It will be very important for the reader to keep this in mind when, later in the session, we encounter a striking "surprise" about Louise's wedding.*

> Paul: Uh huh. Uh huh. Uh huh. Does it feel to you like to feel solidly connected with Ken he would have to not have his family in his life?

* * * * *

I am exploring here, in essence, Louise's *conflict*; that is, whether Louise, although stating that Ken would not be happy without his family being in his life, nonetheless in some ways feels that if he loves her he will choose her *over* them. Put differently, I am wondering if Louise is more conflicted than she realizes over whether to facilitate a reconciliation with Ken's family or to try to pull him away from them and whether such a conflict is making it more difficult for Louise to find ways to achieve that reconciliation. I am trying to open up this topic in a preliminary way so that if this is the case, Louise may work on the conflict in a more consciously accessible way that will enable her better to resolve it.

> Louise: [*Long hesitation, bites her lip*] Well I feel, I feel solidly connected with him now, but I'm afraid that if he cuts his family completely out of his life I'm afraid that he will resent me. That's what it comes down to. I'm afraid that he's gonna blame me. 'Cause he doesn't blame me now, and I believe him. But if the roles were reversed, I would possibly down the line blame him. And I don't ever want him to look at me and go, "Wow, I cut my family out of my life for you." You know, and I don't, he might never do that, and if I had to say, give an answer, I would say no he wouldn't do that. But I just, I don't want him to lose his family that means so much to him, especially his mom, because of me. And this is why I'm trying so hard to mend something that is so difficult for me.

* * * * *

In one sense, Louise here passes over my implicit reference to her own possible *wish* for him to cut himself off from his family in solidarity with her. But her "fear" that he might do so implies some sense that despite wanting to stay connected with his family, he might remove himself from them in order to satisfy Louise. (A complicating factor in all this is that it is also occurring to me that *Ken* may be more conflicted than he realizes in his feelings toward his rather enmeshed and demanding family, and perhaps has unconsciously delegated to Louise the task of addressing his enmeshment with them.)

Paul:	Uh huh. Uh huh. And is the, is the possibility of his losing his family in order to be with you, is that a real prospect? I mean does it feel like there's no way he can be with both?
Louise:	Yes, because, I mean there are many times when I've said, "Why don't you go and be with your family, and you know, I have to do what I have to do." You know—for whatever reason—school, I haven't wanted to go, I haven't felt well. Whatever the case. 'Cause we always fought before we went to see his family, always, big fights. Even if we had fun, you know, I still just remember the fights. And I just think that because they, I mean if he, the few times he did go by himself, such as the Easter, they harass him, they tell him, you know, "She could have come for an hour." And they just make him miserable.

* * * * *

Louise has difficulty seeing that although she is encouraging him to see them, she is also setting it up so that he sees them under conditions that repeatedly create tension. It does seem likely, from what Louise describes throughout the session, that even if Louise were to accompany Ken much of the time, but also reserved the option of not coming with him when she had something she needed to do, there would be tension; that is, that they are a family that "keeps score" and that expects her to accompany him almost ritualistically. But if Louise can be helped to see the ways in which she contributes to the tension Ken feels, she will better understand why "they just make him miserable" and may be in a better position to find a solution that will work for her, for Ken, and for their relationship (a solution, it should be clear, that can include her conveying with strength, and perhaps with Ken's support, her own independence and right to at times pursue her own needs and interests.)

Paul:	Uh huh. Uh huh. Uh huh.
Louise:	So they're not exactly making it easier for us either. 'Cause I'm trying to compromise. You know?
Paul:	Now when they burst into the house just before Christmas and started berating you, what were they . . . and this was while your mother was still there and while you were both grieving over your father . . .
Louise:	Yes.
Paul:	. . . which, you know, is obviously a very hard and painful time. What were they doing? What were they saying? What was, what was their complaint? What would get them to act *that* way at *that* time?

* * * * *

Here, I am seeking a path toward exploring the kinds of issues I just alluded to in my previous interpolated comment. That is, I want to help Louise to better understand how her behavior and her stance look and feel to Ken's family because I think she does not really understand this. But I am aware that here is a line of inquiry that can easily feel to Louise like I am taking their side against her, that can seem, in the term I introduced in Chapter 1, accusatory. So I frame this inquiry in a way that strongly acknowledges and sides with the way Louise has seen things. As Louise describes it, it does seem to me that Ken's family's behavior, occurring right after the death of her father, was insensitive and inappropriate. But I am also trying to engage Louise's curiosity and find a way to invite her to consider some implications of her own pattern of behavior toward them that may contribute to the difficulties she faces.

When I ask, "What would get them to act that way?" (in a tone, as evident on the video, of *what in the world* would get them to act *that* way at *that* time?), I am stating it as essentially a rhetorical question, a question that clearly implies, in sympathy with Louise, that they *should not* have done that. But I am also, at the same time, trying to stimulate Louise to think about it as a *real* question. That is, by conveying my sympathetic understanding of how it felt to her, I hope to make it feel a little safer to actually *consider* why they would have responded in this way and to place this important question in a framework that makes it feel less accusatory, less about it being her "fault" and more about how she might, by understanding how her own behavior has felt *to them*, gain a greater measure of control over how *they* respond to *her*. This example illustrates how one may introduce inquiry into matters that the patient may experience as threatening or accusatory yet do it in a way that is also on the patient's side and acknowledges and affirms her own point of view.

> *Louise:* I wish I had an answer for that. My, my guess is that Denise wanted to clear the air, Ken's sister, the one that thinks she's his mom. And that's, 'cause she had said, "Oh if you don't like my phone message then why don't you call me and let me know?" And it's like it's not that easy for me to call her and say that, because I wasn't sure if it was just me feeling that way, feeling it was inappropriate for her to say on the message that, you know, I didn't have time to call you. And I just, I wasn't . . .
>
> *Paul:* And that was something that she heard then from Ken?
>
> *Louise:* Yeah. Well Ken just, you know, was yelling at his mom because he felt, you know, the family had let him down and let me down.

Paul:	Uh huh.
Louise:	And he was hurt for my sake and for his own sake, and felt like, I mean I'm not saying I was expecting them to bring dinner over every day, but I was still expecting some sort of acknowledgment of my dad's passing. And not just, "Oh, her dad died? Okay, well, whatever." So I guess what she wanted, her goal in some warped way was to get everything out in the open and just discuss everything. But that's not what she was doing. I mean what she was doing was just attacking me and telling me, "Well, we weren't invited to your wedding," 'cause when we got married we chose to get married just me and Ken. We were in Indiana, we had our reasons. That's final. I mean I don't care what anybody else thought. This was, this is our wedding, this is our life, this is how I wanted to get married. And I'm sorry.

* * * * *

I was a little startled to learn at this juncture that Ken's family was not invited to their wedding. It clearly offers an important perspective on why they have been less than warm and welcoming to Louise. And although it was not a *direct* response to my question of "what would get them to act in this way," the fact that this piece of very important information comes up right at this point suggests that indeed, the comment stimulated, even if unconsciously, Louise's thinking about the ways in which Ken's family's behavior is in part in response to her own. Of course, at this point Louise's account is not offered with much reflectiveness, but it did usefully open up the topic for later exploration in the session.

It is also important to notice that here Louise is also talking about her feelings of hurt at how the family responded to her father's death. We may also note that as angry as Louise feels toward them, and as strongly as she seems to be expressing a conviction that they were wrong, she also feels a need to say, "I mean I'm not saying I was expecting them to bring dinner over every day." This comment suggests an internal struggle on Louise's part—on the one hand, an experienced need to defend herself against the perception that she was asking for too much and, on the other, perhaps a secretly cherished fantasy that they would sense her need at that time to be taken care of and *would* care enough to bring dinner over during this trying time.

Paul:	Were you already feeling intruded upon by his family at that point? Is that part of what was going on?

* * * * *

I am here making my first attempt—again in a manner that tries to address a difficult topic in a nonaccusatory way—to examine the sources of the decision not to invite Ken's family to the wedding. By asking if she was already feeling intruded upon, I am implicitly acknowledging that the decision may have reflected hurt feelings that already existed on Louise's part or a need Louise felt to protect herself from their intrusions and taking over. What I am also envisioning here, and wanting (over time and diplomatically) to explore, is an early stage in the evolution of the vicious circle between them in which each of them, responding to the behavior of the other, keeps behaving in the very way that keeps the other behaving in ways that feel hurtful.[11]

Louise: Oh I felt, oh you mean from the beginning? Or when . . .

Paul: When you just . . .

Louise: . . . the wedding?

Paul: . . . in deciding to have the wedding without them being invited.

Louise: Well, I actually never thought I would get married. And then I met Ken and I was like wow, you know, I could actually get, marry him.

Paul: Uh huh.

Louise: And, but I wanted, I wanted the marriage, or the, yeah, the wedding the way that it was. I wanted it to be just him and me. I didn't want a big show. That's not how I saw my wedding. I wanted it to be him and me, and then invite his family. And my mom was in Sweden, and my dad was sick already at the time, so they couldn't come. And I felt like if my mom can't be there, I didn't want anybody else to be there either.

Paul: Uh huh.

Louise: So that was the first reason, and then I realized that it made me really happy that it was just me and Ken. And my mom respected it, you know. She was like, "Okay, well you know, I wish I could have been there. But if that's your choice" . . . it's like she wanted to be alone when my dad died, for example. And I respected her for that. I'm not gonna say, "No, I, I'm gonna be there," you know. So no, it wasn't so much that I felt they were intrusive at that time, but I knew, I was afraid to tell them, 'cause I knew they'd get upset. And I knew they wouldn't understand. And even when I tried to explain to Denise, and I said, you know, when she brought up the wedding I said, "This is

---

[11]I have discussed a similar kind of vicious circle pattern in the ironic structure of racial and ethnic tensions, in which each participant feels hurt or angry and responds to those feelings in ways that evoke the very same behavior from the other yet again (P. L. Wachtel, 1999).

how I wanted my wedding. We all want our weddings differently. Some people want a big lavish wedding and some people don't." And she's like, "Well you're entitled to your opinion." So I . . .

* * * * *

I registered here, for attention at some later point, the experience Louise described of her mother's telling her not to come when her father was dying. I thought it unlikely that Louise was simply fine with that, with no complicated feelings, but I chose for now just to register it, keep it in mind, and see how it applied later. It seemed to me that here was an instance of Louise's having been treated by her own mother with the kind of insensitivity to her feelings that she is so alert to and hurt by in Ken's family. It seems apparent that her image of her mother, so precious and yet so vulnerable and conflicted, is protected by focusing on the quite similar slights from Ken's family, enabling her to express her hurt at being treated this way without having to acknowledge or recognize that her mother has also treated her this way.

This account of her mother's behavior as her father was dying also suggests that her mother's behavior is, unconsciously, a model for her behavior toward Ken's family. Her mother's exclusion of her from the emotionally meaningful participation in her father's last days has noteworthy parallels with Louise's own exclusion of Ken's family from the emotionally meaningful participation in their son's wedding. Although this particular event occurred *after* Louise and Ken's wedding, there are many indications as the session proceeds that this is not the first time that Louise's mother has treated her with little sensitivity to her needs and vulnerabilities. Thus, there is reason to think that part of Louise's behavior toward her in-laws reflects an unconscious identification with her mother's behavior in a fashion similar to that discussed by Anna Freud (1936) under the rubric of identification with the aggressor. This is important to address at some point, because in identifying with her mother's behavior and unconsciously treating Ken's family in similar fashion, Louise creates a source of continuing difficulty and pain for herself that she does not really understand.

I also noted here—and *did* choose to pick up on in my very next comment—that Louise indicated that she did realize that Ken's family would be upset with their choice, that it was a choice made, at the very least, in the face of that potential upset, if not actually *intended* as a kind of finger in their eye. In my inquiry that follows next, I ask about this. But in inquiring into this dimension, I was acutely aware that here was another example of where the therapist must approach the matter very delicately if the patient is not to feel accused by the therapist's comments. Consequently, I framed the question in terms of what made having the wedding in this fashion so *important* to

Louise that she would risk upsetting them. That is, I am not treating it as simply perverse or hostile or foolish. I am conveying that there was a way in which it *made sense* to Louise, had a *meaning*, was rooted in an important concern that must be understood and respected, even as we also begin to look into whether it had problematic consequences and whether there was some other way to pursue the interests and concerns that led to this decision that might have caused her less consequent suffering and difficulty.

> *Paul:* Uh huh. What, help me to understand what made the, 'cause it sounds like that was something that was very important to you. I mean you probably already could at least somewhat anticipate that it would create problems with Ken's family.

> *Louise:* Uh huh.

> *Paul:* But it was really important to you.

> *Louise:* Uh huh.

> *Paul:* What, what was it about it that made it so important?

> *Louise:* The way I got married?

> *Paul:* Yeah.

> *Louise:* To be honest with you, at the time I didn't realize quite what a big deal it would be. Honestly, I didn't think they would be that upset about it. I knew they'd be upset, but I didn't think it would be "you're a bad person." I just feel like getting married is such a big deal, and everybody's entitled to, you know, have the wedding that they want. I'm not gonna, I'm not getting married to make other people happy. I'm getting married to make me happy. And I was planning on having them come, I mean I was planning on having a second ceremony with them and with my parents. So it never, it never really crossed my mind that they would not, after I explained to them, that they wouldn't understand.

* * * * *

In one sense, Louise is communicating here that she was taken by surprise. This is part of the problem she needs to be working on. At times, she doesn't seem to appreciate or be able to anticipate well the impact of her actions on others. As a consequence, she is frequently blindsided by events and feels stricken and confused.

In part, this experience of being blindsided reflects a measure of denial or dissociation; she has said, just before, that "we had our reasons. That's final. I mean I don't care what anybody else thought" and that she "knew they wouldn't understand." And yet she also has the experience that "it never really crossed my mind that they would not understand" and that "I didn't think they would be that upset about it." It seemed to me that part of what happens for Louise is that she is still conflicted about how acceptable it is to acknowledge how angry she is with them and as a consequence she has a hard time knowing when she is being provocative. I noted all this for future reference but did not pursue it directly at this point, choosing to extend the exploration from within the rhythm and content of where our dialogue had been thus far.

> *Paul:* Uh huh. Uh huh. So this was a special time for you, and it was a time that meant so much you wanted it to be for you and not to make other people happy.
>
> *Louise:* Uh huh.
>
> *Paul:* That sort of . . . the, the importance of being able to take a stand that this is for me, this is not to make other people happy, that sounds like there must have been pulls in your life before that to make other people happy that made you finally . . .

* * * * *

This is clearly a comment designed to further *explore* the meaning and implications of her decision, to raise a *question* about it. But it is also framed in a way that *affirms* Louise, by stating it in terms of it feeling important to her to *take a stand*.

> *Louise:* Oh I'm a huge people-pleaser.
>
> *Paul:* Tell me about that.
>
> *Louise:* I'm a huge people-pleaser. I've done nothing my whole life but try to make everybody else happy.
>
> *Paul:* Uh huh.
>
> *Louise:* And I finally decided that there needs to be, there needs to be a limit. I still like to make other people happy, but I realize that I'm not gonna make other people happy to the point of making myself sick. 'Cause that's what I was doing. With his family. I mean I was, you know, like I said, me and Ken were fighting before we went over there, I didn't want to go, I just felt like I was just so pressured and pushed and bullied, and it was like I was back in my childhood again [*stated in a very plaintive voice*]. When I let her, I mean somebody said jump and I said how high. I never took a stand for myself ever.

* * * * *

This is a very poignant statement that offers a therapeutically useful perspective on why she chose not to invite Ken's family to the wedding. It remains a choice that had problematic consequences for her and for her relationship to Ken, but the product of this exploration does help us to better understand why she did what she did. Hearing the story from this vantage point was helpful to me in feeling more sympathetic to Louise after having felt somewhat taken aback when I first heard her mention not inviting them to the wedding.

> Louise: And now, and I never said no. And it's like I was finally, you know, starting, you know, and Ken helped me a lot. My husband really taught me to just, you know, stand up for myself. And then I thought, you know, with his family I was kind of in that stage where I was practicing my standing up for myself, and I wanted to not look back and regret. Because, you know, because my mom and I have talked about it a lot. And she said don't, you know, things that really mean a lot to you, you know, life is too short. Make sure that you do those things the way that you want to do them.

* * * * *

The large number of "you knows" in this passage suggest that we are in the midst of a topic that is particularly conflict-laden for Louise.

> Paul: Uh huh. Uh huh. Now that sounds like your, your mom was really supporting you and what you wanted.

> Louise: Uh huh.

> Paul: The experience growing up of being bullied by the other kids, were there any ways in your own family, where your mom and dad, where you were a people-pleaser with them too?

* * * * *

At the end of the above relatively long statement by Louise, with its reference to painful emotional experiences and signs of struggle with conflicting inclinations and attitudes, Louise presents her mother as an *exception* to the pattern she has been describing. Her mother, here, is presented as siding with Louise, supporting and helping her *not* to just please the other. Perhaps already alerted by Louise's earlier sharp dichotomizing between her "individualist" family and Ken's "collectivist" one, I wondered here if some conflict with *her own* family was being submerged in the way she viewed Ken's family. Note here, by the way, that no interpretation about "splitting" was needed to open up the topic, just the simple question, "Were you a people-pleaser with them too?"

Of course, one is much more likely to ask such a question if one has registered (whether consciously or subliminally) the indications that Louise tends to "split" or sharply dichotomize between Ken's "bad" family and her own supportive one. After reading further in the session, the reader might want to refer back to where Louise talks about the other kids being jealous of her because of how close she and her mother were. I think that by this point in the session I had begun to sense that part of the path toward some kind of reconciliation with Ken's family—and especially, as I took the aim to be, a reconciliation that was rooted not in Louise just acceding to their demands but in a genuine reconfiguring that took *both* parties' needs and experiences into account—lay in a less "split" or defensively dichotomized view of both Ken's family *and* her own.

As will be apparent, this line of inquiry in fact did open up important material that gave a rather different—indeed, a dramatically different— picture of Louise's family life than she had offered up to this point.

> *Louise:* Absolutely, yeah.
>
> *Paul:* Tell me more about that, and how that happened.
>
> *Louise:* Well my dad had a stroke when I was 8 years old. He was 48 so he was very young. It left him unable to speak, read, or write from then on. So I didn't have, from 8 years old on I didn't really have a close relationship with my dad. It was more like he was my brother. And we kind of fought for my mom's atten‑ tion. And I felt like my mom always, you know, took his side, and I was just a kid, you know. And I felt like I wanted my mom, you know.

* * * * *

I had no idea that my line of inquiry in this part of the session would lead to this particular dramatic turn of events (to be followed, rather shortly, with an even more dramatic further revelation). Louise had given no indications whatsoever about her father's stroke previously, or about the particular ways (to be elaborated shortly) that this took on meaning within her family and had its impact on Louise's life. But I think that the emer‑ gence of this material at this point illustrates the importance of the thera‑ pist being receptive to what is sensed unconsciously or implicitly. In this part of the session, I am, in several places, following an intuitive and not fully articulated‑to‑myself sense that there were conflicts and stresses in Louise's family that she has had difficulty in acknowledging to herself or thinking about very clearly. When I picked up on her portraying her mom as supporting her doing things her way and then, a moment later, inquired about whether she was a people‑pleaser in the family too, I was responding to a felt sense, not fully conscious, that there was something useful in this somewhat shifted direction. My line of inquiry did not follow a thread of "logic," but of intuition (cf. Polanyi, 1958, 1967). Had I not asked these questions that to some degree were non sequiturs with regard to the explicit topic at that point, my guess is that the material about the stroke and its aftermath would never have come up in the session. It is unlikely that any "manual" would point the therapist to feel his way into this new and not consciously anticipated material.

In attending to what Louise said, here, it is important to note not only the specific content but the tone as well, which may not come through in a transcript the way it does in a video. Louise's statement that "I was just a kid" and "I felt like I wanted my mom" were again said in a very plaintive tone. She is expressing here, I think, a feeling and need that she still experiences and that enters into her present relationships, including with Ken's family: She is not *ready* yet to be grown up, to think of the impact of her choices and behavior on others; she wants to be taken care of in a way that she wasn't by her own mom.

As I explore later in the session, Louise's difficulties with Ken's family stem not just from ways in which they are less empathic and more demanding and rejecting than her family (as she initially presents them). They stem as well from Louise's sensing that they may be able to offer her something that she *did not* get from her own family and that she longs for. Her wish to join them and to be taken care of by them is certainly a *conflicted* wish, one that she struggles with and that in certain respects she defends against by placing her grievances toward them front and center. But, as the direction the session takes here makes increasingly evident, these wishes are also the product of many experiences she had growing up in her own family, and for that reason they are not easily put to rest.

> *Paul:* It must have been scary to have that happen to your father.
>
> *Louise:* It was scary, but at the same time my mom, I have to say she did a really good job making it normal. So I wasn't, so I mean it felt like, oh okay, you know, she did, she did a really good job. I mean I was always in the hospital, I, you know, I helped my dad learn to walk again. You know, so I was very, very involved. So even though I was scared, she still, when I was 14 for example, she—and then I was really scared, and I will never forget. We were living in France at the time. My mom had a mental, nervous breakdown. She just up and left me, and went to Sweden.

* * * * *

Note how this rather terrifying story unfolds. First I comment that it "must have been scary," a comment that Louise at first mostly rejects, emphasizing that her mom did a really good job making it normal. The thrust of her first few sentences is toward denying or minimizing the terror. And then, in seeming to elaborate on how well her mother had helped her to contain the fear and make things normal, she begins a sentence with, "So even though I was scared . . . " (which seems to evoke expectations in the hearer of the rest of the sentence being something like " . . . she did all she could to help me to cope with it"). But the sentence seems to have a mind of its own, so to speak, changing direction in midcourse and taking her inexorably as it unfolds into the terrifying story of maternal breakdown and abandonment she then relates.

Paul: Uh huh.

Louise: And I didn't know where she went, I didn't know where she was, I didn't know what she was doing. She was gone for like a couple of weeks. And she just *left* me there with my dad. And one day you know, he started getting a nosebleed and it wouldn't stop, and I didn't speak French. And I tried to get a hold of people who spoke English, and I finally got him to the hospital. But, you know, so it was a combination of her trusting me to be able to take care of myself but me going, "What are you *thinking?*" [*spoken in a childlike and plaintive manner*]

Paul: Yeah. That's right . . . [*overlapping*]

Louise: I'm a child!

Paul: That's right, that's right . . . [*overlapping*]

Louise: Don't leave me . . .

Paul: Right. [*overlapping*]

Louise: . . . to take care of . . .

Paul: Right. [*overlapping*]

Louise: . . . my dad, you know.

Paul: Right.

Louise: So, but I never said anything.

Paul: Uh huh.

Louise: I never told my mom how angry I was.

Paul: Uh huh. Uh huh.

Louise: I just did it.

* * * * *

This whole account of her mother's abandoning her proceeded continuously. The "uh huhs," that's rights," and so on, by me were just emotional resonating or supportive bystanding occurring in the midst of a continuous narrative by Louise.

Paul: What, what would it have been like to tell her?

I am trying here to help her create a path toward expressing her feelings and needs as they come up. I am directing it, as it were, toward mom in retrospect, but it is part of a process of helping her to build in potential responses so she can say—to anyone—"you're not treating me properly," "I need something from you," and so on. One might describe this as a form of anticipatory behavior rehearsal.

Louise: Scary.

Paul: Uh huh.

Louise: Because I feel like she never, then she'd, you know, made me feel guilty. Then it was like the guilt trip, you know. "Well, your dad had a stroke, and think about what *he's* going through." And I did, every day of my life I thought about what he was going through. You know, he couldn't, he couldn't talk any more. He couldn't read, he couldn't write. I mean I was aware of that, but I was still just a kid. The past couple of years, we've started to be honest with each other and tell each other the truth, and not holding back.

Paul: Uh huh. Uh huh. So Ken, I would assume, knows a lot about what you've just told me about.

* * * * *

Although Louise responded positively and usefully to the line of inquiry I introduced at this point, it seems to me in retrospect that I moved away too quickly from that really, really heartfelt description of what it was like to be a child in this family and what it was like for her to be with her father and to experience her mother's accusations and inability to recognize the needs of her daughter in the face of all the family was going through. The direction I took the session at this point had its own therapeutic value, and turned out to be of real use to Louise. But there was still a lot of feeling there about the experiences we were directly addressing, and I think in retrospect I would have liked to have stayed with it a bit longer before shifting the topic some.

Louise: Most of it, yeah.

Paul: And so when you were feeling this is gonna, about the wedding say, this is gonna be one of the first times in my life where I'm not taking care of everybody else, where I'm really able to just say, "*I've* got a place in this world, too."

Louise: Uh huh.

Paul: And he respected that, and honored that, and went along with you on it. Do, does his family understand that that was part of what led to your making that decision?

* * * * *

Having now heard about the trauma she had experienced in her childhood (which I did not know about before) and about the prominent role of "people-pleasing" in her makeup, I am beginning to understand, in a way that I could not before, why it was so important to her to not submit to the needs and demands of parental figures. In stating out loud for her "*I've got a place in this world too,*" I was helping her to give voice to an experience in a way that facilitates both her self-understanding and her ability to represent herself more effectively with Ken's family. This giving voice to the patient's experience, articulating what we have heard the patient say but doing so in a stronger or clearer way, is one of the most useful things we do as therapists. On the one hand, it enables the patient to feel understood and affirmed, while simultaneously, it implicitly models for the patient a somewhat different way of representing herself that she may take in and use without feeling she is copying someone else's words or thoughts. Because I am presenting what I am saying as simply a restatement of what I have heard *her* say, it can still feel like hers, even though it is put in words that she has never quite used. This is an aspect of what I have called the *attributional* dimension of therapeutic work, which I have discussed in some detail elsewhere (P. L. Wachtel 1993). Thus, the aim of these comments is at least twofold—to help Louise better understand her own motives and experience and to help her find a way to communicate with Ken's family about what had happened.[12]

With regard to the first aim, I felt that although Louise seems in *certain* respects to be able to state quite powerfully her wish to do things her way and its rationale in her life experience ("I never took a stand for myself ever"; "I'm not getting married to make other people happy. I'm getting married to make me happy"; "That's final. I mean I don't care what anybody else thought. This is our wedding, this is our life"), in other respects it seemed to me that Louise was quite conflicted and uncertain about this, that it was often a *defensive* assertion of her right to self-determination, not a *secure* one. I felt that in fact she was not all that sympathetic to or comfortable with her own needs and experience and still struggled with the inclination to override them and "people-please." In restating what she had told me in the way I did ("*I've got a place in this world too!*") I was aiming both to stand behind and help her to sympathetically regard her own experience and to offer a form of modeling for her further communications with Ken's family.

Regarding the second aim, helping Louise better express herself with and represent herself to Ken's parents, it seemed to me that if Louise had a less conflicted and clearer way of understanding and expressing why she made the choice she did, she might be able to discuss it at some point with Ken's

---

[12]It should also be noted that in elaborating my comment, I was also trying to help Louise strengthen her bond with Ken by highlighting his "honoring" her needs and feelings.

family in a somewhat more effective way, or at least to open up the topic as one that could be spoken about rather than as one she shrank from because she felt she was not equipped to communicate effectively about it with them. This is in part why I also asked her if his family understood that some of her experiences growing up were part of what led her to make the decision she did. I was implicitly encouraging her to find some way to open up this topic and represent herself to them more three-dimensionally rather than as just someone who had treated them badly, which is how they presently view her.

This does not mean that an apology to Ken's family, some taking into account of how it felt to them, may not also be a part of the healing process. But I think that Louise would be unlikely even *to be able* to apologize or feel an apology is in order without having achieved a secure sense of the *legitimacy* of the needs and feelings that led to her behavior. Moreover, what might be called the *effectiveness* of the apology would likely depend in part on whether Louise was able to convey to them an understanding of her behavior that communicated the *meaning* of her choice, that it was not just an expression of hostility by someone who completely disregards them and their feelings.

Here is an illustration, I should also note, of how the therapist can use his or her own subjective experience to help the patient potentially anticipate the reactions of others. That is, I must confess that my initial response to hearing that Louise had not invited Ken's family to her wedding was one of being rather startled, maybe even shocked, and to feel (if only in part), "Oh, *that's* why they are so hostile to her. Now it makes more sense. They are not ogres or overly demanding, but were understandably furious at what they experienced as a totally unjustified slight of them." For me, the experience of then hearing about her father's stroke and her mother's leaving her in Paris offered me a *different* perspective on what she did. Louise herself did not fully articulate this different way of understanding her decision about the wedding, but I articulated it for her in the comment I made. In doing so, I was also trying to help her frame or formulate her own understanding of what had happened in a way that could enable her to communicate more effectively to Ken's family.

Louise's account of the rather extreme circumstances and events she had to endure as a child and of the degree to which her mother was not up to the task of protecting her in this rather overwhelming situation also sheds further light on why Louise had to direct her negative feelings so exclusively toward Ken's family. Her splitting, the sharply dichotomous line she drew between her family and Ken's, served to protect her image of her mother from the painful recognition of how much her mother had failed her at such a crucial time in her life. The feelings of anger, abandonment, and isolation that threatened to emerge were potentially overwhelming, and the fear of losing whatever connection she did still have with her mother if she let herself see more clearly how things had been was potentially unbearable (cf. Fairbairn, 1958). By experiencing those feelings in relation to *Ken's* family, she could give some expression to their powerful and urgent push while still keeping "pure" the image of her mother that—if the floodgates were to be opened—was potentially so vulnerable to being "spoiled," to use the language of Melanie Klein (1952).

> *Louise:* No. They just see it as you know, me shutting out the family, and how could I do that and how could Ken go along with it, and you know. There's just, even when I tried to explain, it was like, whatever. Don't want to hear it. Because they, they, I mean they don't say no to each other. It's like, as I said, they don't have any boundaries. They walk all over each other and nobody stands up to anybody else.

* * * * *

Here, Louise shows that she has not yet taken in my message in the fashion I intended. That is, she takes my question of "does his family understand?" as a simple factual question, whose answer is no, rather than as a hint as to how she might begin to *lead them* to understand.

Does this response to my comment indicate that I should have framed it differently? I don't think so. I framed it as "do they understand?" because that way of framing it maintains, and even bolsters, my position of being on her side, standing beside her. This is a position that *in general* one should try to occupy vis à vis the patient whenever it is possible (i.e., without being insincere or airbrushing important realities).[13] But it is perhaps especially important with Louise, and especially important *at this point* with Louise, because she has just been telling me about a very significant trauma in her life, and one marked especially by the failure of a parental figure to take her needs and her experience into account. The implicit message (i.e., the suggestion regarding how she might more effectively and sympathetically present herself to Ken's parents) was still communicated, I believe, even if it did not bear fruit at the first saying. It will be apparent below that I further follow up on it and that Louise begins to "get" this other side of what I am conveying as the session proceeds.

> *Paul:* Uh huh. Uh huh.

> *Louise:* So when I'm trying to be my own person and stand up for myself it's like, "What are you *doing*? What do you think you're doing?"

---

[13]I say "whenever possible" because it is important to be clear that taking such a stance if it is insincere is not likely to be very helpful. However, as I have discussed in detail elsewhere (see especially Wachtel, 1993, 2008) the "harder" or "darker" comments that we offer patients are not necessarily "compelled by the data"; the therapist's comment is usually but one of several equally "true" or "accurate" statements one could make in response to what the patient has conveyed. But if several different responses may be equally "true," they are not necessarily equally *therapeutic*. Much of the talent of being a good therapist is developing a mind-set in which the formulation that occurs to one, or that one chooses, is the one that not only fits the facts of experience but points in a direction that is genuinely therapeutic and liberating.

Paul: Uh huh. So you tried to explain to them.

Louise: Yes. And during the confrontation I tried to explain to her. She, she, you know, she apologized about Easter when I was telling her. She's like, "Well, you know, I'm sure you took an hour to eat." I'm like, you know, "I was eating while I was doing my exam. I'm sorry. I don't really think I should have to sit here 2 years later and explain this to you." But apparently I did. So . . .

Paul: You know, one odd thing that occurs to me is that in some way Ken's family lives the way you lived growing up.

* * * * *

As will be apparent, here begins a key intervention.

Louise: Oh, *yeah*.

Paul: You know?

Louise: Yeah.

Paul: You know what I mean?

Louise: Yeah, I never thought about that. That's a great way of putting it, because that helps me be more sympa, empathetic to them, actually. That's a good observation.

Paul: Yeah, they really seem caught in the same . . .

Louise: Yeah [*overlapping—Louise still affirming and responding to what I am saying*]

Paul: . . . thing. There's no time to really even have any time to think about "what do *I* want to do?"

* * * * *

Even though Louise has agreed with what I said, I'm actually still not sure at this point *what* she is agreeing with. That is, she does seem to have gotten what I was getting at from the very first phrase ("lives the way you lived growing up"). But I want to be sure that she understands that phrase the way I intended it, so I here further spell it out, even though she has already seemingly assented. It will be evident that I in fact continue to do this because I *also* want to stimulate further reflection on it and experiencing of it, not simply agreement. The therapist's aim is not to be "right" but to stimulate and maintain an active process whereby the patient can rework some of the patterns in which she has been entrapped.

Louise:	Uh huh.
Paul:	It's what *should* I do?
Louise:	Uh huh.
Paul:	How do I . . .
Louise:	Exactly.
Paul:	Yeah.
Louise:	It's always you should, you should, you should.
Paul:	Right, yeah.
Louise:	Family, family, family.
Paul:	Yeah, right.
Louise:	And it's like when you married Ken you married the family.
Paul:	Right.
Louise:	And that is so foreign to me. So foreign to me.
Paul:	It's so foreign to you, and at the same time it's so central to you.

* * * * *

This whole sequence constitutes a key intervention. Given how significant it turned out to be, it should be mentioned that my aim in making it was not so clear until *after* I said it. Here is another example of the trust in and openness to intuition I discussed just a few pages earlier. What I offered was another partial non sequitur, a comment that did not necessarily logically follow from the topic she was talking about, and that is introduced by me as "an odd thing that occurred to me." Once again, the example reveals, I believe, the limits of "manuals," which are often based on a rather programmatic approach to the work that assumes that each step can be made rather explicit. But as Polanyi (1958, 1967) highlighted, often our most important advances come from attention to what he called *tacit* knowledge, that which we have begun to grasp but have not yet consciously articulated.

Here, when she says, "That is so foreign to me," her defenses are coming back into play as she attempts to ward off the implications of what she had just so enthusiastically agreed to. The very point of my earlier comment, to which she responded, "That's a great way of putting it," was that their way was *not* so foreign to her.

In my response to this resurgence of the defensive, dichotomizing vision, I do not make a "defense interpretation." I do not tell her she is being defensive, or inconsistent, or going back on what she acknowledged just a moment ago. Nor do I contradict her statement, suggesting that it is *not* foreign.

Instead I say that it was "foreign *and at the same time* so central." This enables me to embrace and affirm her experience at the moment even while bringing her back to the other side. It is one more example of the distinction between comments that address what the patient is "really" feeling and what she is "also" feeling discussed in Chapter 2. The "really" comments are adversarial and convey that the patient's conscious perception is wrong, that she is out of touch with her real feelings. The "also" comments convey, as I noted in Chapter 2, that there is "*more to you*" than you have experienced thus far. They are expansive and friendly, yet they point to the very same omitted experience and seek to make room for it.

"So foreign and yet so central" was clearly experienced by Louise as a helpful and friendly comment that resonated with the experiences she was describing, not as a *challenge* to her self-understanding. Perhaps for that very reason, it was also a comment that contributed to *changing* her self-understanding. It *got through* to her, was taken in in a way that the more traditional defense interpretation might not have. And it is interesting to note that just a short while later, she says, "I'm thinking . . . when you said even though that's so foreign to you, that's still always been central . . . " Thus she brings up my comment spontaneously, indicating that the comment is still resonating for her, making sense to her, and illuminating her experience. She has continued to *think* about it; it was a comment that did not just get filed and put aside but—I think because of the very "both–and" structure I am highlighting here—worked to further the process of self-examination and reappropriation of experience. It will also be evident in Chapter 4 that Louise returns to this comment still again in the second session.

> *Louise:* Right, yeah.
>
> *Paul:* You know what I mean?
>
> *Louise:* Yeah. 'Cause I'm caught in the middle of it.
>
> *Paul:* Yeah, yeah. And were all through growing up in a way.
>
> *Louise:* Uh huh.
>
> *Paul:* I mean you couldn't be, I would even wonder whether some of the difficulty you had with other kids growing up was because there was some way almost in which you *weren't supposed to* make those connections outside, because you had these duties in the family to this very wounded . . .
>
> *Louise:* Yeah. [*stated very affirmatively, as a spontaneous expression in the midst of my sentence*]
>
> *Paul:* . . . family.
>
> *Louise:* I'm thinking, because when you said that, when you said even though that's so foreign to you, that's still always been central.

I never, you're right because I always, I was always told to be loyal to the family, and never talk to anybody about my problems. And now I'm like telling everybody. You know, in classes and stuff I'm always sharing and I'm always very open. Because it's like, screw you, I'm just gonna tell everybody, because you told me my whole life I should never open up.

Paul: Right, right. So you've . . .

Louise: So, *wow!* [*strong affect*]

Paul: . . . broken out of that.

Louise: Yeah, I have. [*laugh of almost glee, excitement*]

* * * * *

Here, and through the whole sequence that begins a bit earlier and continues for a while, Louise is very excited by the ideas she is exploring.

Paul: And they almost like represent what you, what the, the trap you were in for so many years.

Louise: Yeah.

Paul: Sort of like they're so familiar.

Louise: Wow, I never thought about it that way, it makes it easier for me to understand why I'm so, you know, it totally makes more sense to me now. 'Cause that's what I've been trying, but maybe it's, 'cause they always, I don't know if it's the same, but I always hear that, you know, if you haven't dealt with something it keeps coming back in your life. And I guess I never dealt with that, and that's why unfortunately I have this family to deal with. But if, yeah, I need to face it. I just don't know . . . again, it's just working on how.

Paul: Yeah. Well let's think together about how. What would you, how would you *like* to approach them? What would you *like* to say to them? If you, if you had a little room for them to listen, and I know that's not easy, and we can't assume that. But what would you like to say to them?

* * * * *

Here I do something that most therapists whose work is strongly rooted in the psychoanalytic tradition do not feel comfortable doing or think is likely to be worthwhile. I *take seriously* Louise's "I just don't know." I also take seriously what she says more incidentally and indirectly, perhaps almost evasively: "It's just working on how." To be sure, she is not directly *asking* for help on the how, which for some therapists might mean it is presumptuous for me to *offer* any help on the how. But I think she is not asking for help in good part because it does not even occur to her that anyone (including me) *would be willing* or *is able* to offer her help. There is a certain resignation in not really asking for help with the how, and my response is intended as a counter to this resignation. It is intended to convey that she *can* get help from others and *deserves* that help. It is also an affirmation that people *do* need help with complicated emotional issues, that she does not need to solve everything alone.

My choice is rooted as well in a conviction that the "how" is often as important as the "why." That is, successful psychotherapy is usually not just a matter of insight, of gaining an understanding of *why* one has been stuck in the patterns that constrict one's life. It also usually entails *doing something about* those patterns (see P. L. Wachtel, 1997). Many therapists believe that if the patient fully "understands" her motivations, or gains insight into the childhood roots of her difficulties, what to do about her present situation and how most effectively to do so will follow more or less automatically. Once the brush is cleared away, in this view, the rest is easy.

In my experience, this is not necessarily the case. Dealing effectively with complex emotional and relational experiences requires a good deal of *skill*. Most people acquire that skill through a long process of trial and error—thousands, if not millions, of transactions in which one learns how to express anger, love, or need in a way that "works" in the real world of human transaction. One must learn how not to be *too* angry, too needy, or cloyingly affectionate, and also, when there are inevitable rebuffs and failures, how not to retreat too far in the opposite direction so that the feeling is not effectively expressed or gotten across. One must also, over developmental time, learn how to move from being an "effective" 2-year old, to being an effective 4-year-old, and so on. What works and is appropriate at age 3 is problematic behavior at age 6, and so forth through the developmental eras. All of this is constrained or prevented when the person learns early to defend against or shrink from a particular kind of affective constellation, and as a consequence, from lack of opportunity to hone one's skills in socially expressing emotion, the emotion becomes *genuinely* dangerous. That is, when we don't know how to express an emotion in a way that works in actual personal transactions, then expressing that emotion *is* disruptive of whatever security and gratification we *have* managed to achieve, even if it is compromised.

Put differently, my response to Louise's "it's just a matter of how" is a reflection of my participation in and commitment to the integrative movement in therapy that I have alluded to previously in this book. I am working in a fashion that has clear roots in the psychoanalytic tradition, and especially the relational version of that tradition, but I am also guided by the insights and methods of the behavioral tradition. That tradition points to the importance of helping the patient to take on new behaviors, to activate in practice the new understandings they have achieved in the therapeutic work, and it also has methods and a consonant philosophy that *directly address* the "how" question and the overt changes in behavior that are a crucial part of therapeutic change.

Louise: Well, first of all I'd like them to return my phone calls. [*smiles*]

Paul: Right. That's . . .

Louise: I want them to just respect me for who I am.

Paul: Uh huh.

Louise: When I, not just tell me what to do, but also do what they tell me. 'Cause they're like do as I say, but don't, you know, not as I do.

Paul: Uh huh.

Louise: Because, and if I make a mistake or if I say something that hurts you, you know, tell me right away instead of you know, waiting 2 years to tell me.

Paul: Uh huh. Uh huh. Right.

Louise: Understand that it's not that I don't want to spend time with you, it's just that I honestly, you know, I . . . women who have kids and a job and go to school, I hold them on a pedestal because I could never do that. And I don't know what it's like to have kids, but please don't tell me that, you know, I don't know what it's like to be busy because I don't have kids. 'Cause I, I mean when someone says, "Wait until you have kids and then you'll find out." I hate that.

Paul: Right. Uh huh.

Louise: So just the biggest thing is respect. And try and, and when I try and explain to you, hear me.

Paul: Uh huh. Uh huh. One thing I'm wondering about is . . . I, one thing I understand clearly, and that you've described, and I, it makes sense to me, that there's a way in which there's this pull from them that you feel the need to resist and that creates conflict, because they want to pull you in, and you want to keep some boundary. But I'm also wondering, is there another part of it that is, that there's something about—after all you grew up in a very small family; you were the only child, and in a certain sense the family was even smaller because your father wasn't fully there, either—whether there's something about this large enveloping family that's in some way appealing and attractive.

* * * * *

Here I am opening up the issue of *conflict.* I fully acknowledge that there is a pull from them that she wants to resist (so she does not feel that I am denying her experience or failing to understand what her experience has been). But then I use that as a platform for *adding* something else—that she might also feel *attracted* to aspects of Ken's family (and, implicitly, that in part she is fearful of her own *desires,* which can feel dangerous because they potentially could lead her into the very web of obligation that she had to contend with growing up. Those obligations, after all, are also a part of what Ken's family represents for her).

As this sequence proceeds, it becomes apparent that Louise is surprisingly receptive to an idea that might seem, on the basis of how she *first* presented things, like something that would be totally alien and unacceptable to her. This is, I think, one more indication of the clinical value of framing one's comments in terms of conflict and of what the patient may "also" be feeling rather than trying to persuade the patient that what she is "really" feeling is something quite other than what she had thought.

> *Louise:* Absolutely.
>
> *Paul:* But maybe feels a little too . . . sort of almost like *threateningly* appealing.
>
> *Louise:* Uh huh.
>
> *Paul:* You know, like you could get sucked into it because there is something that you could like and could want in it.

* * * * *

Here I am elaborating on the implications of what I had just said a moment before, making sure, as I have a number of times earlier in our interactions, that when Louise was assenting she was in fact responding to the meaning I had intended. I am also here further *clarifying* what I was pointing to, amplifying on the point I had just made. It is common in the training of therapists to emphasize the importance of being brief, of not saying too much. But it is equally important to make sure one is not being cryptic to ensure that the patient really understands what you are getting at.

It is also worth noting that as I am saying these things, the video reveals that there is an expression on Louise's face of joy and fascination, like I am saying something both excitingly new and excitingly *familiar,* something coming out from under cover and being given room for the first time.

> *Louise:* Yeah, that makes sense. Because I've always wanted a big family. I've wanted you know, maybe two or three kids. I don't know if that's big, but you know.

Paul: Uh huh. Uh huh.

Louise: I've always, the idea of family, big family like them has always appealed to me.

Paul: Uh huh.

Louise: But that doesn't mean that you know, come over whenever you want, and you know, walk all over my boundaries and that kind of thing.

* * * * *

I am pleased here to see her affirming the other (originally more evident) side of her conflict, standing behind the experience of not wanting to have her boundaries trampled. This indicates that she is not just being compliant, that she is *integrating* what I have said rather than *substituting* it for what she previously felt. And, as I too further elaborate right after this exchange, it is the very combination of opening herself to them *and* maintaining her boundaries and prerogatives that offers a potentially viable new way of being with them in a genuine fashion.

Paul: Right.

Louise: So yeah, it makes sense what you're saying.

Paul: Right, right. So it's really not just how do you keep them away, but how do you *move into* the family *while* being respected, you know. And not just respected, 'cause that's, that's too abstract. But while being able to say, "There's things I want for myself. And I don't want to be just taking care of other people and living a life of obligation."

Louise: Uh huh.

Paul: Yeah.

Louise: Yeah, 'cause I mean I'm, we are very different, not just, you know, I mean I don't care to cook, I don't care to have, you know, parties at my house.

Paul: Uh huh.

Louise: And you know, I wish that we could just reach some sort of compromise instead of, I mean, I'd rather pay them to not have to cook for them, you know. And I don't, I feel like my house is too small, we're moving, so we're gonna get a bigger house. So it's like I just wish that they would instead of telling me do this, this is the only option you have, if we could just talk about some sort of compromise. And they could say well, you know, "We notice that you don't really like to cook so what else do you think you can do?"

Paul:	Uh huh.
Louise:	So.
Paul:	I'm also wondering, I certainly hear ways in which you're very different. But I'm wondering is that the part that's a little easier to sort of see, to notice, to feel comfortable with, more than the ways in which you might be similar.

* * * * *

I am responding here to her immediately preceding statement that "we are very different," but I am also responding to it in the context of the already introduced theme of her being *attracted* to them as well as wanting to create barriers and ward them off. Depicting them as very different is another way to ward them off or, put differently, to ward off *her own* inclination to move closer to them (which, as we discussed, also feels dangerous to her)—if they are so different, then there is no basis for them to relate to each other.[14]

Louise:	Uh huh. Yeah, it's always easier to talk about what's different . . .
Paul:	Yeah, yeah.
Louise:	Well we're similar I think, me and Denise are similar because I think she's a very insecure person. And I can be very insecure still. Because she feels the need to control everybody else. I have a need to control my environment too, so I know what's, what's going on to make me feel less vulnerable.

* * * * *

A moment before, when I was saying that it's been easier to notice the ways in which they were different than the ways in which they were alike, the video showed Louise once again with a wonderfully responsive, receptive smile. What we were talking about was reaching her on an affective level, not just cognitively. But because we are talking about feelings that are highly conflictual for her, the degree to which she can stay with the newly emerging experience, and let it be fully felt, can be expected to fluctuate.

Here it feels to me like she is giving a "contrast and compare" exam answer, rather than, as in some of her previous responses to my comments, responding with affect and a sense of real personal involvement. At the same time, she certainly is taking up the theme I have introduced and is considering it seriously. In a moment, the fuller sense of having actually assimilated emotionally what is the theme of this part of our collaborative dialogue

---

[14]Louise had earlier defended against the desire to be closer to them in a somewhat similar fashion, by stating that they are the "collectivist" family and hers the "individualist," again drawing a sharp distinction between them.

becomes apparent when, as the reader shall see next, Louise recalls an emotionally meaningful detail regarding Ken's mother that surprises me a good deal and suggests that a real path toward opening up blocked channels of affect and desire has begun.

> *Paul:* Uh huh.
>
> *Louise:* I feel, I think she's the same way. His mom and I are very much alike, too. I mean we, I felt, and it hurts, because I felt we had a really good connection. 'Cause she was telling me, you know, she doesn't really, she likes her alone time. And she was not being respected for that either. And she just went along with it, she never stood up for herself.
>
> *Paul:* Uh huh.
>
> *Louise:* And I was trying to work with her to help her stand up for herself. And I said, you know, "If you have to, you know, tell them you're at my house. You know, if you want to be left alone, tell them you're at my house. You know, I'll say you're here." So yeah, you know, and his other sister Maria, she's not really that much in the picture. But yeah, I can, I can definitely see, I never actually had to say it out loud, but yeah, I can see the similarities.

* * * * *

So here is a rather dramatic recollection in its way, a revealing of a bond with Ken's mother that, in the affect state with which she began the session (the affect state that seems to have largely dominated her experience of his family for some time), was barely visible, not only to me but to Louise. Louise herself, I believe, had lost contact with this aspect of her relationship with Ken's mother, and her regaining it seems to me one fruit of this session and one useful indication that we have seen a genuine shift and not just compliance or change merely at the verbal level. When the patient elaborates and carries forth the theme of the session via concrete, affectively meaningful memories or experiences, especially bringing up experiences that point in a different direction from how she had previously felt and seen things and that signify a different experience of herself or another person, that is a good sign that something genuinely therapeutic has occurred.[15]

This example also illustrates well how the older conception of "the unconscious" needs to be refined to include a more differentiated account of

---

[15]It should be clear that I am not implying that a "permanent" change has occurred or that now that she has had an "insight," everything will be different. There is still a lot of work to be done. But one very important brick has been laid in the foundation of further change. And what is being constructed, brick by brick, is not a merely cognitive change but one that integrates new ways of viewing things with new ways of feeling, experiencing, and behaving.

many different ways in which experiences may not be accessible to consciousness at any given moment. The memory of her playful collusion with her mother-in-law was not unconscious in the way that psychoanalysts have traditionally conceived of that term. That is, I have little doubt that, if I had asked her at any point, did you ever say to your mother-in-law, "You can say you're with me," she would without a moment's hesitation have said yes. What was inaccessible was not the memory per se but the associative links that *called up* the memory (for more on this phenomenon, see P. L. Wachtel, 2005). But notwithstanding the ready path to awareness *if* the question were to be asked, it is nonetheless important to recognize that this memory *was* blocked, that it did not "fit" with the state of mind that Louise has been in. In that sense, its "release," the way it was able to become spontaneously accessible, represents a significant therapeutic advance given that we are talking here about just a single session. Louise is here, in essence, reweaving the tapestry of her subjective experience and her subjective map of what goes with what, and such creating of new *connections between* experiences is an important part of what creates more enduring therapeutic change. Attending to the differences between such experiences and merely verbal or cognitive events is, I believe, an important element in promoting meaningful and significant therapeutic change.

> *Paul:* Well, 'cause it sounds like there's a lot to talk about . . .
>
> *Louise:* Yes! [*interjected in the midst of my comment with almost a* chortle *of joy*]
>
> *Paul:* . . . between you, and a lot to share, but because you can get pulled it's sort of hard for you to make contact with those feelings, so it's hard for you to let the warm feelings toward them even emerge because they feel like a threat. And then when that happens it's very hard to approach them.

* * * * *

Throughout this entire sequence, Louise looks and listens with rapt attention, and has a look on her face that often seems either joyful or serene.

> *Louise:* Uh huh.
>
> *Paul:* You know, how do you approach somebody when you've sort of decided that all the good feelings and the longing feelings I have toward them are dangerous? You know, so part of the job you have to do in some way is to figure out how to make those feelings, which are not the only feelings, I, I'm clear about that, but make that part of those feelings safer.
>
> You know, we can't, we have to stop in a minute so we can't go in right now to how to do that. But maybe we can sort of at least end on the note of that that's an important thing to do; that in

some way, part of what happened is that certain parts of your experience were acceptable and other parts of who you are kind of had to be pushed aside.

* * * * *

The question I introduce, "How do you approach somebody when you've sort of decided that all the good feelings and the longing feelings I have toward them are dangerous?", frames her dilemma. It also further moves to the foreground the good feelings, the longing feelings, and again does so in a way that does not brush aside the at least equally strong (and equally important) feeling that to acknowledge the first set of feelings is dangerous and perhaps unwise. This way of stating it also partakes of what I have called "attributional" comments or interpretations (see P. L. Wachtel, 1993, 2008). Instead of my comment having the implicit structure of my "telling her what I know but she does not," which is all too often the structure of interpretations if one looks closely, it instead refers to something she *already* knows; it *acknowledges* her feeling this rather than *informing* her that she feels it.

Notice also that I refer to her "job" and to her reconciling these two aspects of her experience as "an important thing to do." The approach I take includes not just the patient having "insights" but her *doing* things differently, having tasks to achieve in the process of change. But far from it being a "taskmasterish" telling her what she needs to do, it is rooted in a sympathetic appreciation of her conflict and dilemma and a respect for *all* aspects of her: "Certain parts of your experience were acceptable and other parts of who you are kind of had to be pushed aside."

Louise: Uh huh.

Paul: You know, the part of you that longs for more connection felt threatening, because there's also a very real part of you that wants the safety, the comfort, the self-integrity of being able to make your own choices. But in doing that, the part of you that wants connection got sort of squeezed out. And then it becomes very hard to reach out to them.

Louise: Yeah.

Paul: And it's really also a loss for you.

Louise: Uh huh.

Paul: Because that part of you is just as much a part of you and deserves as much space, as much room. So that's sort of like your, your next task in life so to speak. [*said in a tone of affectionate joking*]

Louise: You have absolutely given me so much more insight than I thought was possible in so little time. So I thank you.

Paul: Good. Well, we worked well together.

Louise: Thank you, I agree.

Paul: Okay.

* * * * *

I am obviously gratified that Louise felt she gained so much insight from the session. I am, of course, also aware that she has described herself as "a people-pleaser" and so am wary of that element in her positive response to the session. But I also believe that she *really has* gained some important insights and important new perspectives and experiences in the session. The shifts in emotional attitude in the course of the session and the emergence of meaningful and concrete images that pointed to a quite different portrayal of the cast of characters in her life and her relation to them—such as the image of covering for her mother-in-law in order to help her ward off the family's intrusive demands, or her account of her mother's abandonment of her in Paris, which represents such a departure from the image of the family she offered earlier in the session, when she was talking about her family being "there for each other" or the kids in school being jealous of her because her family was so close—seem to me to point to a very genuine emotional reworking having gone on in the session.

I do believe that some of this positive response had to do with the therapeutic approach this book is intended to illustrate, and in that sense I am pleased with how the session went. But I also *meant it* when, in response to Louise's compliment at the end of the session, I said we worked well *together*. This *was* a two-person process in at least two senses. First, it depended, as I think *all* therapy depends, on processes that are intersubjective, not simply a matter of one person using expertise to "operate on" the other. Second, and a very important matter of contextualization, the session went well because the *pairing* of Louise and me "worked." Therapy occurs in a *relationship*, and like any relationship it depends on the intersection of the particularities of the two parties. I will next be turning to a second session I had with Louise, but I think it is important to alert the reader at this point that the third session I will be examining in this book is with a different patient with whom the pairing was not as salutary and where I was *not* as able to forge an effective working alliance. My comment to Louise that "we" worked well together may be, ultimately, the most important takeaway message not only for her but for the reader as well.

4

LOUISE: SESSION 2

Session 1 with Louise ended with the expectation, on both our parts, that that would be the end of our opportunity to interact with each other. As it turned out, however, a technological deus ex machina intervened that led to a second session. Shortly after the session ended, the director who had been filming the session came in and told us that he had "bad news" for us. Apparently, there was some sort of electrical glitch in the sound system, and there was a hissing sound that made the audio track of the DVD potentially problematic. He asked if we would be willing to have another session right then. We both agreed, and so there was a second session just 15 minutes or so after the first.

As it turned out, the technical glitch was not nearly as severe as it had first seemed—it was just a subtle buzz that lasts little more than a second or two and does not prevent a single word of the session from being heard clearly. Indeed, this turned out to be a "good glitch" because it afforded Louise and me an opportunity for a follow-up session, which is presented with my commentary in this chapter.

In my own experience, second sessions are often the hardest. Although I know colleagues who find that it is the first session that is the hardest—a reflection of the fact that the two parties do not know each other at all, and hence the session is an encounter between strangers with all the anxiety that such encounters usually bring—my experience is generally quite different. I *enjoy* first sessions. They usually seem to me to bring a certain air of excitement and positive anticipation for both parties. The very same fact that some find disconcerting—that we both are encountering each other for the first time—seems in my experience to create a very positive frame to the session. There is a feeling that this is the beginning of a process of *change* in whatever has been troubling the patient, and there is often a sense of unlimited potential, of looking at all the ways in which the person can overcome constricting anxieties and inhibitions and begin living more fully and satisfyingly. In the first session, there has often been much less opportunity for disappointment of these expectations, much less intrusion of the limits inevitably introduced by "reality." I recall, in this connection, a comment made to me by the distinguished psychoanalyst Merton Gill in a private discussion we were having about psychoanalysis: "The trouble with psychoanalysis is that we can always still recognize our friends after they have been analyzed." Gill, in his usual witty way, was pointing to both the fantasies of complete transformation that almost always accompany participation in the analytic process and the reality that even when real and solid gains are achieved, they are in fact usually rather far from complete transformation. We remain who we were, though hopefully a better version of who we were.

Remaining the same is not necessarily a bad thing. It is hoped that one of the things that results from an analysis, or from any good psychotherapy, is feeling better about *who one is*. One is *pleased* to be oneself, not longing to be someone else (or, in the case of some patients, to be godlike or a superhero). But there is also always some sobering appreciation that life is inevitably lived with limits and compromises. Acceptance of those limits and the ability to thrive within their boundaries is an important result of a good therapeutic experience. So too, of course, is some considerable *extending* of those limits. But extending is not the same as abrogating.

The second session, I find, is often the beginning of the process of coming to terms with the *limits* of what psychotherapy can accomplish. The "honeymoon" of the first session is behind us, and the long period of hard work on the relationship and on the problems that brought the person in is beginning. Adding to the difficulties of a second session, in my experience, is often the very fact that the first session has been so positive and encouraging an experience as well as an experience of surprising *connecting*, given that we really don't know each other very well. In the second session, we *still* don't know each other very well, but there may be more of an expectation that it should feel that we do. I often find that there is difficulty in picking up the thread of the first session and that the awkwardness that some therapists experience in the first session is, for me, stronger in the second. It is the third session, in my experience, when we most often sit down together and go to work as if this were "normal."

One interesting element in the different experience I have of first and second sessions is that it has seemed to me that the impressions I get of the patient and his or her dynamics in the first session are often surprisingly on the mark, and my understanding of the patient's key issues and of how to work with them is in certain respects clearer than it will be again for some time. Often, what I need to do in the "middle" stages of the work is to periodically revisit those initial impressions in order to recreate for myself my sense of the patient in the very first session. There is a certain "purity," one might say, to the initial impressions that is in some ways obscured and muddied by our further immersion in the complexities of the person's life and, importantly, by the further development of the countertransference reactions that draw us in as "accomplices" in the pattern (P. L. Wachtel, 1991) rather than as mere observers.

I do not mean here to make a case for a truly "pristine" perception in first sessions. Far from it. From the very first moment, we are inevitably drawn into the patient's force field, inevitably immersed in and becoming a part of the relational matrix that frames the patient's experience (Aron, 1996; Mitchell, 1988; P. L. Wachtel, 2008). Nor do I mean to draw an overly sharp distinction between first and second sessions, or a distinction without exceptions. There are certainly times when I am more confused in the first session than the second, when the opportunity to interact further with the patient has the consequence that might seem more obvious or expected to most people—helping me to know the person better. But I do want to mention this experience that I frequently encounter with first and second sessions because it is probably another part of the frame of the sessions discussed in this and the previous chapter. In some ways, I entered the first session with Louise with an expectation that it would be a good one (though certainly with the increment of anxiety that came from its being taped and potentially available to many people to watch), and I probably entered the second session with an expectation that I would have a harder time following up. In my own view of these two sessions, these expectations were to some degree confirmed. It is not that I think of the session about to be presented as a "bad" session. As I will discuss, I think some valuable and useful therapeutic work was done. But it does seem to me that the first session accomplished more.

To be sure, the session's coming just 15 minutes after the prior session, rather than after a day or two or a week, most likely contributed to what transpired in the session as well, as did the fact that it was not originally planned but was the product of a "rude shock" that our first session might be unusable for demonstration purposes. I had sensed by the end of the first session that in my view it was a "good" one, and I had been feeling pleased that it might be the session that would represent my work in the APA video series. So—

since I did not know at the time that in fact the video of the first session would turn out to be absolutely fine technically—the second session began with a sense of loss for me and an additional increment of anxiety. For Louise, the experience seems to have been a different one. She expressed delight at the opportunity to have a second session. There was no burden on her to demonstrate her skill in her profession, and she had already had some experience of being exposed to the camera, so the second session probably felt less strange or intrusive than the first. (This element of the sessions being taped did not become a part of the content of either session—one of the many important things that are always and inevitably left out in the very process of addressing *other* important themes.)

These are some of the background considerations that the reader should take into account in reading the transcript and comments on Session 2 with Louise. Certainly the session is of interest in its own right as a piece of therapeutic work with a beginning, middle, and end, as any session has. But it is also usefully understood both in relation to the experience of the first session *and* in relation to my particular idiosyncratic experience of first and second sessions as described above. The larger context in which experiences occur is always important to consider, as are the expectations with which either party enters the transaction since such expectations so frequently become at least in part self-fulfilling.

THE SESSION

Paul: Well, Louise, we . . . we covered a lot of ground in the first session and I think, you know . . . accomplished a lot, but I'm interested to know what of that most stayed with you? What was the most important to you of what we talked about?

* * * * *

Although in this instance the session followed almost immediately after the previous one, I proceeded as I often do in second sessions. I (and, I think, Louise) experienced the first session as an unusually rich and full one, and knowing what, of all the things we focused on, most left an impression on Louise felt like a useful place to start. It also ensured that we would be starting with a topic that had some emotional resonance for Louise.

Louise: The way that you helped me connect my feelings now to my feelings in my childhood, and I was aware of how much what's going on now is triggering stuff from before but I never really saw how it connected. So that stays with me the most.

Paul: And what connections in particular?

* * * * *

I wanted to be sure that we went beyond the general and abstract idea that feelings in her childhood were influencing her reactions in the present and instead went to specific, affectively alive experiences.

Louise: That . . . that it's so foreign to me that family means too much, even though it's been central to me in my whole life, and that I never realized how important my own family was because I've always felt like, yeah, family is important, but, you know, these people are going to the extreme. But still . . . you know, my family went to the extreme too. I mean, we never see each other. We never get together, it's all phone conversations and stuff like that, but yeah, there was, you know, "Don't tell other people about our problems."

* * * * *

Louise here seems to be connecting with the absence of connection in her family, something she had explicitly denied at the beginning of the first session (and that I think she probably has chronically tried to keep out of her awareness). She also seems clearly here to be experiencing some real anger and resentment at this. That is, it is an affective experience, not a purely cognitive one.

Paul: Right.

Louise: So that was, right, that was . . . those, also a connection I never saw before.

Paul: Right. Right. And it sounds like it was also . . . even though there were seemingly certain ways in which you had a lack of connection or lack of that kind of connection with them, there was also a time when you were *too intensely* connected, when you had to take care of your father. I mean, you were, you know, right there and in a sense not allowed to leave. Right?

* * * * *

I was probably going too fast here, too eager to introduce the full complexity of the different sides of her difficult childhood. I think in retrospect that it would have been better to let her stay for a while with the sense of, "We never see each other. We never get together." That is, she was experientially going into the feelings of abandonment and loneliness, and I introduced the additional (but distracting) theme of her being given too much responsibility as a child. This does, it will become apparent, lead her to an important reexamination of a similar taking on of responsibility for the care of Ken and to further useful considerations of the impact of that on her relationship with Denise. But

I nonetheless think it would have been best to stay for a while with the experience she had just begun to get into, the sense of loneliness, isolation, and lack of connection.

Louise: That's true . . . that's true, I never thought of that 'cause he couldn't . . . obviously he couldn't care for himself.

Paul: Right.

Louise: Oh, yeah.

Paul: Right.

Louise: And it's interesting, because my husband had two back surgeries, and he'd already hurt his back when I met him, so I knew that he had a hurt back, and then he had a first . . . we got together in January moved together very quickly because we moved together in . . . in . . . this is in 2001. We've been together in May, then he has his first surgery in August, and then a year later, his second surgery in September. So he was . . . I was in the same situation among those who was . . . caring for him.

Paul: Right.

Louise: In . . . in every . . . you know in every way, so I think that even though I was telling you last session that Denise feels like his mom, I kinda took over that role as his mom in a way, and I was saying, I'm his wife but I've also been his mom a lot. So I think she felt like I crowded her out.

Paul: Right. Right.

Louise: Which is making her angry, I think.

Paul: Yeah . . . yeah.

Louise: Because he's listening to me and he is not listening to her anymore.

Paul: Right. Right.

* * * * *

Here it seems that Louise is going on to create further insights for herself without my providing much input about it. That is, the things she is seeing now, with a feeling of some freshness and of seeing them virtually for the first time, are not ideas that I had said anything about. This may be an instance in which, having had an experience of being encouraged both to explore her experiences more reflectively and to be more accepting of her experiences and perceptions, Louise was liberated to carry forth some of the work on her own.

In this sequence and throughout the transcripts, I notice that the "words" I use frequently are "right" or "right, right." I hope it is clear to the reader that in most of these instances I am not commenting on whether Louise is "right" or wrong. Rather, the verbal notation in the transcript reflects what is more evident from the video, a verbal equivalent of nodding my head and signaling that "I hear you, go on."

Louise: And she like, I know she . . . she often belittles and . . . you know, and she thinks she is funny when she says things to him but, you know, I feel like she is more putting him down and kinda putting him in his place, and I feel like she wants to do the same thing with me.

Paul: Right. And you feel protective of Ken?

Louise: Oh, yeah! I feel very protective but I . . . I also feel angry with myself because I don't stay enough for him with his family, because it's hard for me that . . . because I don't know . . . I don't have any brothers and sisters, and I talked to my mom about it and I said, you know, I don't like how they are to Ken. She said, "What you have to remember, you don't have any brothers and sisters. You don't know." And there's a 6-year age difference between her and her sister. So she is basically trying to just tell me that, you know, the way that they interact, you don't know what's inappropriate because you don't have that kind of experience. So there are a lot of times when they have said things to kinda . . . and I feel like mom had areas, you know. But I also find out that I'm not the only one who can say things about Ken to his mom without his mom getting upset so . . . it's just . . . it's . . . it's hard, you know, because there's a lot of times I wish I would just start saying something. I shouldn't let her talk to him like that.

Paul: How does Ken feel about it?

Louise: About the way they talked to him?

Paul: Yeah.

Louise: I guess he's used to it, so he doesn't react to it so much until I point it out to him. I think he is very . . . I think there's a lot of things he doesn't want to see. He doesn't want to see how they treat him. He kinda paints in this picture for me of this, you know, great family and . . . you know, they're so loving and so fabulous, and then once I met them, their picture is just gonna fall apart and I think that's hurt him a lot because he keeps telling me how do you think I feel? How do you think I feel? And it's like . . . and you know, I'd always say, "I'm not you but I'm trying to understand."

It seems that Louise is seeing things in Ken's family that Ken would prefer not to see and so doesn't want Louise to see. In a way, Ken has maintained an idealized picture of his family just as Louise has. Or at least this is one speculation at this point.

Paul: Uh huh . . . and when he says, "How do you think I feel?"

Louise: Uh huh . . .

Paul: What is he mainly pointing to?

* * * * *

I am here trying to put flesh on Ken's saying, "How do you think I feel?", trying to stimulate Louise to think further about just what Ken is wanting her to understand.

Louise: Well, when I get upset with him because [*breathes deeply*] when I feel like he's not . . . acknowledging me or when I feel like, you know, he is just, "Oh, I'm so tired or blah blah blah," they're so, I feel like he always excuses . . .

Paul: Uh huh . . .

Louise: And then, or when I talked about his family, for example, and I'd say, "Why won't you let me talk about them?"

Paul: Uh huh . . .

Louise: Or when he gets upset with me and I get upset with him because I'm just trying to fix the problem.

Paul: Uh huh . . .

Louise: And he says, well, you know, "How do you think I feel?" and you know, "This is my mom," and basically that's what he means.

Paul: Uhm-mm . . . I was . . . what I'm still not quite clear about was . . .

Louise: Okay . . .

Paul: . . . was when you were going back to when you were being protective of Ken . . .

Louise: Okay . . .

Paul: And you were feeling his sister wasn't treating him well, for example. How does he feel about that? Like when you . . . when you have felt she is not treating him well . . .

Louise: Uh huh . . .

Paul: . . . does he say . . . what does he say when you have talked with him about that? Does he say that "No, that's fine," or does he say, does he act like, "Oh I . . . I felt fine about it but now that you said it, suddenly I am feeling bad," or what . . . what happens?

* * * * *

I think that both Louise and I have still not gotten our feet back on the ground after the impact of being told that the first session had not recorded properly. Louise reacted to the news with pleasure, being eager to have another session. But the session's coming so soon after the first and so unexpectedly, before either of us had gotten our rhythm or worked through what had transpired in a very rich and full session, it seems to me that neither of us is as sharp. We both are evidencing more sentences that begin in one direction, break off, go in a different direction, and so on. I was confused about where the session was going and having difficulty at times following what Louise was saying. But my own comments were also a bit incoherent, and as I read my own words I find them hard to follow.

Louise: Uhm . . . like I said, he doesn't really notice it, so when I do point it out to him, he says, "Oh, that's just Denise."

Paul: Uh huh . . .

Louise: So then, he just wants to makes excuses for her.

Paul: Uh huh . . .

Louise: But I think I make him upset about it like you just said, and we never talk about that actually, so maybe I shouldn't say anything. 'Cause he just does not notice it. But I notice, and then when I point it out to him, at first he's just kinda like, "Well, whatever that is, it's just her," but I think it kinda stays in the back of his mind.

* * * * *

I'm thinking here that on the one hand, Louise is seeing something going on that she wants to be able to communicate to Ken and to have acknowledged by him. But at the same time, she senses that the way she is going about it isn't working. It's leaving her more alienated from Ken rather than closer. I cannot know, of course, just from this report, which of them is closer to "the truth" about his family (recall here especially the discussion of constructivism and objectivism in Part I of this volume). But it is clear that there is conflict generated by what goes on, and one of my thoughts at this point is, how can I help Louise be true to her own experience and at the same time not alienate Ken? Is there some way that she can express her experience of what goes on that is more likely to make some contact with Ken's experience? Is there something she is seeing that Ken wishes he could acknowledge, and if so, how might that be framed more effectively? Just as I believe that the therapist's framing of his or her observations is a crucial element in whether they will be therapeutically useful (P. L. Wachtel, 1993), I also believe that *the patient* needs to learn to frame and express her experience in a way that evokes responses from others that enable real communication and mutual understanding to occur.

Paul: Uh huh . . .

Louise: And then when we talk, he gets more and more upset about it. So I think it's kind of my fault too, because even though I'm noticing, since *he* is not noticing, maybe I shouldn't be pointing it out.

Paul: When you say it's kind of your fault too, was that what you're feeling, or what you're afraid Ken feels, or . . . ?

Louise: That's more what I feel. Uhm, again, I am . . . my constant fear is that he will turn around and go, "Wait a minute, I had no problems with my family until you came along."

* * * * *

This brings us back to the experience and concerns with which Louise started the first session. It again suggests that it is very important for the state of their marriage that Louise find a way to reconcile with his family. But the progress that had seemed visible at the end of the first session now seems rather far away, and neither of us at this point is creating a connection to what was happening in the first session. The challenge I am feeling here is to figure out how to do that. I am, at the moment, too immersed in and bogged down in the immediate topic without having a broader perspective on it.

Paul: Uh huh . . .

Louise: And why didn't I pick somebody who was more like my family?

Paul: Uh huh . . .

Louise: And why didn't I pick somebody who, you know, lives up to his idea of what a wife should be?

Paul: Uh huh . . .

Louise: 'Cause I don't. [*laughs*]

Paul: Uh huh . . .

* * * * *

Louise's laugh here is a poignant and rueful one, not a laugh of pleasure or humor. She is feeling like a failure (as am I, for the moment).

Louise:	And he doesn't, uhm . . . I mean, it's not like he says it to me you hurt my feelings but I think he thought he'd have a wife who was like his mom . . . that's for, I mean, he often . . . he often tells me . . .
Paul:	Uh huh . . .
Louise:	I am a lot like his mom.
Paul:	Uh huh . . .
Louise:	But I think he expected me to, you know, like to cook and like to clean the house and, you know, being a typical wife, uhm . . . by American standards, while where I come from men and women are equal and we do equal things in the house.

* * * * *

Here, in contrast to Louise's comment in the first session about individualist and collectivist families, I think that the cultural dimension she is introducing is quite relevant and one part of the overall dilemma. At least as she describes it, Ken's expectations of her differ from what her own expectations of herself were growing up in Sweden. But I am struck in reading over this transcript that I missed an opportunity to draw her back to the experience she reported in the prior session of connection and solidarity with Ken's mother, the episode of offering to help her out by saying that she was with Louise. Here is the other side of the dialectic of difference and similarity, and Louise is not in touch with it here because she is feeling lost and discouraged. Somehow that feeling has also overtaken me, and I am unable to think to bring her back to the experience with her mother-in-law that so struck me just a little while ago.

Paul:	Uh huh . . .
Louise:	And I say to him, "Yes, I know you worked all day, but what do you think I did all day?" [*laughs*]
Paul:	Uh huh . . .
Louise:	And no, I didn't just sit on my butt all day.
Paul:	Uh huh . . .
Louise:	I did stuff.
Paul:	Uh huh . . .
Louise:	So . . .
Paul:	Uh huh . . .
Louise:	I'm just afraid that he is gonna think, you know . . . he is 12 years older than me, so there is a big age difference too, which does not bother me at all but I know it probably bothers his family.

Paul:	Uh huh . . .
Louise:	Uhm . . . because you know, they haven't exactly asked me why we don't have kids yet, but we have been together for 5 years now, and I know almost all people have kids by now.
Paul:	Uh huh . . .
Louise:	But it's like my education comes first.
Paul:	Uh huh . . .
Louise:	That's what's important to me, and Ken is very supportive of that.
Paul:	Uh huh . . .
Louise:	Uhm . . . But again, I am always thinking, you know, maybe if I didn't make such a big deal, out of everything . . .
Paul:	Uh huh . . .
Louise:	Maybe it's me.
Paul:	Uh huh . . .
Louise:	And I need to stop.
Paul:	Uh huh . . . well, certainly, you, you know, it would be useful to be clear about what he is experiencing . . .
Louise:	Uh huh . . .
Paul:	You know, to listen to him in the sense of if he is truly not feeling treated badly, and it feels that way to you, uhm . . . you know, to reflect on that.
Louise:	Uh huh . . .
Paul:	But it sounds also like there is a feeling that he can't quite speak for himself.

* * * * *

This whole sequence has felt a bit lame on my part. I have been unable to find a useful handle for Louise. Here is the first point where there is something potentially promising. I am trying to help Louise to reframe and reconsider what Ken's experience is. We are potentially moving toward a consideration of whether some of Louise's feelings toward Ken's family are expressing for Ken what he cannot permit himself to express. This is, of course, a common dynamic in couples, and clarifying it may be useful to both of them.

Louise:	Uh huh . . .
Paul:	Understand?

Louise:	That's true, yeah. I feel that way. I feel like he . . . I feel like I'm always telling him, "Why don't you say something?"
Paul:	Uh huh . . .
Louise:	"Why don't you ask?"
Paul:	Uh huh . . .
Louise:	"Why don't you? Why don't you? Why don't you?"
Paul:	Uh huh . . . And that's, that must be something that you're especially attuned to and sensitive to, because you grew up in a home where there was a person who couldn't speak for himself.
Louise:	Uhm-mm. And it's interesting that you were saying that, because I could always understand what my dad was trying to say even though he couldn't say the words . . .
Paul:	Uh huh.
Louise:	. . . I understood.
Paul:	Uh huh . . .
Louise:	And even my mom doesn't have that, and I don't know if that's because I was his daughter . . .
Paul:	Uh huh . . .
Louise:	But I'm very, very sensitive, which is . . .
Paul:	Uh huh . . .
Louise:	. . . helping me now when I counsel other people.
Paul:	Right.
Louise:	But it is very difficult in my own life because I am so sensitive to people's little . . . little things.
Paul:	Right.
Louise:	And I pick up on things right away.
Paul:	Right.
Louise:	So, so, yeah. I am very sensitive to them.
Paul:	Yeah. And you're somebody who sort of speaks up for people who can't speak for themselves.

* * * * *

Here I am for a second time coming back to her father's inability to speak. I'm not sure if this was the most productive direction to try to point things at this point in the session, but it was one route to seeing some coherence or convergence in the material, and it was directed toward further opening up the topic of whether some of what is going on between them has to do with Louise being the designated partner who expresses what Ken may be feeling but is unable to say or even fully to acknowledge to himself.

Louise: Uh huh . . .

Paul: And . . .

Louise: And I'm trying, 'cause I think I enabled him in the beginning a lot, because I, you know, I carried him.

Paul: Uh huh . . .

Louise: Like my mom carried my dad.

* * * * *

It seems that Louise literally carried Ken when his back was injured, just as her mother literally carried her father when her father could not move.

Paul: Right.

Louise: But there is a big difference always I see between him and my dad.

Paul: Right.

Louise: He can take care of himself.

Paul: Right.

Louise: He took care of himself.

Paul: Right.

Louise: While my dad couldn't.

Paul: Uh huh . . .

Louise: So, and my mom said this to me: She said, "You're kind of taking over my role."

Paul: Uh huh . . .

Louise: And my mom was concerned about that, because she did not want me to live my life the way she did.

Paul: Right.

Louise: Especially when it is not necessary.

Paul: Uh huh . . .

Louise: Because she was telling me that the day before my dad had a stroke, she actually would have divorced him.

* * * * *

It now seems that the groping in the dark that I have been experiencing, looking for a handle that would lead us in a useful direction, has begun to touch on a very important topic. This news about Louise's mother having decided to divorce her father just a day before he had a stroke is another dramatic new revelation. It gives still further poignancy to the family's painful circumstances and points to still further dimensions of psychological bind. Moreover, as Louise relates the story, it is evident that there was a rather explicit message from Louise's mother that caretaking can be a dangerous, entrapping role.

Paul: Uh huh . . .

Louise: So she had chosen divorce.

Paul: Uh huh . . .

Louise: And then she felt obligated to stay.

Paul: Right.

Louise: And took care of him for the rest of his life.

Paul: Right.

Louise: And I'm sure she loved him. I have no doubt that if she didn't . . .

Paul: Right.[1]

Louise: But sometimes I'm scared that I've gotten myself wrapped up in the same situation, that I feel that he needs me and I can't, you know, I can't leave him because of who would take care of him.

Paul: Uh huh . . .

Louise: And that's not a healthy marriage.

* * * * *

This additional painful dimension to her father's stroke, and the burden, further, of having been told by her mother of the contemplated divorce, has left Louise very wary of commitment. (Recall her having said in Session 1 that she had never thought that she would get married.) This hyperalertness to compromised choice and freedom has perhaps made it more difficult for her in sorting out just what she does feel. It has also likely contributed to her discomfort with and resistance to the demands made by Ken's family.

Paul: Do you have doubts about him? About how you feel about him?

---

[1] Here again, in this series of saying "right," the word *right* has nothing to do with right or wrong, correct or incorrect, but is simply an utterance to convey that I am hearing her and am with her as she speaks.

* * * * *

Here I take up directly what is seeming perhaps to have been the developing theme of some of the foregoing parts of the session.

Louise: Sometimes. But I don't know if that's because I have these unrealistic expectations of him, or if I don't . . . if I'm so angry and just upset that I . . . instead of seeing the good things, I just see the bad things. But I think we'll make it.

Paul: Uhm-mm.

Louise: But there's just been, I feel like there has been, and I feel it's been there right from the start, and this thing with his family is just, I feel like it's kind of tearing us apart.

Paul: Uh huh . . .

Louise: It's bringing us closer together in one way but in another it's just like, I don't know how we're gonna make it.

* * * * *

One question that arises here for me is whether some of the conflict with Ken's family is a function of conflict between the two of them, and whether, indeed, the conflict with his family is a kind of diversion from that. I am not *assuming* that this is the case at this point, but the question has arisen for me more focally as something to explore as we proceed.

Paul: You know, one other thing that occurs to me about you and him in relation to his family is you're very worried, and he sort of falls into a somewhat similar view, you know, that you're tearing him away from his family . . .

Louise: Uh huh . . .

Paul: And that, you know, he was so close to his family and it's "your fault," so to speak, that, you know, he is *not* anymore.

Louise: Uh huh . . .

Paul: But after all, he chose to marry you.

Louise: Yeah.

Paul: What do you think about that, for instance?

Louise: I think, I know he loves me.

Paul: Uh huh . . .

Louise: I believe in relationships, in my opinion, that one person loves more than the other.

Paul:	Uh huh . . .
Louise:	I think it is rare that both people love equally.
Paul:	Uh huh . . .
Louise:	And I think he loves me more than I love him, even though I do love him.
Paul:	Uh huh . . .
Louise:	But there's always gonna be a part of me that holds back.

* * * * *

Here the link she has mentioned between her feelings about Ken and caring for him and the trap that her mother felt in and the message that her mother gave to her seems even more important to further explore.

Paul:	Uh huh . . .
Louise:	And I tried to explain that to him, and it's not, that it does not have anything to do with him, it's more me and my insecurity and me thinking that people are always gonna leave me.

* * * * *

Here, and in what follows, we began to see more of the painful core of Louise's "internal life," the long-standing, persistent insecurities and self-doubts that have contributed to the difficulties we have been discussing thus far and that are perpetuated and exacerbated by such difficulties. "Why in the world would you marry me?" (see the following dialogue) is a wrenching statement of self-disparagement that would obviously be close to the heart of what needs to be addressed in further therapeutic work. Some of what follows immediately is a part of the healing dialectic, not denying Louise's painful self-experience or attempting to argue her out of it but making room for her to find the other side of her experience to build a more stable and accepting sense of self. In this effort, the work needs to be more than purely "internal." The interactional feedback loops that were the focus of the work in the first session are an essential component of what keeps Louise stuck in the painful, self-derogatory state of mind that she has been describing here.

Paul:	Uh huh . . .
Louise:	And yeah, he chose me but my insecurities tell me why in the world would you marry me?
Paul:	Uh huh . . .
Louise:	You know. Yeah, I think I'm a good person and all that kind of stuff, but uh, I'm difficult and [*laughs*] you know, and I can be

mean and, you know, my hair like this in the morning [*laughs*] you know, and . . . but he just . . .

Paul: Is that the whole story?

Louise: [*laughs*] It is amazing 'cause he just still loves me for who I am.

Paul: Uh huh . . .

Louise: It doesn't matter if my hair, you know, and I'm in my pajamas and I look like crap. He still loves me.

Paul: Uh huh . . .

Louise: And then, it's so unconditional for him. So, I am, and he's seen me at my worst, absolute worst.

Paul: Uh huh . . .

Louise: And he still wants to stick around so . . .

Paul: That's pretty powerful.

* * * * *

This has been a poignant part of the session in a number of different ways. I did not have an "interpretation" to offer here, but I did want her to know I was listening intently and to highlight what she has just said.

Louise: Yeah. Yeah, it is.

Paul: Really is . . .

Louise: And I guess I have seen him at *his* worst, and I still manage to forget, like we can have this big, big fight right before we go to bed. Because for some reason, I like to talk to him when he is really tired and he can't respond and he just pulls the covers over him, but in the morning, it's like he still, you know, puts the covers over me and he is still, you know, gives me a kiss before he goes to work and I forget that I'm angry with him.

Paul: Uh huh . . .

Louise: Or at night, I just wanna roll over and have him hold me or something.

Paul: Uh huh . . .

Louise: Like damn it, I was mad at him [*laughs*], I forgot I was mad at him. I'm not supposed to be talking to him [*laughs*].

Paul: Uh huh . . .

Louise: So, and I never had that one with anybody before.

Paul: That's how good relationships work.

* * * * *

I have heard her insecurities and her fear that she does not love Ken enough, but I have also heard some rather detailed and affectful accounts of their being very good together, and I want to acknowledge and underline this here.

Louise: [*laughs*] Yeah. I guess I just don't wanna. Again, I think it's just that being afraid of acknowledging, you know, what we have.

Paul: Uh huh . . .

* * * * *

I think that Louise has actually put her finger on something valid and important here. Her fears and insecurities do seem to interfere with her seeing that in many ways their relationship is very good. And, it should be noted here, a central concern in the much more intense and affect-laden first session was Louise's fear that if she did not repair the relationship with Ken's parents she would lose him, something that she was indicating strongly in that session she did not want to happen.

Louise: And Ken has told me, and now he is trying to tell his family, how good our relationship is.

Paul: Uh huh . . .

Louise: But it's like, I don't know if because they don't have a good relationship themselves, maybe they're . . . you know, they have some sort of resentment because we have this relationship, because we like to spend time together.

Paul: Uh huh . . .

Louise: You know, even if it's, you know, I prefer when he is in a different room so I can have the TV by myself, but we want to do things together.

Paul: Uh huh . . .

Louise: And when he starts . . . tells his family, that's then they say, well, like two trimesters ago, I . . . basically, we went to the movies once a week. You know, that's basically the time we saw each other, and his sister was like, well, you know, you should take that hour and go, you know, the hour that you go see a movie, you should spend that with us, you should come over to our house.

Paul: Uh huh . . .

Louise: And Ken is like, that is the only time we have together.

Paul: Uh huh . . .

Louise:	And she didn't care.
Paul:	Uh huh . . .
Louise:	It's like our relationship as husband and wife didn't matter as much as . . .
Paul:	Uh huh . . .
Louise:	As spending time with them.
Paul:	Right. But it mattered to Ken, it sounds like.

* * * * *

It's not quite clear why this is the only time they have to spend together. Is it their work and studies? Is it her wanting to watch TV alone? Is it some preference on his part? At some point that needs to be explored a bit more. But here, what seems most important to me, and is a link to the first session, is that Ken and Louise are connected and that Ken's family represents the third point of a triangle that threatens that connection—and, conversely, perhaps in certain ways also *strengthens* the bond between them, enabling them to stand together against a common foe or obstacle.

Louise:	It mattered to Ken that, that . . . I'm sorry?
Paul:	To have time with you . . .
Louise:	Oh, yeah, yeah, yeah.
Paul:	Not just with them.
Louise:	Absolutely. And she knew that, but it didn't matter, though.

* * * * *

Louise is again getting mired in her preoccupation with Ken's family and what they are doing to her. This is the same point of view with which she began the first session and that the first session had some success in modifying and expanding. But, as is often the case, that success was temporary, and further work on the issue is needed. In this part of the session, I am trying again, in a different way and a different context, to help Louise shift away from a simple or singular focus on what "they" are doing—a focus that has helped keep her in the uncomfortable position she has come to therapy to change.

Paul:	And he was having, and still has in some way, difficulty not getting sucked into the family.
Louise:	Uh huh . . .
Paul:	And . . . he chose a woman who could help him establish some of that boundary.

Louise:	Yeah.
Paul:	You know, he probably also chose a woman he could then blame for it, so to speak.
Louise:	[*laughs*] Yeah.
Paul:	That's true, that's a piece of it.
Louise:	Yeah.
Paul:	But you know, it . . . you know, he could have married someone who just wanted to spend as much time as possible with his family.

* * * * *

The implicit message here—that Ken may in part have chosen Louise because she can help him to set boundaries with his family, which he finds difficult to do—is a complement to the perspective introduced in the first session that Louise may actually want *more* connection than she has let herself experience, that there is something attractive to her in the enveloping family. The combination of these two perspectives reduces the either–or division between Ken and Louise in much the same way that addressing the "individualist"–"collectivist" dichotomy points toward reducing the either–or split between Louise and Ken's family. Louise's understanding that Ken is not as unconflictedly opposed to her boundary setting as she fears can help to open up possibilities for reconciling the competing sides of each of their feelings about their relation as a couple to Ken's family.

Louise:	Okay.
Paul:	He didn't.
Louise:	Yeah, that's true.
Paul:	And I don't think that's an accident.
Louise:	That's true, and I don't think about that. I don't give him enough credit sometimes. I know that, so, that's true, that's true. I think we do a lot for each other. I mean he's just . . . he's raised me up.
Paul:	Uh huh . . .
Louise:	I know that's sounds really easy but he really has.
Paul:	Uh huh . . .
Louise:	He has made me feel really good about myself.
Paul:	Uh huh . . .

Louise: And I always say I still have my days when you know I think I'm fat and ugly and all that kind of stuff, but he always, always makes me feel like it's okay.

Paul: Uh huh . . .

Louise: No matter what.

Paul: Uh huh . . .

Louise: And I'm . . . [*laughs*]. But it's . . . I don't think about that enough, 'cause I let that other stuff crowd in on us.

Paul: Uh huh . . .

Louise: And you think, you know, even my mom said, you know, this is a good guy.

Paul: Uh huh . . .

Louise: You know, and when I say even my mom, I mean you know often parents . . . you know, my mom had never met him. My mom met him for the first time in person, actually after my dad died.

Paul: Uh huh . . .

Louise: She'd never met him, and she said, "You know what? If he treats you well and you're happy with him, that's all I care about."

Paul: Uh huh . . .

Louise: And then when she met him, she is like, I can tell he really cares about you.

* * * * *

Note that these are concrete memories that seem to have been stirred by my line of comments about Ken. Here again, the point is not that the evocation of these memories reflects a permanent change. Therapy usually requires *multiple* reconfigurations before changes get consolidated, and in fact, notwithstanding the very considerable improvement that can result from good therapy, almost never is the old way of experiencing completely eradicated. It remains one of the potentials the person retains. But if the therapy is successful, what happens is that the old way emerges much less frequently. And this is no small matter.

Similarly, in saying that these concrete memories are being stirred, I am not implying that they were previously unconscious in any dynamic sense. But here too, when a different set of memories and thoughts begins to be stirred than was previously, that is no small matter either, but is, rather, close to the very heart of what constitutes an effective therapeutic process and of therapeutic gains per se. That is, as I discussed in Chapter 3 (see also P. L. Wachtel, 2005), many of the memories that are brought up by the therapeutic process are not memories that, strictly speaking, were inaccessible to consciousness. Here too, if I had asked Louise if her mother had said these things, she could easily have acknowledged it. But it would not necessarily *have occurred to her* to think of them. It is access to the associative networks that would *call up* the memory or make it likely to be evoked that is more often blocked, rather than the memory being kept permanently unconscious and inaccessible even if the right question were to be asked. As I noted in a different context in Chapter 2, Freud himself commented on the common experience of disappointment among his patients that little came up in their analyses that felt like they could not have remembered it if asked about it. Rather, he said, "When the patient talks about these 'forgotten' things he seldom fails to add: 'As a matter of fact I've always known it; only I've never thought of it'" (Freud, 1914/1958).

Paul:	Uh huh . . .
Louise:	And she said, "You know what, I'm very happy," and that meant a lot to me. But you know, you'd think that a family would see that and you would think that his family would be happy for him, but it's like they're not happy for him because, I don't know, I mean, Ken was saying it's because they wanna see me and the kids love me, and that's great, I mean I love the kids too, but when I only have so much time, then I wanna spend it with him.
Paul:	Uh huh. How do you think Ken would feel if you suddenly started to say, "Let's not go to the movies together, let's go over your mom's." How would he feel?

* * * * *

This is obviously a paradoxical intervention, designed to promote further thought on Louise's part and to point to ways in which the self-perpetuating cycle between Louise and Ken can be interrupted. As things stand now, they are caught in a pattern in which they both are driven to give voice and action to just one side of their conflicted feelings about their relation to Ken's family and to fight the other side of their feelings in the person of the other. The comment provides a kind of platform to stand outside that seemingly inexorable state of affairs and view it from a different angle. They have been so immersed in a single-minded view of their struggle that they have not been able to see around the corner, so to speak, and thereby to recognize that part of their struggle with each other is actually a struggle *within* each of them, a struggle to contain and reconcile competing feelings and inclinations. Approaching the struggle in a fresh and surprising way can potentially interrupt the cycle in which they each pull on opposite ends of the same rope and continue to feel a tug from the other end to which they need to respond (for more on the use of paradoxical interventions; see E. F. Wachtel & P. L. Wachtel, 1986; P. L. Wachtel, 1993).

Louise: I think he'd be happy at first. I mean I think . . .

Paul: At first?

* * * * *

I am highlighting this phrase here, which could otherwise get tucked into the comment and pass by without her noticing it. I am working to call her attention to her implicit sense that he would not "simply" be pleased she was cooperating. And I am stimulating her to consider that he might *not* be so happy if she did not provide him with an easy foil to address his own conflicted feelings about his enmeshed family (Minuchin, 1974).

Louise: Yeah . . . I mean I think he'd appreciate that I took the initiative to wanna see his family.

Paul: Uh huh . . .

Louise: But maybe . . . I don't know. I never thought about it. Maybe, after a while he'd . . . he'd want . . . you know . . . you go, hey! Wait a minute! You know why aren't we doing something together?

* * * * *

It seems Louise gets my point here.

One aim of this line of intervention is to take the entire weight of maintaining contact with Ken's family (*and* of resisting them) off her shoulders, to enable the burden to be shared more equally. This is not just a matter of justice or equity. It is also that the way they have implicitly divided up the tasks of family maintenance has led to each of them suppressing or denying a significant part of his or her own wishes and feelings. Ken has suppressed his desire for autonomy from them because that has been implicitly delegated to Louise, and Louise (as discussed toward the end of the previous session) has suppressed her desire for more contact with them. This results not just in conflict between Ken and Louise but also in each of them individually being impoverished, in a way, because an important part of their experience is not given expression. Enabling them each to accept and incorporate "the lost half" would likely result not just in more effective strategies for balancing and expressing the full range of their needs but would enable them each to feel more whole and alive as well as more united.

Here again, of course, I am describing and calling attention to *one small piece* of the therapeutic process. This is how I would aim, through *multiple* interventions over many sessions, to help rebalance the dynamic between them and enable them to find room for the varied sides of their experience and desires. I do not intend to imply that one or two such interventions would "do the job."

Paul: Right . . . right . . .

Louise: So . . .

Paul: Could be?

Louise: Yeah.

Paul: Yeah.

Louise: But I think he'd be very happy . . . I mean he . . . you know, pushed the standard down my throat . . . uhm . . . I think he'd be very happy about . . . The few times, like once after we walked my dog, his mom literally lives a couple of blocks away, so I walked over there and I showed them my dog . . . but she didn't seem interested and stuff, so I don't know. But this was . . . this was before my dad died, so I don't know if anything happened . . .

* * * * *

Louise's speech is somewhat more fragmented and lacking in coherence here. I think that the new perspective I have introduced has, we might say, therapeutically discombobulated her. That is, old and smooth ways of seeing things are being interrupted, and we are seeing the struggle to make sense of a new way of seeing things that is not so readily assimilated into her existing schemas. Here again, we must assume that whatever changes become evident here are very fragile and provisional. The old schemas are powerful, and we can anticipate that even where some new way of experiencing things emerges, it will be "resubmerged" many times before it becomes comfortably and reliably available or well integrated with the previously existing way of experiencing things (which, it is important to remember, is not "wrong" but only partial).

Paul: Uh huh . . .

Louise: And it's . . .

Paul: So there was some way in which . . . when you try to enter into the family . . .

Louise: Uh huh . . .

Paul:	There were . . . there were barriers?
Louise:	Yeah.
Paul:	Yeah?
Louise:	'Cause I don't know if . . . I talked to Ken about this, I said, you know, did I do something that was misunderstood?

* * * * *

I am thinking again at this point of the decision not to invite them to the wedding. Louise still does not understand the impact of that on them, I think.

Paul:	Uh huh . . .
Louise:	Prior? Prior to my dad's passing? You know, and he said, "Not that I know of," but I always felt like, you know, I was trying to get closer with his sister. She came over a couple of times, you know, we're sitting in the kitchen and I'm trying to open up and talk about myself, because that's a constant complaint, which is hilarious to me, that I won't talk about myself. [*laughs*] It's like a . . . I talk about myself. *If you give me a chance* to talk about myself, I *won't stop* talking about myself.
Paul:	Uh huh . . .
Louise:	But I just feel like, you know, when they're talking about their kids and taking their kids to school, it is not really appropriate for me to say, "Well, when I spent 4 months in Australia . . . "
Paul:	Uh huh . . .
Louise:	You know what I mean?
Paul:	Uh huh.
Louise:	It's like, where do you find the connection there? And I'm trying to find the connection, but then it's like . . . well, you don't have kids. You don't know what you're talking about. Then I try and say, "Well, you know, I heard at school . . . " and then it's like "Whatever."
Paul:	Uh huh . . .
Louise:	You know, so . . . yeah . . . you're right I mean there are these barriers because I feel like when I try to make the connection it's always like . . . I don't know.
Paul:	Uhm. It sounds like this, this issue with kids feels like another one of these things that is a way that they are trying to push you around, so to speak. Right?

Louise:	Yeah. Because these kids . . . the kids are gonna get upset. The kids . . . the kids . . . the kids.
Paul:	No, but also that you are supposed to have kids.
Louise:	Yes, oh yeah.
Paul:	Right?
Louise:	Oh! Absolutely. Yeah.
Paul:	Yeah.
Louise:	Absolutely. Because I don't know anything until I have kids.
Paul:	Yeah.
Louise:	But it's probably gonna be if I have one kid that's gonna be . . . "Well, you won't know until you have *two* kids."
Paul:	Right.
Louise:	And then it's gonna be, "You don't know until you have three kids."
Paul:	Uh huh . . .
Louise:	So, I don't think it's ever gonna end.
Paul:	Right.
Louise:	But I, you know, as I was saying, I mean I do, as far as the kids are concerned, it's not, I just feel . . . oh yeah, when Denise was dropping by . . . uhm . . . and I was trying to open up and I was trying to talk about myself and she kept cutting me off and she kept returning the conversation to her. And I, and I brought this up when they came over . . . uhm . . . with a whole confrontation thing and I said you know, "I was trying to talk to you, I was trying to open up a dialogue with you." I'd asked for help with the family tree for school . . .
Paul:	Uh huh . . .
Louise:	And then . . . and then she kinda threw that in my face like, "Oh! Well I was good enough when you needed my help." And . . . and that really hurt me, because that wasn't me using her. That was me trying to connect with her.
Paul:	Uh huh . . .

* * * * *

I think I should have said here something like, "So you really felt misunderstood," or "So you really felt like your motives were being distorted, and it felt like a real rejection."

Louise: Uhm . . . and I said, "When we sat here and we were in the kitchen and you just cut me off. I'm telling you a story about myself that you claim that you wanna hear and it's like you bring it back to yourself." And she said, "Well, that's called a conversation." And I'm like, "I'm sorry. How is that a conversation when you're . . . you're, I mean badgering me to tell you about myself but then when I tell you about myself it's like, 'Well, I just want to talk about me'?" You know, and I even said to her, I said, "You are not a shy person, why don't you ask me questions? If you wanna know something about me, ask me."

Paul: Uh huh . . .

Louise: Because again, I don't wanna make them feel like I feel like I'm better than them. I mean I have more education than any of them do. I have traveled more than any of them have.

Paul: Uh huh . . .

Louise: I've had a lot more experiences than they do. But I don't feel like I'm in any way better or . . . than them, and I wanna be a part of them.

* * * * *

"I wanna be a part of them." This is a very clear and moving statement. Perhaps I should have emphasized that here, that she wants to be a part of them and feels rejected, feels hurt. But again, in order to be able to join them, she also needs to be able to see and understand why they behave as they do toward her. The wedding is one part, but there is also a systemic vicious circle that they are all caught in now, where each complains about and sees the hostility/rejection from the other and does not see her own rejection/hostility.

I wonder here if, on the one hand, Ken's family felt insecure in the face of Louise's international background and greater education and experience of having seen the world and reacted defensively in response to this. I also wonder, on the other hand, whether Louise was more disdainful or condescending toward them than she realizes. I wonder as well whether each of these attitudes fed off the first signs of such feelings from the other, so that what was initially only incipient or a minor part of the picture became increasingly predominant as they evoked more and more extreme responses from each other.

Paul: Uh huh . . .

Louise: But it's hard for me when . . . when, you know, when I'm trying to find the connections and it's like, well, you don't know what you're talking about.

Paul: Uh huh . . .

Louise:	Because you don't have kids. Sorry. Whatever.
Paul:	Uh huh . . .
Louise:	So.
Paul:	So they keep emphasizing how different you are from them?
Louise:	Yes. Yeah.
Paul:	In a lot of different ways, they keep saying in a way, you are the outsider.
Louise:	Uh huh . . .
Paul:	You're different.
Louise:	Uh huh . . . and my sister-in-law . . . it's interesting that you should say that, because my sister-in-law used to say in words . . . uhm . . . Ken's brother's wife . . .
Paul:	Uh huh . . .
Louise:	She said, you know, "We, as outsiders, we have to kinda stick together."
Paul:	Uh huh . . .
Louise:	And that surprised me to hear her say that, and I realized, oh the last time you asked me if I had any similarities with the family, and I . . . the similarity I have with her is she is, she also felt like she wasn't accepted by the family.

* * * * *

Here Louise is remembering a part of our exchange in the previous session and elaborating further on that. I view that as a positive indicator that Louise has engaged seriously in our interaction and is still mulling it over. Some patients leave the session and can barely recall by the next session what went on. When the patient has been thinking further about the session, when what transpired reverberates in her head, this is a very positive indicator of the potential to really gain from the therapeutic work. In this instance, of course, this conclusion must be tempered by the fact that this second session is occurring only a matter of minutes after the first. But it nonetheless indicates an inclination to be thinking further about what we talked about, not just placing it in a mental circular file.

Paul:	Uh huh . . .
Louise:	But she has done nothing but bow to them.
Paul:	Uh huh . . .

Louise:	To the point of now it's like impossible for us to stand up to them.
Paul:	Uh huh . . .
Louise:	So I think maybe she feels like, "You go, girl." But she will never say that to me.
Paul:	Uh huh . . .
Louise:	So I think that she might be supportive of my trying to.
Paul:	All right. So there's a lot of people who are sort of letting you be their representative.

* * * * *

Here I am returning, via an expanded context, to the theme I introduced earlier of Louise expressing feelings that Ken has a hard time expressing.

Louise:	Uhm. Yeah.
Paul:	Right
Louise:	Because Ken's other sister . . . uhm . . . her name is Maria, she said to me, she said, "You need to do what's best for your relationship."
Paul:	Uh huh . . .
Louise:	And I was like, wow! That means so much to me that somebody would say that.
Paul:	Uh huh . . .
Louise:	But then, I don't trust her really either, because I know she said some things that had been inaccurate.
Paul:	Uh huh . . . uh huh . . .
Louise:	But I believe that she . . . she really meant what she said, though.

* * * * *

We can see in this sequence one more element in what leaves Louise conflicted and uncertain how to proceed. From one sentence to the next, she goes from "Wow! That means so much to me," a kind of almost naive enthusiasm, to "I don't trust her," to "But I believe she really meant it." She is not sure what is the solid ground to stand on.

Paul:	Uh huh, right. May I ask you? Over the time that you've been with Ken . . .
Louise:	Uh huh?

Paul:	Have there been some occasions, even if they have been few, when you actually *enjoyed* being with his family?

* * * * *

Here I am coming back to a theme that had seemed to be very productive to explore at the end of the last session.

Louise:	Uhh . . . yeah. And that's what hurt even more, because I felt like . . . the last 6 months prior to my dad's passing . . .
Paul:	Uh huh . . .
Louise:	I felt like we'd really gotten along well and I felt like we were having a good time.
Paul:	Uh huh . . .
Louise:	And uhm . . . you know, just walked away thinking "Oh! Well Denise said *this*, and I think she likes me, Therese said this," and you know . . . so I really felt like that we were building this relationship, and then, because I've made some comment about how I was hurt because I felt like nobody acknowledged me, then, instead of thinking . . . I would think that they will go, "Well, you know, she is grieving and she is not really in the . . . in the right place right now, so she is probably just thinking things to . . . "
Paul:	Uh huh . . .
Louise:	And they know I'm sensitive and all kinds of stuff.
Paul:	Uh huh . . .
Louise:	But instead it was like all that we built, you know, was just smashed to pieces.
Paul:	Uh huh . . .
Louise:	And then that's . . . you know . . . I don't know where to start again.
Paul:	Yeah. Yeah. Because somehow in reconnecting with them, the fact that you were hurt needs to be part of the conversation.

* * * * *

I take Louise's comment that she doesn't know where to start again both as an expression of a *wish* to start trying again to reconnect with them and as a feeling of being stymied in *knowing how* to pursue that wish. (She also, of course, as I have been discussing throughout, is *in conflict* about whether she wants to make the connection, struggling to reconcile quite different feelings that include anger, mistrust, feeling intruded upon, and fear that she will get hurt again.) Here, in this and the following comments, I am trying to help her to link the various sides of her experience. That is, reconnecting does not mean leaving out the hurt she felt, and attending to that hurt does not mean ignoring the wish to reconnect. I am trying to help her weave together the two sides of her emotional experience and to model for her ways to think about it that do make room for both sides.

Louise: Yeah.

Paul: You, you know, it's important to find out how they felt about it too.

Louise: Oh, yeah.

Paul: But the fact that you were hurt can't be lost.

* * * * *

In this sequence, I am again, from a slightly different angle, emphasizing the need to pay attention to Ken's family's experience, to attend respectfully to what they are feeling and try to understand them better. But again, I am introducing this not at the expense of Louise's respecting her own feelings or expecting her feelings to be heard and attended to. For some therapists, this sequence may feel somewhat more didactic than they are comfortable with (e.g., "It's important to find out how they felt about it too"). I do not share with many of my colleagues in the psychoanalytic world a reluctance to be didactic per se. This in part reflects my simultaneous immersion in the world of psychotherapy integration, in which a wider range of ways of helping people is considered. It reflects as well my conviction that a crucial part of change occurs outside of the therapy room, and that without breaking the vicious circles in the patient's life, even very good work in the session will be repeatedly undermined by the feedback loops that keep old patterns going. Thus, directly helping patients to change their behavior toward the important others in their life is an essential ingredient in effective therapy. But perhaps most of all, my comfort with being somewhat didactic lies in the tone that I try to achieve and the attitude that I try to genuinely embody. What matters is that the didactic element not be a condescending one, not have a tone or message of "I know how to handle things in life and you don't, so I will teach you." One useful means of ensuring that this is the case is the employment of attributional comments (P. L. Wachtel, 1993, 2008). This way of approaching things enables the therapist's input to be experienced as part of the patient and therapist standing side by side in the struggle against the patient's difficulties.

Louise: Uh huh . . .

Paul: Yeah, I think that's . . .

Louise: And I think it is. And I'm . . .

Paul: Uh huh . . .

Louise: And I'm afraid that . . . that, you know, they want an apology from me.

Paul: Uh huh . . .

Louise: Because my mom was there and I didn't tell them. And if I give . . . because she came back with me from Sweden and I chose not to say anything because my mom felt like I can't, you know, I just I can't.

* * * * *

Here is another instance of the vicious circles that Louise gets caught in. One can readily understand Ken's family's indignation at Louise not even telling them that her mother was there from Sweden. And one can readily understand Louise's own shock and outrage at how they behaved when they barged in. What none of the parties seem to understand is how each of their behaviors is bringing out in the other the very behavior they object to.[2] From the vantage point of helping Louise to be less vulnerable to thoroughly unanticipated eruptions and rejections, it is important to help her to see the underlying structure to these experiences of hurt and outrage. To the degree that she can better understand how Ken's family experiences the choices she makes, she will be better able not to encounter unpleasant surprises and better able to create a kind of relationship with them that meets her varied needs.

Paul: Uh huh . . .

Louise: You know, my mom needed time to herself. She is just crushed . . .

Paul: Uh huh . . .

Louise: And I respected that, and I felt like, you know, it's probably not the best time to meet the family.

* * * * *

Here we may surmise that Louise was also caught in a still older pattern with her mother, a pattern we have heard about in a number of ways already in the first session. (Even apart from the traumatic abandonment in Paris—which one might attribute to an isolated acute breakdown but which was likely but an exaggeration of many other instances in which Louise's needs were frighteningly disregarded—we may recall her conveying to Louise that she did not want Louise there when Louise's father was dying.) Here again,

---

[2]For an examination of similar dynamics between racial or ethnic groups, in which each side repeatedly evokes in the other the very behavior they object to, see P. L. Wachtel (1999).

her mother's need for her own private form of solace takes precedence over and disregards Louise's needs. She says Ken is wonderful for Louise but completely fails to recognize the bind she puts Louise into regarding Ken's family when she asks Louise not to tell them she is there.

In proceeding with exploring these dynamics, however, it is important not to simply demonize her. She clearly is herself very much a soul in pain, however much pain she ended up inflicting on her daughter as a consequence. In working with patients to help them understand the ways in which their parents have hurt them or let them down, even at times in very gross or extreme ways, there is almost always a need for—and a possibility of—offering at least some counterbalancing perspective. The parent, after all, is for better or worse embedded in various ways in the person's sense of self.

When the parent's behavior has been egregiously sadistic or abusive, this may not be possible to do. But in considering Louise's mother, for example, there will come a time in the work when some understanding of what has *driven her* to respond so problematically to her daughter's needs can be sought. This must not be introduced to "excuse" her behavior toward her daughter or to minimize in any way its impact. But Louise has clearly indicated that she has a need to see another side of her mother, and indeed that there *was* such an other side. Helping patients to see their parents more three-dimensionally can help them to reconnect with the positive qualities in themselves that are associated with the "other side" of the parent's behavior. But again, this should not be done in a way that glosses over what has been painful for the patient or insensitive or hurtful on the parent's part.

> *Paul:*   Uh huh . . .
>
> *Louise:*   And I knew they wouldn't respect that.
>
> *Paul:*   Uh huh . . .
>
> *Louise:*   So I just said to Ken, "Would it be okay if we just didn't say anything?"
>
> *Paul:*   Uh huh . . .
>
> *Louise:*   And then when his mom and Denise came over . . .
>
> *Paul:*   Uh huh . . .
>
> *Louise:*   He came in and said, "Oh, it's just my mom." And I thought, "Oh, well, if it's just her, I'll go get my mom."
>
> *Paul:*   Uh huh . . .
>
> *Louise:*   And then, you know, Denise comes running in saying, "Shut off the TV. We need to sort it out."
>
> *Paul:*   Uh huh . . .

Louise: And I was just like, "Hah," how soon are they leaving, you know.

Paul: Uh huh . . .

Louise: And I just forgot my mom was there for a second. You know, my mom had said, you know, "I was thinking about coming out but I didn't want to in case you wanted to deal with this on your own."

Paul: Uh huh . . .

Louise: And then when we finally calmed down enough, I brought my mom out so they got to see her. So now they want an apology from me because I hurt them so bad by hiding my mom.

Paul: Uh huh . . .

Louise: And I like . . . I wasn't hiding my mom. It was just that if you'd given me a chance, I would have explained to you, you know . . .

* * * * *

Here is another instance in which Louise finds herself bewildered by what is happening vis-à-vis Ken's family. Clearly one important part of the work with her will be to help her to not be caught unawares so frequently and to have a better understanding of what they experience as a provocation.

Paul: Uh huh . . .

Louise: But it was just the same, and they said, "We chose to go Niagara Falls. We drove up to Niagara Falls for . . . on December 17." And that's usually when the family celebrates Christmas, because that's when they can all get together, and that's when they give gifts and stuff. And I said to Denise, "You know what, even if my mom and I could have gone to Niagara Falls," I said, "I wouldn't have wanted to go, because I just didn't feel like celebrating Christmas," and she said to me, "Well, you know, we would have cheered you up."

Paul: Uh huh . . .

Louise: And I'm like . . . excuse me . . .

Paul: Uh huh . . .

Louise: You know, that kind of just sums it up in a nutshell, I think.

Paul: One of the other things that sounds like . . . that also was happening around that particular moment, that must have made it even harder, is that you were . . . you were protecting your mother.

Louise: Uhm-mm.

Paul:	I mean, you were grieving yourself. So it was a hard time even for you, but then you were sort of cast into this role where you probably sensed that this could potentially be difficult vis-à-vis Ken's family.
Louise:	Uhm-mm.
Paul:	But you had to protect your mother.

* * * * *

I am here trying to help Louise to see how her mother's choices put her in a bind. In being loyal to her mother, she had to act in a way that created further anger and alienation vis-à-vis Ken's family.

Louise:	Uhm-mm.
Paul:	. . . so you were sort of caught between these two families in a sense.

* * * * *

Here I am again employing the phrase Louise found apt and useful in the first session, the "two families." It is important, in making room for Louise's experience of autonomy, that she not be forced to wear blinders that only enable her to see how Ken's family has hurt her. In that direction lies further alienation from them and further difficulty in achieving her therapeutic aim. She is feeling assailed from *two* directions, and not acknowledging that to herself is part of what leaves her vulnerable to being blindsided by Ken's family's reactions.

Louise:	Yeah, 'cause I didn't wanna hurt them. Same thing with my wedding, you know, it was never to hurt them. It was because that was how I wanted to get married. Final. You know . . .
Paul:	Uh huh . . .
Louise:	You don't like it, then you don't like it, but please don't make me feel like I'm less of a person.
Paul:	Uh huh . . .
Louise:	Or that I intentionally tried to hurt you, because I am telling you, I didn't.
Paul:	Uh huh . . .
Louise:	And if you don't believe me there is nothing I can do.
Paul:	Uh huh . . .
Louise:	But it still hurts me.
Paul:	Yeah.

* * * * *

As I read this portion of the transcript, I see that at this point I am doing a lot of acknowledging and affirming of Louise's experience ("uh huh," "yeah") in the midst of her articulating what she has to say. I think I was sensing the intensity of Louise's feeling here, along with her feeling of *vulnerability* regarding how safe or acceptable it was for her to be expressing these feelings, and as a consequence, I was implicitly lending my support to her in her struggle with these issues. Therapists are rarely aware consciously of saying "uh huh" or some variant to a greater degree at some points in the session than in others. More often we are aware of some shift in the intensity of our listening and our engaging, perhaps of leaning forward in the chair or of making eye contact in a more intense way that says, "I am with you on this. I hear what you are saying." Such "noninterpretive" interventions are a bigger part of what contributes to the success of the therapeutic effort than was appreciated until rather recently (Lyons-Ruth, 1998; D. N. Stern et al., 1998).

> *Louise:* And it was the same thing in this situation, unless you were saying . . . yeah, I needed to protect my mom, and that was my number one priority.

* * * * *

Here Louise is affirming part of what I was trying to bring into sharper focus for her. My aim was not to decide which choice she should make in this complex set of demands and loyalty pulls. It was, rather, that she be clearer that there *was* a choice to make, a difficult choice. It was also, more provisionally, that she recognize that whatever she chose, part of the difficulty is that her mother has expectations of her that clash with her ties to Ken and his family and *their* expectations toward her.

> *Paul:* Uh huh . . .
>
> *Louise:* That was all I cared about.
>
> *Paul:* Uh huh . . .
>
> *Louise:* And Ken was supporting me. And it was like, they were not open to any kind of explanation to that.
>
> *Paul:* Uh huh . . .
>
> *Louise:* And that was part of the reason his mom has not talked to me.
>
> *Paul:* Uh huh . . .
>
> *Louise:* Because I hurt her so much. And she said . . . you know, I was gonna get up and leave but I didn't wanna offend your mom, because you hurt me so much by hiding your mom.

Paul:	Uh huh . . .
Louise:	Instead of, you know . . . like . . . I'm thinking . . . any other person would think, you know, if I just get an explanation, even if I don't understand.
Paul:	Uh huh . . .
Louise:	At least . . . if family is so important to them . . . then why are they doing nothing but nit-picking and I call and they don't return my calls?
Paul:	Uh huh . . . and what I actually thought you, you were gonna say just then was . . . why aren't they appreciative of this, of how you were being a good protective daughter?

* * * * *

This *is* what I thought she was going to say. But it also is a kind of tool I am giving her, a way to think about herself more positively and to present herself to Ken's family in a way that they might understand a bit more.

To be sure, from what I have heard thus far, I would not expect them simply to understand. They would probably be involved in the kind of in-law loyalty tug of war that is, sadly, far from uncommon in families and that might be particularly likely in this family, given what Louise has described. But at least Louise would be better equipped to defend herself and, indeed, to use their own language of family loyalty to do so.

Louise:	Yeah, I like that, but I never thought of that . . . yeah, you're right. Because I was . . . I was . . . that is what I was trying to do at once.

* * * * *

I think Louise liked what I said because I was responding on the basis of what I really did think she was going to say and on the basis of what perhaps she was trying to say but couldn't get to, in part because it implied acknowledging to herself that her mother was difficult and did need protecting.

Paul:	Uh huh . . .
Louise:	Yeah, I wanna tell them that!
Paul:	Well, how *could* you tell them that? In a way that would . . . let . . . how could you tell them that in a way that might . . . not just "put them in their place" but help you to *connect* with them?

* * * * *

I am here building on Louise's enthusiastic response to my comment and also offering explicit help. Techniquewise, this reprises what I did in the first session, when Louise responded enthusiastically to my reframing that the patterns in Ken's family, which she had described as so foreign to her, were "so foreign and yet so central," but then said, "I just don't know [how to deal with them]. It's just working on how." She said this in a way that implied that *someday* she'd have to work on how, but with little expectation that we would do so right then in the session. I responded, however, by saying, probably to her surprise, "Yeah. Well let's think together about how . . . how would you *like* to approach them? What would you *like* to say to them?" Here again, in the second session, I focus quite directly on what she could actually *say* to them, on how she could follow through in the real world of daily interaction on the fresh way of seeing things she has just achieved. And once again, my response reflects an integrative approach that combines psychoanalytic and cognitive–behavioral sensibilities. I am willing not only to respond to a request for help but even to spontaneously offer it as part of the evolving collaborative relationship.

Note here also that I refer to telling them "in a way that might not just 'put them in their place' but help you to *connect* with them." This too is part of the integrative nature of the work here. I am aiming not just to help her to "express" what she is feeling, not just to "get it out" or be true to herself. It *is* important that she be true to herself—*crucially* important—but as a constructivist epistemology suggests (see Chapter 1, this volume, as well as Hoffman, 1998; P. L. Wachtel, 2008), there are *multiple* ways of being true to oneself, multiple ways of expressing what one is experiencing. Each of those different articulations of one's experience, each way of constructing and making sense of what one sees and thinks and feels has somewhat different consequences and implications, both for how one feels about oneself and for the interpersonal transactions that constitute much of the texture of one's life and that are so central to the feedback loops that maintain problematic patterns—or permit them to change. Louise had indicated right at the beginning of the first session that a central aim of therapy for her was to find a way to reconnect with Ken's family, something she was finding very hard to do. Here I am trying to point her toward ways of expressing herself that are more likely to help with that aim while simultaneously affirming her wish for firm boundaries and enabling her to express feelings of hurt or anger when that is what she is feeling.

Louise: [*sigh*] Yeah.

Paul: 'Cause that's what you . . . all in all—with mixed feelings, but still all in all—want to do.

Louise: I would try to . . . I would try to say to Denise, for example, because she is angry with me for hurting her mother obviously too . . . so I would start with her, and I would say to Denise, "The way that you protected your mom, when you felt like uhm . . . I hurt her or can hurt her . . . "

Paul:	Uh huh . . .
Louise:	" . . . that's the same way I am protecting my mom."

* * * * *

Louise is picking up the ball here, and doing well.

Paul:	Uh huh . . .
Louise:	So, I would ask her if she could see the similarities there. And say, "Can you understand where I'm coming from, since you would do the same?"
Paul:	Uh huh . . .
Louise:	And I would say to Ken's mom that . . . my . . . I was a parenti-fied child.
Paul:	Uh huh . . .
Louise:	So, I often felt like you know . . . I was the one and . . . because of my dad obviously, 'cause I took over the . . .
Paul:	Uh huh . . .
Louise:	The parent role of my dad.
Paul:	Right . . .
Louise:	But also with my mom many times, when she was overwhelmed.
Paul:	Uh huh . . .
Louise:	She put me in charge.
Paul:	Right . . .
Louise:	Uh huh . . . so . . .
Paul:	Including . . . this most recent event?

* * * * *

Here I am making sure that we are also still talking about this particular event, her mother's asking her not to tell Ken's family that she was visiting from Sweden. I don't want the conversation to get too general. Staying with the specific event enables the discussion to be more affectively alive.

Louise:	Yeah, yeah! Because she just . . . my dad was her backbone.
Paul:	Uh huh . . .
Louise:	And she just, I've . . . I felt like I had to take her side . . .
Paul:	Uh huh . . .

Louise:	And she couldn't you know . . . do anything. She couldn't shower . . .
Paul:	Right.
Louise:	You know . . . anything without me.
Paul:	Uh huh . . .
Louise:	And it scared me . . . it was scarier to me . . .
Paul:	Uh huh . . .
Louise:	'Cause I was afraid she might hurt herself.

* * * * *

We see here more indication of the serious fragility of her mother's mental health. The horrific incident in Paris that Louise reported in the first session was likely not just an isolated instance. This kind of fragility, and Louise's having had to take care of the caretaker, seems to have been a chronic part of her life experience and one that has a significant impact on her difficulties with Ken's family.

Paul:	Right.
Louise:	For a while.
Paul:	Uh huh . . .
Louise:	And I was . . . and I called my aunt and it has . . . has brought my aunt and I closer.
Paul:	Uh huh . . .
Louise:	But it's still scary. I said to my aunt, you know, keep an eye on her 'cause I'm afraid she might hurt herself.
Paul:	Uh huh . . .
Louise:	And I don't think my mom would do that. But still, you know . . .
Paul:	Uh huh . . .
Louise:	Uhm . . . I was afraid mom would have this breakdown, but I was hoping she will have it when I was there so I could hold her and take care of her . . .

* * * * *

Both a sign of caring, something admirable about Louise, and a further indication of her having internalized the role of the parentified child.

Paul:	Uh huh . . .
Louise:	And so, what I say to Denise, I would say . . . you know . . . my mom is in many ways like my daughter.

Paul: Uh huh . . .

Louise: So, I needed to protect my daughter.

Paul: Uh huh . . .

Louise: Just like you would protect your child.

* * * * *

This series of statements represents a powerful and poignant expression of Louise's experience with her mother and, implicitly, of the painfully complex set of feelings and inclinations it brings out in Louise.

Paul: Uh huh . . .

Louise: So I think maybe that's how I would try and connect.

Paul: Uh huh . . . one other thing that occurs to me about the several different things that you just said . . . as you were imagining talking to them . . .

Louise: Uh huh . . .

Paul: . . . is . . . that you were . . . asking them to understand you.

Louise: Uh huh . . .

Paul: And you were in a way imagining talking to them . . . assuming it might be possible for them to understand . . .

* * * * *

I am here trying to offer a gentle nudge of support for the possibility of approaching the world in a way that assumes she can be understood and that therefore communicates in a way that makes it more likely that she *will* be understood. The comment can be seen as a variant of the attributional comments I have referred to in earlier discussions in this and the previous chapter (see also P. L. Wachtel, 1993, 2008). It builds on her implicit and emerging strengths, and in attributing those strengths to her in a fashion that highlights and magnifies them, it aims to make it more likely that they will be expressed further.

Louise: Uh huh . . .

Paul: . . . whereas the conversation with Denise that didn't go well . . .

Louise: Uh huh . . .

Paul: Was one where you were trying to make a point with Denise.

Louise: Yeah.

Paul: To show her what she had done wrong.

Louise:	Yeah.
Paul:	And she gets very defensive.
Louise:	Yes.
Paul:	And it crumbles.
Louise:	Yeah.
Paul:	And you know, you . . . very largely were correct in what you said . . . accurate.
Louise:	I think so . . .
Paul:	Its not that you weren't accurate.
Louise:	Yeah.
Paul:	But it didn't serve you . . .

* * * * *

Here I am both offering affirmation of the accuracy or truth of what Louise had said and, at the same time, *in the very context of supporting her,* also helping her to reexamine just how she said it so it can work better for her in her life. Working with patients on how they could have said something differently always has the potential of leaving them feeling criticized and not appreciated or understood. Thus, in such instances it is especially important to combine one's comment with an affirmation, as I did here.

Louise:	Yeah.
Paul:	Because all it did was make Denise defensive, almost *because* you were right, you know . . . when you hit somebody, you know, if you hit a glancing blow, people can recover, but when you hit them right where they're vulnerable . . .
Louise:	Yeah.
Paul:	You know . . . they get very defensive.
Louise:	Yeah.
Paul:	But what I'm struck by is . . . you have in you . . . a whole other way . . . you know, that's not a matter of taking on somebody else's way. You just spoke about how you could, you spoke as the Louise who could say, "Look, I really want you to understand and I think I maybe I haven't made certain things clear. I really would like you to understand. And I wanna understand your experience."
Louise:	Uh huh . . . that's true.

Paul: You know, and . . . and . . . you did it. You know, it wasn't an alien thing.

* * * * *

The foregoing represents again an attributional intervention that, as many of them do, highlights and attempts to amplify the patient's strengths. I am calling attention here to the Louise who could, respectfully *and* self-respectingly, ask to be heard and understood. I am emphasizing that this was her own statement, that it was not something that came from someone else but something she herself came up with. This is especially important to do at this juncture because of the way I am working here, actively making suggestions and working collaboratively with her. It is important for her (perhaps for us both) to see that in this collaboration it is not just her taking on something from me but also building on her own *already existing* resources, resources that had been suppressed by the conflicts she had been struggling with

Louise: Yeah. I feel better now. It makes me feel good that I know I can do that.

* * * * *

There may be some element of compliance here, of "people-pleasing" as she called it in the first session. But I believe her comment also reflects how patients feel when their therapists are genuinely responsive to their strengths even while helping them to further bring them out and see where they may be inhibited or buried. It is crucially important that Louise "know she can do it." Only then can the examination of what impedes or inhibits her in doing it be helpful and growth promoting. and only then can the therapist's efforts to help her fine tune her communications with others be comfortably embraced rather than feeling demeaning or a source of shame.

Paul: Uh huh . . . but you know, what's also important to me, what I worry about just a little bit is . . . because you've always had to take care of people, I worried just now that you were taking care of *me* a little bit. I mean, that you were . . . it's not that I don't believe that what I said was helpful.

Louise: Yeah.

Paul: But you were . . . you know, kinda letting me know what a good job I had done.

* * * * *

Here I am expressing a caution on the other side. I am concerned about the people-pleasing, especially in light of still further evidence that she has had to be the caretaker. I don't want her to feel burdened with taking care of me. But at the same time, I don't want simply to dismiss her expression that it has been helpful or minimize the value of what has transpired, which could undermine it. Just as the therapist needs to be alert to taking too much credit, he or she needs to be aware of the potential drawbacks to being too modest, both in the sense that it can devalue (and hence actually diminish the impact of) what has been accomplished and in the sense that the therapist is always, among other roles, a model for the patient. No amount of ideology about autonomy or differentiation can eliminate this model role, and if we are too modest, there is a danger that this will convey to the patient that this is how *she* must be, that even healthy pride in what one has accomplished is not acceptable (cf. Crastnopol, 2007). Clearly this is not a message we want to convey to the patient—and especially one that we do not want to convey "between the lines," where it is harder to bring it out into the light of day and examine it.

> *Louise:* Yes, I do that.
>
> *Paul:* You know what I mean?

* * * * *

I think my comment "You know what I mean?" here reflects some anxiety about my previous comment and how Louise has perceived it. I say "You know what I mean?" because I am concerned about the very issues I was discussing in my last interpolated comment. The implications of my comment to Louise that perhaps she was *taking care of me* by saying that she felt better and that my prior comment had been helpful could be experienced by her in a variety of ways, some not so helpful. So I am trying to take a closer look at, and possibly to examine with her, what she takes from this additional comment about her taking care of me.

> *Louise:* Yeah. I didn't . . . I wasn't doing it consciously . . . but yes.
>
> *Paul:* Uh huh . . .
>
> *Louise:* I wanted . . . I want people to know when they are helping me.
>
> *Paul:* Right. And that is a great thing. And I appreciate it. It's you know . . . I . . . I . . . got . . .

* * * * *

Our dialogue is beginning to be a bit incoherent, and it continues to be for a few more exchanges after this. I think that in my comment a few exchanges back about her taking care of me, I was trying to be a little *too* sophisticated in addressing the different facets of her conflicts, a little *too* aware of the complexities. Louise was not ready to take all of this in at this point; I was running ahead of myself. This is probably part of what led Louise to say, in her next comment, "In what way?", a statement that did not quite seem logically connected to what

I had just been saying but that reflected her (quite appropriate) confusion. In trying to get us out of the tangle I am sensing we have entered, I have gotten a little convoluted and continue to be for a few more exchanges. This tangle was primarily of my own making; I had been trying to do too much at once.

Louise: In what way?

Paul: I don't want to discourage you but . . . but I . . . [*simultaneous talking*] . . . I guess where I worry about it is just this . . . I worried was there some part of what we were talking about . . .

Louise: Uh huh . . .

Paul: . . . that maybe wasn't feeling right on. Like maybe a feeling of . . . "Yeah, that's easy to say, but I don't feel so confident I could do that," or something, and that just when you have that doubt . . . you feel the need to reassure me. I don't know if that was the case, but I worried.

* * * * *

Here is an illustration of what it means to work in a two-person fashion. I am thinking out loud in front of Louise, sharing my thoughts with her and putting myself on the same plane. (In this regard, see Aron, 1996; Renik, 1995; Safran & Muran, 2000.)

Louise: Well, when you asked me what I would do, uhm . . . to try and connect what I was thinking in my head, even though I didn't say it aloud, I was kinda putting my counselor, my training so far in the counseling field . . .

Paul: Uh huh . . .

Louise: I would take the role as the counselor . . . so, but I think. So you . . . you have very good instincts because I do . . . I do that. I mean, I want . . . you know . . .

Paul: Uh huh . . .

Louise: However, it was more of a . . . I can do as a counselor, if I take on that role.

Paul: Uh huh . . .

Louise: And protect myself, but me . . . just make it kind of . . . and as of just . . . you know, face to face, and that's part of the reason I didn't . . . I couldn't see her mom face to face . . .

* * * * *

Louise is obviously less clear or coherent at this point in the session. She is struggling with something that is difficult for her to articulate. Her statement that "you have very good instincts" certainly may have an element of the very people-pleasing that I had commented on earlier—and that I had in part contributed to this tangle by doing so. But I think it also did reflect some feeling of being understood in an important way and perhaps an unformulated (D. B. Stern, 1997) sense that although we had *both* been a bit less coherent and clear, we were both groping for a potentially shared understanding of something of consequence. At this point, it can't all be put readily into words; there is too much that needs to be conveyed and taken in simultaneously. But in her confused speech pattern here, mirroring or paralleling my own confused speech pattern of a moment before, Louise is resonating, I think, with the larger message that there are many sides to this tangle and that although it may be hard to see them all at once or talk about them all at once, the "correct instinct" is to be sure to make room for all of them.

Paul: Uh huh . . .

Louise: And why I needed to see her on the phone, and why I needed that protection, kinda as I needed the protection of a counselor. It wasn't easy for me to find the words.

Paul: Uh huh . . .

Louise: Uh huh . . . I'm so extremely hurt by them. So, I would need to get past that hurt first.

Paul: Uh huh . . .

Louise: And I think I have no doubt that you understand that at all.

Paul: Uh huh . . .

Louise: But I think it would just . . . for some reason . . . just Denise just represents . . . you know, this bully from my past that's come to life now . . .

* * * * *

Here is a clear link to an important topic from the first session. But, thankfully, I *did not* explicitly make the connection at this point. I had already been doing "too much" and sensed that here it was best just to listen.

Paul: Uh huh . . .

Louise: Like in a nightmare kind of thing.

Paul: Uh huh . . .

Louise: You know, like when you have a nightmare, one of the figures comes out in a nightmare.

Paul: Right . . . right.

Louise: That's what she is to me.

Paul: Uh huh . . .

Louise: And I understand that it sounds very extreme, but I feel like I would love to be able to face her . . .

* * * * *

Rather than sounding extreme, this sounds to me like it conveys very clearly and strongly the uncanny or eerie dimension to the experience of Denise and dealing with Denise. The links of the experiences with Denise to her mother and to being bullied as a child seem increasingly important to explore (though again, at a pace that enables Louise to assimilate where we have been) because the contemporary experiences are stored in and linked to neural circuits that intersect with older, more affectively dominated schemas (Gabbard & Westen, 2003; Westen & Gabbard, 2001a, 2001b).

Paul: Uh huh . . .

Louise: And not hide behind the mask of . . . you know, my education . . .

* * * * *

Louise seems to be alluding here to something she mentioned earlier—that she uses her greater education defensively to cope with the distressing feelings and experiences she has in relation to them. But the defensive disdain she feels toward them becomes a part of the vicious circle between them that she is struggling to find a way to break: When Ken's family picks up this disdain, whether consciously or not, it contributes to their hostility to her, thereby increasing her discomfort and insecurity in ways that evoke in her the same defensive disdain to cope with it, perpetuating the pattern still again. Louise will have to come to terms with the sources of this disdain and find a way to master and transcend it if she is to effectively repair her relationship with them. Nonetheless, it is impressive that at this point Louise can spontaneously refer to her "hiding behind the mask of her education." This is both insightful on her part and, as a spontaneous, unbidden remark, an indication that the process in which we have been engaged is bearing fruit.

Paul: Uh huh . . .

Louise: But be able to confront her.

Paul: Uh huh . . .

Louise: Does that make sense?

Paul: Well, what I'm hearing is that . . . is that what's important for us both to be clear about . . .

Louise:	Uh huh . . .
Paul:	Is that, yes there is a way in which you want to connect with her, but you want to do it in a way that says, "I want you to understand me and I want to understand you."

* * * * *

Here we see another example of an attributional comment. I am, in one sense, simply restating what I have heard *Louise* say, but I am also, at the same time, implicitly offering her a way to state it more effectively or—because it will be best if she can express it in her own words—to *think about it* more effectively. She can take this implicit suggestion or leave it—the very way it is presented makes it easier for her to have the choice—but if she does make use of it, the way it is presented makes it easier for her to feel that whatever she says comes from her, not from me.

Louise:	Uh huh . . .
Paul:	But there's also a way, and you don't want me to miss it and you don't want to have it taken away from you . . .
Louise:	Uh huh . . .
Paul:	There's a way in which . . .
Louise:	Uh huh . . .
Paul:	There's a way in which she represents those bullies from your childhood . . .
Louise:	Uh huh . . .
Paul:	And you wanna be able also to sort of tell it like it is.
Louise:	Uh huh . . .
Paul:	But that is another part of what you were feeling there. And, and let's not brush that under the rug, so to speak.

* * * * *

Here again, I am working to bring whatever has been pushed aside to the surface. The side of Louise that is visible—and, importantly, that feels acceptable to Louise—keeps shifting. Processes of dissociation and shifting self-states seem to be of importance here (see Bromberg, 1998a; Crastnopol, 2001; P. L. Wachtel, 2008).

Louise:	Yeah. And, and as I said, I think part of me was telling you that . . . I understand . . . and I, and I, and it's good to know that I have it in me. I feel proud of myself.

* * * * *

Here again, I think there is a very real way in which Louise does appreciate—and gain something important from—the approach that highlights what she has done and can do. And at the same time (and one more instance of what I was referring to above regarding the shifting self-states and need to find a way to make all sides available and acceptable) she also wants known—so they are *also* acceptable and able to be talked about—her *inabil-* ities, the fears and inhibitions that prevent her from acting effectively with Ken's family. This is clearly evident as the next few exchanges unfold.

Paul: Uh huh . . .

Louise: So you help me feel proud of myself . . . but at the same time I'm far away from being able to actually put into place what I can say to you that I'm able to do.

Paul: Right.

Louise: But knowing that I can do it is so huge for a start.

Paul: Uh huh . . .

Louise: Because I hadn't actually, I know, I keep thinking of myself, you know, I should know better, you know, I have the training and . . . but it's always when you're in the situation . . .

Paul: Uh huh . . .

Louise: And you're just being a person then it's hard.

Paul: Right.

Louise: No matter how much you know.

Paul: Right. So, it sounds like it might be actually easier as a start . . .

Louise: Uh huh . . .

Paul: To try it with Ken's mother.

Louise: Yeah.

Paul: More than with Denise.

Louise: Yeah.

Paul: Because Denise is sort of like, you know, that's the finals.

Louise: Yeah.

Paul: First you've got to get through the early rounds.

Louise: Yeah. She's the PhD. [*chuckles*]

Paul: Yeah. Yeah.

Louise:	Yeah.
Paul:	Right.
Louise:	So, yeah, yeah. But it hurts now that she hasn't . . . I feel like I took the stuff . . .
Paul:	Uh huh . . .
Louise:	I mean, I'm being very, you know, very hurt, very easily right now.
Paul:	Uh huh . . .
Louise:	And started just being able to, like with my friends.
Paul:	Right.
Louise:	You know, but with her, it's like every little thing that she does, and like I react to it.
Paul:	Uh huh . . .
Louise:	Some very reactive basis to these situations. What I'm trying to say . . .
Paul:	Uh huh . . .
Louise:	Ummm . . . I just, you know, now I took the first step and now I called her and she hasn't called me back.
Paul:	Uh huh . . .
Louise:	So, that's like, you know, putting more salt in the wound.
Paul:	Right. Right.
Louise:	You know?
Paul:	Right. And, and it hurts.
Louise:	Yeah.
Paul:	It hurts, and one thing I wonder about with Ken . . .
Louise:	Uh huh . . .
Paul:	Ummm . . . there have been ways in which when Ken has intervened, and it has felt not good to you.
Louise:	Uh huh . . .
Paul:	You know, you've talked about that in the first session.
Louise:	Uh huh . . .
Paul:	But, in some way, you know, you are feeling hurt. You're so often the one who is the caretaker.

Louise:	Uh huh . . .
Paul:	Maybe sometimes you also need to be the one who is taken care of.

* * * * *

Here I am following up on themes introduced earlier in the session and that I have further highlighted in my interpolated comments. I am adding a new link here in tying it to her experience with Ken and am thinking that in this there is a potential to open up and enrich their relationship.

Louise:	Uh huh . . .
Paul:	You know, and it may be, some of it . . . you know, I know you have spoken about it with Ken . . .
Louise:	Uh huh . . .
Paul:	It's not like you've never spoken about it with him, but maybe some of just a feeling of, "I feel hurt," "I feel stymied," "I don't know how," "I want to get from here to here and I don't quite know how" . . .
Louise:	Uh huh . . .
Paul:	Ahhh . . . is something that might be useful to talk about with Ken.
Louise:	Uh huh . . .
Paul:	Letting yourself be the one who's taken care of.
Louise:	Uh huh . . .
Paul:	You know, 'cause I think you, you want to be independent.
Louise:	Uh huh . . .
Paul:	And that's obviously then, in many ways that is very important.
Louise:	Uh huh . . .
Paul:	But, you know, the other thing that suddenly strikes me and, and we're gonna have to stop shortly . . .
Louise:	Oh, yeah.
Paul:	Now that I mention this, what I'm thinking about . . .
Louise:	Yeah.
Paul:	Is you being taken care of
Louise:	Uh huh . . .
Paul:	You've got closer to your aunt . . .

Louise: Uh huh . . .

Paul: When you asked her for help . . .

Louise: Uh huh . . .

Paul: You know, and I remember reading once that good politicians, when they offended somebody . . .

Louise: Uh huh . . .

Paul: What they usually do to repair it is they don't apologize, they *ask for something* from the very person that supposedly they should be in less of a position to ask.

Louise: Okay.

Paul: And in asking for something . . .

Louise: Uh huh . . .

Paul: You give the other person an opportunity to connect with you because you let yourself depend on them a little bit.

Louise: Right.

Paul: Which you did with your aunt, by the way . . .

Louise: Yeah. Yeah, that makes me . . .

Paul: And if you think about doing that with Ken . . .

Louise: Uh huh . . .

Paul: And even . . . it would be complicated to figure out just how . . .

Louise: Uh huh . . .

Paul: But even with his mother, and maybe when you get to the finals . . .

Louise: Uh huh . . .

Paul: . . . with Denise, you know, to be able to ask them for something. That actually sometimes is easier.

Louise: Uh huh . . .

Paul: You know, I want something from you, can you do me a favor?

Louise: Uh huh . . .

Paul: You know. At least the politicians say it works.

Louise: Why, I mean, I could ask Jane, Ken's mom, to help me with Denise?

Paul: Uh huh . . .

Louise: To reach out to her that way.

Paul: Very interesting.

* * * * *

I mean it when I say "very interesting." Louise has clearly heard what I said and run with it, taking it in a creative direction that is "her own." In that sense, it is also a good illustration of the combination of relying on someone and relying on one's own resources—and, further, of how the very act of relying on someone can bring out one's own resources further.

Louise: All right.

Paul: Great! Creative idea. Maybe this is the perfect place for us to stop.

Louise: Okay. Good.

Paul: Good

Louise: Good. Thank you.

Paul: I hope this proves helpful.

Louise: This is great. This is great. Right said. [*giggles*]

Paul: Okay. Right.

* * * * *

This second session with Louise did not have the narrative arc of the first. There were fewer new revelations and no dramatic surprises. It also differed from the first in that I was less noticeably active in the second session; I said less and listened more. In good part, I think this was a response to Louise having gotten a good deal out of the first session, having had much to assimilate and work on. That she was doing this was evident from very early in the session. When I asked her what most stayed with her from the first session, she again highlighted an idea that she had at first had difficulty assimilating in the initial session but then returned to spontaneously later in that session, making it a key metaphor for her in thinking about her family and Ken's—"so foreign and yet so familiar." In the second session, in responding to my question, she says similarly that what stayed with her was the idea that "it's so foreign to me that family means too much, even though it's been central to me in my whole life, and that I never realized how important my own family was because I've always felt like yeah, family is important but, you know, these people are going to the extreme."

Here, we may note, she is not only bringing forth again the idea that what she had viewed as foreign had actually been central to her life experience, but she also is beginning to sense the way that she has used her perception of Ken's family to help her distract herself from aspects of *her own* family that have been uncomfortable to acknowledge. As she puts it as she proceeds, "My family went to the extreme too."

In the immediate elaboration of this newly available experience, she at first maintains some version of the "difference" emphasis. What she is highlighting here is not only that her family went to extremes also (something they had in common with Ken's) but that they went to extremes *differently*. Where Ken's family was excessively enmeshed and bound up in demands and obligations, what characterized her family was "we never see each other. We never get together, it's all phone conversations and stuff like that, but yeah, there was, you know, 'Don't tell other people about our problems.'" This is an important expansion of perspective for her, very much in contrast to the presentation, at the beginning of the first session, that "we were always there for each other." And, in important ways, her family and Ken's *are* different, and Louise is now able to look at those differences in a more clear-eyed way, without her family being all good and Ken's all bad. But there is another side to "so foreign and yet so central" that was more of the focus in the first session—the ways in which there was something *similar* in the structure of obligation in Ken's family and in her own, the way that her family too placed enormous demands on her. The fidelity demanded by Louise's mother was certainly not exactly the same as that required in Ken's family, but even beyond the requirement of loyalty through secrecy, we can well imagine that it was difficult for Louise to go out and play or to go through preadolescent and adolescent growing, rebelling, and differentiating when there was such a need for help with the family's desperate situation. "How can you go out and enjoy yourself when I am stuck in the house with your paralyzed father?" may well have been a demand—whether explicitly stated or *not needing* to be stated—that had a somewhat similar emotional resonance to Ken's family's "How can you not visit us on Easter just because you have an exam to study for?"

In the beginning of the session, I was a little premature in attempting to help Louise see this other side. In immediately stating that "even though there were seemingly certain ways in which you had a lack of connection or lack of that kind of connection with them, there was also a time when you were *too intensely* connected, when you had to take care of your father . . . and in a sense not allowed to leave," I gave short shrift to the experience that Louise was talking about at that moment—the experience of "we never see each other, we never get together." That lonely, disconnected feeling was where Louise was at emotionally at that moment. Moreover, it is clearly as much an aspect of what was painful in her upbringing as the demands were. And, it seems clear, despite the similarities that I had highlighted in the first session and that were indeed important for Louise to be able to acknowledge, there also clearly *were* major differences.

I think there were several factors that led me astray here, in the sense, as I view it retrospectively, that it would have been best to just stay for a while with Louise's experience of "we never see each other, we never get together," especially because it was not only important and strongly felt but was indeed a new perspective in its own right, and even one that helped to reduce the black-—white, all-good/all-bad images that exacerbated her alienation from Ken's family. First, I was trying to help Louise achieve a more complete and balanced picture. In highlighting the ways that her family was disconnected and Ken's was enmeshed, Louise was certainly pointing to a real and important difference between the two families. But it was a partial truth, as it were, and I wanted to flesh out the full picture. In jumping so quickly to connect the dots, however, I did not give Louise sufficient opportunity at that moment to immerse herself in, elaborate on, and *feel* the important new understanding that she *had* achieved.

A second factor that probably influenced my choice at that point was that in the first session, highlighting the ways in which Ken's family was more familiar and less foreign had seemed to generate an emotionally experienced reconfiguration. When I said to Louise, "You know, one odd thing that occurs to me is that in some way Ken's family lives the way you lived growing up," Louise responded with a strongly felt affirmation and then said, "Yeah, I never thought about that. That's a great way of putting it, because that helps me be more sympa, empathetic to them," and much of the rest of the course of the session followed up on this vector of change. Similarly, later in the session, in a different version of "less foreign than you've thought," when I mentioned that it was easier to see the differences between her and the members of Ken's family than to notice the similarities, Louise eventually got to the recollection of having offered to "conspire" with Ken's mother to say she was at Louise's house in order for her to have some time alone. Here again, it seemed to me that this focus yielded emotionally important results; an important bridge to an affective connection or reconnection to Ken's mother was being built. I think that as a result of these experiences resonating for me outside of awareness as I began the second session, I was overvaluing this particular dimension of new experiencing on Louise's part and trying too hard to lead her back to this dimension rather than staying with where she was at the moment.

Fortunately, as I have noted at several points in this book, the process of therapy is a relatively forgiving one if the therapist is willing and able to reflect on what has gone right and what has not. This false step early in the session did not "ruin" it, as beginning students of psychotherapy sometimes fear. Missteps are inevitable, and what is important is that the process proceeded in a useful manner. It may even be that I sensed rather early that I was trying to do too much too soon here, because it is evident that as the session proceeded I embraced more of a listening stance, intervening less than I had in the first session (where I still think it was useful and helpful) and less than I did early in the second session (where it was considerably less useful and helpful). As the session proceeded, our collaboration took on a somewhat different look than it had in the first session, but the exploration of alternative ways of understanding and experiencing both her early life experiences and her experiences with Ken's family, as well as of alternative ways to approach Ken and Ken's family more successfully, continued in a useful way. By the end, I felt that Louise had gained a good deal from our contact, and I wished that it had been possible for us to have had a more extended therapeutic experience together.

5

MELISSA

My session with Melissa, the patient to be presented in this chapter, had a rather different character from my sessions with Louise. For much of the session, I had difficulty finding my footing with Melissa. There was a sense of our being at cross-purposes, of our not really collaborating in the fashion I am accustomed to. Reaching the point where it felt like we were genuinely working together and on the same page took longer than it did with Louise, and the session never felt quite as productive or well conducted as the sessions with Louise did.

There are, of course, inevitable differences in the way the work proceeds with different pairs of participants. Our field has paid far too little attention to the question of what enables a therapist to work better with one patient than another or a patient to work better with one therapist than another. In part, Louise and I may have been a better "match" than Melissa and I. But a number of complicating factors make it difficult to know if that was the case in this instance. First of all, of course, the fact that the therapeutic interaction was set up as a one-time demonstration session clearly adds a layer of complication to the complexities that already inhere in the therapeutic relationship. Although this was the case for Louise as well, the arrangement may have different meanings for different participants. It is possible that if Melissa and I had had the opportunity for further sessions in which we could have followed up on and explored the difficulties we had had and built on the connections we did experience, we might have built a stronger therapeutic alliance that enabled considerably deeper engagement and considerably more thorough and meaningful collaboration. Indeed, in my experience, sometimes difficulties encountered in connecting at an earlier stage of the work turn out, in retrospect, to be an experience that actually enhances the therapeutic work, providing patient and therapist with a kind of "laboratory" or "workshop" that enables a fuller and more direct encounter with the issues that underlie the patient's difficulties. In such instances, a smoother initial course might have actually impeded addressing effectively the most important issues.

A factor that may have had a particularly strong impact on the meaning to Melissa of the therapeutic encounter's being a single demonstration session was revealed to me by the video series organizers shortly before the session began. It turned out that this was not Melissa's first encounter with this format or, indeed, with the American Psychological Association (APA) video series. She had participated in a similar one-session videotaped encounter a year earlier with Diana Fosha, a therapist I know well and greatly respect. I tried to approach the session as I would *any* initial session—not knowing what kind of experience awaited me and trying to be as open as possible to making it a good and useful experience for the patient—but this special circumstance (i.e., that Melissa had had a similar session previously) became an additional factor in the session that complicated our task together.

Adding to the impact of this unusual state of affairs, Melissa's session with Diana had been a particularly meaningful experience for her. As the reader will see in reading the transcript, Melissa refers very positively to her session with Diana in my own session with her, and Diana, for her part, selected the session with Melissa to be the one that was included in the APA video series. Thus there is a sense in which I came into the session as more of a "stranger" than I otherwise might have. I was, one might say, the "non-Diana" in the room.

Further complicating the import of Melissa's having previously done an APA video with Diana (in the very same studio in which we were now recording our session) is that, as she describes in the session with me, she *attributes her divorce* to the session with Diana. She describes this as a good thing and is grateful to Diana for having sufficiently clarified her feelings that she gained the courage to pursue the divorce. But it is nonetheless the case that as Melissa experienced it, just one session with a visiting therapist brought to Chicago by APA changed the very foundations of her life. It would be very understandable if Melissa, whether consciously or not, was determined not to let herself be similarly touched or shaken by another therapist from New York who would be seeing her just for a single session.[1]

One way in which this caution on Melissa's part may have been manifested is in the way she framed the issue she wanted to work on in the session. Melissa was clearly in conflict—a state of mind that therapists are certainly not unused to. But the conflict she focused on was one largely limited to very concrete choices about whether to continue in her current job as a waitress—which did not utilize or develop the skills and knowledge she had acquired in college—or to find a job in the career for which she had trained and which was still a part of her aspirations for the future. Her discussion of this conflict was rather narrowly focused on concrete economic issues such as salary and health insurance, and she did not stray very far from this focus for most of the session.

These are by no means trivial concerns in contemporary American society. But the narrow way that Melissa framed her dilemma actually impeded the exploration of a range of other issues that may have been contributing to the very difficulty she was having in resolving her conflict in this realm. As the session went on, its scope widened some, and Melissa's relationships and conflicts with key people in her life became more of a focus. But all in all, the framing with which Melissa entered the session was one more suited to career counseling than to the kind of psychotherapy, focused on relationships, conflicts, and experienced and warded-off emotions, that I more typically practice—and that is characteristic of Diana Fosha's work as well. Put differently, Melissa seemed implicitly committed to making sure she did not experience another "Diana-type" (and, it so happens, "Paul-type") session.

Over the course of the session, a number of additional themes did begin to emerge that are closer to what a dynamic or integratively oriented psychotherapist can be helpful with. As a single mom with a young daughter, Melissa was understandably loathe to risk her health benefits, but the impact of having been recently divorced and of now being in the role of single mother were probably creating stress for Melissa on other levels as well. The challenges and conflicts included continuing to figure out what will be the nature of her relationship to her ex-husband, who clearly remains an important figure in her life, both in broader emotional ways and just by consequence of being the father of her child. Relatedly, she is faced with the question of whether she wants to pursue a new relationship at this juncture or to focus for now rather exclusively on her child and her work issues. These themes were

---

[1] As it turned out, enough was stirred by Melissa's single session with Diana that Diana volunteered to follow up that contact with a number of telephone contacts from New York, to which Melissa alludes in the session with me. Thus, strictly speaking, Melissa did not have just a single contact with Diana. The point being made here, however, remains relevant—perhaps even more so.

all potentially useful ones to explore with Melissa, but they were not as fully or richly addressed in the session as I am accustomed to seeing happen in my work. The discussion in this chapter examines why this was the case.

Looking at the session in overview, I think my participation was impeded by two factors in particular. The first is the general bias of therapists, especially dynamically oriented therapists, toward looking "underneath" and finding more complicated, hidden issues rather than staying with the more "surface," practical concerns. I have, in many ways, been a critic of that tendency, or at least of the ways in which it can become problematically one-sided (e.g., P. L. Wachtel, 1997, 2003), but I also think I succumbed to it to some degree here. In retrospect, I think I underestimated the degree to which the life-changing impact of Melissa's session with Diana Fosha a year earlier had affected her feelings about herself, her life, and most of all, about the therapy experience itself. In certain ways, Melissa was seeking help from a therapist in dealing with what help from a therapist had previously wrought. From Melissa's account, the changes that resulted after the session with Diana were important and positive ones for her. But they were still large changes, and she was still struggling to assimilate them and reorganize her life in the stressful circumstance of being the single mother of a young child.

The second factor that made it difficult to provide the kind of assistance that *Melissa* was seeking, rather than attempting to offer her what *I* wanted to give, is that this session was being recorded and was potentially going to be made into a video. As a consequence, I wanted the session to be *interesting* to a potential viewer and to illustrate well the way I work. It is important for us, as therapists, to be aware that although there is probably a positive correlation between interesting and helpful, it is by no means an airtight connection. Sometimes, what the patient needs is not necessarily what the therapist needs, in the sense that she may not be seeking an especially "interesting" or intellectually challenging mode of participation but just a calm, steady, kind, supportive presence. The presence of the camera had more of an impact on me than it has had in other recorded sessions (including Louise's), I think because I was sensing from very early in the session that this would be a difficult session in which to demonstrate what "usually" happens in my sessions. As a consequence, it took longer to find a mode of engagement with Melissa that was genuinely collaborative.

Over time, even in this one session, Melissa and I did find some common ground and begin to work together more productively. I think the second half of the session was much more productive and interesting than the first half. In particular, as the session proceeded, it became possible to highlight for Melissa the degree to which she *wanted* to remain in her current job for now and was mainly thinking of changing because of pressures from others, both in their actual demands and in the "shoulds" in her head that were a residue of prior experiences. Melissa's complex role in the family system was clarified as well, pointing to ways in which she may have been receiving mixed messages that were hard to sort out. The tone of the session became both more supportive and more exploratory. Often, in discussions of the therapy process, these two poles of the process are treated as antithetical. In my own work, I view the two not as antithetical but complementary and mutually facilitative—one can only be effectively exploratory by being supportive, and vice versa (P. L. Wachtel, 1993, 2008). As will be apparent in the session with Melissa, for example, part of what enabled us to begin to explore the more complex and less conscious elements contributing to her difficulties in making a decision about what job path to pursue for now—and to the decision that, de facto, she *had* made but felt unable wholeheartedly to endorse *as* a decision—was my standing behind her choices and inclinations and framing them, in a positive fashion, as doing things "the Melissa way." Ultimately, it was finding a way to conduct the session itself in a "Melissa way" that was the primary challenge of our work together. Although the element of struggle in achieving this is not always as apparent as it was in this session, that is also ultimately the task of *every* therapeutic encounter.

THE SESSION

Paul: Hello, Melissa.

Melissa: Hello.

Paul: Tell me a little bit of about what brings you here today.

Melissa: My biggest concern right now is just getting a job in my field. I was recently—well, I'm in the counseling program.

Paul: Uh-huh . . .

Melissa: And I was in the marriage and family track, but I've decided to switch to school counseling.

Paul: Uh-huh . . .

Melissa: So, and I'm waitressing right now and I've been waitressing for—I don't know, for going on 5 years.

Paul: Uh-huh . . .

Melissa: But the biggest thing is just quitting my job and finding another job in my field. Like, I've been wanting to quit my job for a while, and—but it's like, it's hard because it's quick, fast, easy cash. It's not a job I take home with me. The hours are great, but I just need to start filling my resume for, you know, my career down the line.

Paul: Uh-huh, uh-huh . . .

Melissa: So, that's like my biggest struggle right now is just trying to decide, you know, what it is I can do that's gonna go with school counseling now.

Paul: Uh-huh . . . uh-huh . . . so, some part of that is just sort of practical and external and life decision stuff. And then some part of it you have an intuition, which brings you here, that there's something else that's sort of impeding that decision. And when you think of it that way, any hunches at all?

* * * * *

I have been hearing so far a rather practical concern, important but not yet something that a psychotherapist could be very helpful with. Since she *was* discussing this with a psychotherapist (and, indeed, presents it as the reason she is here), I am trying to open up the question of *what else* is involved in this decision that I might be able to help her clarify or work on. In saying to her, "You have an intuition, which brings you here, that there's something else that's sort of impeding that decision," I am trying to help her to pay attention to and get more in touch with that intuition. In saying it this way, I am offering what I call an attributional comment (see P. L. Wachtel, 1993), crediting her with the intuition that she has not yet voiced, and possibly not yet had.

Even at this very early point in the session, I am beginning to worry that there will be nothing that I can meaningfully engage as a therapist and especially—since this was meant to be a demonstration session—nothing that will be of interest to a viewer who is training to be a psychotherapist or to an experienced therapist who is interested in learning more about or thinking more deeply about the therapeutic process.

Melissa: You know, my biggest concern is just—because I'm recently divorced and I have an apartment now with my daughter. So, my biggest concern is taking a pay cut.[2]

---

[2] I don't notice it yet here, but in fact Melissa is already, at this early point in the session, introducing a broader context for her conflict about whether or not to stay in her current job as a waitress. Her spontaneously introducing the fact of being recently divorced and having to take care of a daughter on her own provides an opening to explore the very kinds of issues and experiences—difficulties in relationships, experiences of loss, conflicted emotional responses, and so forth—that are standard concerns in my work. But it is not until a bit later in our dialogue that I pick up on these themes, or even notice that Melissa has introduced them. At this point my perceptions are still dominated by the anxiety that the session will have too restricted a focus to make a good demonstration video.

What I have already begun to think in the session itself, and am certainly thinking as I sit here reflecting on the session afterward, is that the problem here is going to be finding a common agenda, finding a problem that is one that I can help her with and to which my skills and experience are suited. Her concerns are, of course, completely legitimate. And obviously she has every right to be concerned about what *she* is concerned about, not what a therapist might find of interest or suited to his skills. But there is beginning to be a sense of a mismatch, of her coming to the wrong person, to someone who has no particular expertise in the problem, at least as she has framed it.

Since we have committed ourselves to spending some time together, my own agenda is, on the one hand, to stay with *her* experience, to respect her as the expert on what she is feeling and wanting but, on the other hand, also to try to see where there may be additional dimensions of the conflict she is experiencing that are not purely external and practical. What I can offer her, after all, is not expertise about medical benefits but expertise in helping her to see if there are thoughts and feelings that are impeding her decision making that are not in her focal awareness and that are impeding it in part *because* they are not fully conscious.

My view of unconscious processes, and of how to discuss them in the therapeutic setting, differs some from that of many dynamic therapists (P. L. Wachtel, 2005, 2008). I view the unconscious not as some totally separate realm about which the patient does not have a clue and that only the therapist can see but rather as consisting of aspects of the person's experience that are difficult to look at focally, usually uncomfortable to acknowledge, and hence either marginalized at the edge of consciousness or kept out of focal awareness at all (cf. D. B. Stern, 1997). The expertise that the therapist brings consists in large part in *noticing* the various hints that something is being left out (hints that include certain absences of content; changing the subject at certain points; speech hesitations and other affective cues, including those given nonverbally altogether as well as, of course, phenomena such as slips of the tongue). It consists as well in knowledge or experience that give him or her some ideas about what the missing experience might be.

The good therapist also needs a second kind of expertise that often is not part of therapists' training—expertise in how to *present* these observations and provisional hypotheses to the patient. If the implicit thrust or tone of the therapist's message is that "you are thinking and feeling things that you know nothing about, you are clueless about your own experience, you think you want one thing but 'really' you want something else," then it will not be therapeutic.[3] If, on the other hand, one acknowledges, affirms, and follows along with what the patient *is* experiencing and then explores if the patient might be *also* wanting or feeling something *additional*— that is, *expanding* the patient's sense of herself rather than challenging it (P. L. Wachtel, 1993, 2008)—a therapeutic result is more likely.

As this particular session proceeds, it will be apparent to the reader that the attempt to expand the patient's vision of herself and her dilemma was not nearly as successful as was the case with Louise. I will consider at various points as the session proceeds whether I was too impatient and impeded the development of a therapeutic alliance, making it more difficult for us to collaboratively expand on the problem as initially framed. I will consider other ways as well in which the relationship with Melissa unfolded differently from that with Louise. (I will further discuss these differences and their implications in Chapter 6.)

> *Paul:* Uh-huh . . .
>
> *Melissa:* And, so financially speaking, I don't wanna take a pay cut, but I have a very good feeling that whatever job I get with the bachelor's in psychology is gonna be a pay cut compared to what I'm making now. So, that's like my biggest concern, you know, but that's what—that's what keeps me there, plus I wanna make sure that if I am gonna change jobs, that it is something that it is going to be good to have on the resume.
>
> *Paul:* Uh-huh . . .
>
> *Melissa:* I don't just wanna get out of waitressing just because I'm getting out of waitressing, you know. And then the other concern is insurance. That's another really big factor why I don't wanna quit waitressing, you know.
>
> *Paul:* Right.
>
> *Melissa:* So, it's just about the money, you know.
>
> *Paul:* And that is obviously very realistic.
>
> *Melissa:* Uh-huh . . .
>
> *Paul:* And nobody can make a good decision without taking that kind of thing into account.
>
> *Melissa:* Uh-huh . . .
>
> *Paul:* But, here the two of us are, so there's some thought you have that maybe there's something about making that decision that's more than just sort of adding up the numbers, right?

---

[3]Unfortunately, this is in essence the tone of therapists' comments much more than is commonly appreciated (Wile, 1984).

$$* * * * *$$

Here I am again pursuing the line of inquiry that I began earlier and was discussing above. I start with affirming the reality and appropriateness of the concerns—about money and career opportunities—that she has expressed. But I then try to expand the lens, so to speak, to see if there is any way I can help her better understand why making this decision has been as difficult as it has been.

Melissa: Uh-huh . . .

Paul: You've mentioned being recently divorced, having a child, does any of that enter into it any way?

$$* * * * *$$

Here I am picking up on something she had mentioned earlier as part of the context for her decision. I am, in essence, trying to help her think about whether this might be part of the *emotional* context for the decision, not just the practical context.

Melissa: I'm not sure. I mean, it doesn't bother me to switch jobs. I'm not afraid of that. It's not a big concern of mine. But I guess my focus is just doing something that, you know, is gonna be good to follow through with, like with school counseling, because before I had thought about getting a job in a hospital. I was like, oh the hours are good, the benefits are great, you know, the insurance is there, and I thought that that would be good if I was staying in the marriage and family track. But now that I'm switching, I was thinking, well maybe now going into the hospital wouldn't be such a good thing.

Paul: Uh-huh . . .

Melissa: It wouldn't tie me in any way, so, I don't know. I mean, I've had enough of stress over the last 2 months, so it's like there's a bit of comfort there for me to stay in my job for now.

Paul: Uh-huh . . . uh-huh . . .

$$* * * * *$$

One thing that is occurring to me now as I write this that I did not say or think to say at the time is that perhaps it would have been useful to her here to address the sense of internal pressure, the "should," that is making this decision more difficult for her. One might say something like, "So it sounds like in many ways you're feeling that staying with the waitressing is really what feels best to you right now. But there is some nagging voice in your head that is saying you're 'not supposed to' do that." Then, if she responds in a way that indicates that that captures her phenomenological experience, one might follow it up in a variety of possible ways. Depending on her response, and the affective dimension of it, one might, for example, ask, "Has that kind of nagging inner voice been around putting pressure on you before?" Or one could ask more about the experience directly: "Tell me more about what that voice is like. What else it says. What kind of tone of voice it has. Whether it sounds familiar, like the voice of anyone in your life growing up. How it *feels* to hear that voice." (Any of these questions might be useful, with the others kept in reserve, so to speak, for further expansion or if the first ones chosen don't elicit very much.)

One might also envision exploring whether there is a part of her that is *angry* at that voice, that wishes it would go away. If so, one might ask, "What would you like to say to that voice?", thereby helping her to explore and implicitly rehearse responses that might enable her to at least partially *liberate* herself from an inner demand that is getting in her way.

<blockquote>

Melissa: But I mean, I'm willing to switch, you know.

Paul: Uh-huh . . .

Melissa: So . . .

Paul: Tell me a little bit more about that, that, the experience of stress and then the feeling of comfort right now.

</blockquote>

* * * * *

Although in reading the transcript it may appear that I am going back to something she said a comment or two before, I am actually responding to what she said in the statement that immediately preceded my comment. This may be obscured in reading the transcript both by my interpolated comment above, which of course was not part of the dialogue in the session, and by the "uh-huh's" that are noted in the transcript but that are just verbal "nods" as I was listening to what was essentially a continuous statement by Melissa about the stress over the last 2 months and the waitress job as a bit of comfort from that stress.

In my comment here, I am trying to enter more into the affective realm. Melissa has described feeling stressed and also that the decision she is making by default, to stay in her waitress job, leaves her feeling *less* stressed. By focusing on her experiences of stress and relief, I am again making an attempt to enter into her experience in a fashion suited to promoting the aims of the psychotherapy process. It is worth noting that were I not relating to her as a therapist but, say, as a friend, I might well have stayed with the level of career opportunities versus medical benefits.

<blockquote>

Melissa: The feeling of stress is just—it's like there's just anxiety a lot, you know. There's just a lot of tension, you know. A lot of

</blockquote>

things you don't wanna think about, you know, and for just the comfort, like the only area of comfort I have right now, I'd say, is just knowing that I still am waitressing and that the money is still stable and it's consistent. So in that way I do have comfort.

* * * * *

Here again, as I am writing these comments, I am thinking of that inner voice that *isn't letting her* just be comfortable, and I am again thinking that perhaps it would have been helpful to have made a comment in the session that addressed that.

Paul: Uh-huh . . . uh-huh . . .

Melissa: You know, but I mean there are so many aspects of my life that have changed recently, and I thought what's one more?

Paul: Uh-huh . . . uh-huh . . .

Melissa: You know, why not switch jobs too, and just change everything? So, you know, I mean, I'm willing to do it, but I guess there was a piece of me that does have comfort in staying there. But I'm also willing to go. Because I know that, you know, especially for insurance purposes, you know, I mean to quit.

Paul: Uh-huh . . . uh-huh . . .

* * * * *

As I reflect further, in writing these comments, on her statements, "There are so many aspects of my life that have changed recently, and I thought what's one more. . . . why not switch jobs too and just change everything?" it occurs to me that there is a self-punitive tone to this. Is she unconsciously feeling guilty about her divorce and feeling she should "pay" for it by having a hard time, by piling one thing on top of another? Alternatively, is this a somewhat despairing statement, a sense of "it's going to be one thing after another anyway, what's the difference?" One might explore these possibilities with statements such as, "So, so much has already happened that has been so stressful, why would you feel you deserve to have still one more thing added to the pot?" Or, "It feels like it's just one thing after another, what's the difference anyway?"

Melissa: So . . .

Paul: Is there some worry about making the wrong decision? Is that . . . ?

Melissa: I'd say the advantage I have in terms of worrying is that right now with my job I know that they would take me back. If I were to quit and then I needed to go back, they would take me. So, you know, that wouldn't be a big deal. But I just wanna make sure that if I do quit, that I'm gonna quit and go somewhere that's gonna benefit me in the future.

Paul: Uh-huh . . . uh-huh . . .

Melissa: That's like my biggest concern.

Paul: Uh-huh . . . uh-huh . . .

Melissa: You know, I even started getting my resume together like a month ago and then I was trying to—try [for a] master's [degree], and then they got set aside and, you know, more of just trying to talk to people to see, you know, who knows who or can maybe—someone can maybe make some suggestions, you know.

Paul: Right. So, being somewhere where they support you and they will take you back, that feels very important.

* * * * *

This comment, another effort to reframe the focus from the level of simply practical dollars and cents and career issues to one more psychological in nature, alludes to the level of attachment phenomena, the secure base from which to explore (Bowlby, 1988; Wallin, 2007).

Melissa: Yeah, yeah. I mean, I have a lot of comfort knowing that, you know.

Paul: Yeah.

Melissa: But, again, I mean, I'm willing to go.

Paul: Uh-huh . . . uh-huh . . .

Melissa: You know, it's just a matter of, if I go, I just wanna make sure it's the right thing, 'cause I don't wanna bounce back and forth.

Paul: Uh-huh . . .

* * * * *

I am thinking here that this thought of Melissa's may be related to her having recently gotten divorced and perhaps having more doubts about that choice and its consequences than she is comfortable letting herself experience. The concern about bouncing back and forth and not being sure she is doing the right thing could be a displaced expression of doubts about the more consequential decision she recently made and an allusion to the temptation to bounce back and forth in *that* decision. It could allude as well to concerns about whether, being unmarried, she will have a home or safe harbor or will just "bounce back and forth."

Melissa:	You know, I just wanna make sure that, if I go, I mean, you know, I thought, well . . . even if got a job in my field and I took a pay cut.
Paul:	Uh-huh . . .
Melissa:	Even if I waitress like a couple of weekends out of a month just for some extra money.
Paul:	Uh-huh . . .
Melissa:	I know I could do that, too. So, you know . . . but the biggest thing is just financially, you know, what's the money gonna be like and then, if I change jobs, is it gonna be something that's gonna benefit me down the line with what I'm going into, you know. I don't wanna get a job that doesn't tie in with something, you know, later on.
Paul:	Now, you've just been through a very major change in your life. You were divorced . . .

* * * * *

Here I do begin to take up with Melissa some of the line of thought I was alluding to in my interpolated comment above. I change the focus some from her financial concerns to the divorce itself.

Melissa:	Right, right.
Paul:	Tell me a little bit about what the divorce was like.
Melissa:	Fast. Like that. We filed in February, we were done in March.
Paul:	Uh-huh . . .
Melissa:	It was that quick.
Paul:	Uh-huh . . . how long had you been married?
Melissa:	Three and a half years. We were going to 4 years.
Paul:	Uh-huh . . . and when did you know that . . . because you said that the divorce itself happened very fast. How did you know that the divorce was coming?
Melissa:	What was scary is that when I was here in November with Diana, and I've gotten so much out of Diana, and it was like she was, talking with her for that session was such a huge

eye-opener for me. Now, I realized and recognized so many things about myself and a lot of things have seemed to have been holding me back and I understood reasons why I was contemplating, do I stay or do I go.

Paul: Uh-huh . . .

* * * * *

Melissa's session with Diana is clearly an important part of the context for the present session in a number of ways. On the one hand, she had a very meaningful and powerful session with Diana, which could mean that now seeing a different therapist, also for a single session, might leave her feeling that I was a poor substitute, that it was really Diana that she wanted to be seeing. It could also stir the feeling that therapists just come and go, that no matter how powerfully they move you, they are not there for the follow-up. Both of these feelings would be likely to make her less receptive to participating deeply in the therapeutic possibilities of this session.

At the same time, the experience with Diana is likely affecting this session in a different way as well. In addition to having experienced the session with Diana as meaningful and helpful, Melissa is likely also feeling that therapy just might be a little *too* powerful an experience and, as a result, she is likely as well to be limiting the degree to which she gives me access to any of her deeper experiences. After all, it was her experience that her one session with Diana played a significant role in her getting divorced, and even if that felt like it was ultimately a *good* thing, it clearly was also a wrenching experience—as reflected, for example, in her describing the consequences of the session with Diana as "scary." If every session with a therapist can lead to her whole life being pulled out of its orbit, it would not be surprising that she would be motivated to limit the impact of this one.

(Also useful to note at this point in the session, Melissa's phrase "do I stay or do I go," referring here to the decision about the divorce, is also a bridge to the conflict Melissa introduces as the presenting issue of the session. That is, "do I stay or do I go?" is also the question Melissa is asking herself about the waitressing job, and the consonance between the presenting conflict and the question raised in deciding whether to divorce her husband further suggests that some of her difficulties in making the more concrete job decision may be linked to still unresolved feelings about the divorce.)

Melissa: And it was like, I found a little bit of peace in myself knowing that I knew why now, you know. It was like, I finally had some answers. And so, when I left the session with Diana, a couple of weeks later I told him.

Paul: Uh-huh . . .

Melissa: And now, I'm divorced.

Paul:	Uh-huh . . .
Melissa:	So, I don't know what today's therapy is gonna bring, but— then these feelings will all be nervous.
Paul:	You don't wanna allow yourself . . .
Melissa:	So, I've had enough of changes, but . . .
Paul:	. . . to destabilize or what.
Melissa:	Yeah, you know it would be nice to just sit still, not move for a while.

* * * * *

Here we see still clearer indications that Melissa feels that after the experience she had in opening up to Diana, she is going to be much more cautious this time around:

> When I left the session with Diana, a couple of weeks later I told him . . . and now I'm divorced. . . . So, I don't know what today's therapy is gonna bring. . . . So, I've had enough of changes . . . it would be nice to just sit still, not move for a while.

This all points to a very understandable state of mind on Melissa's part of not wanting to risk the prospect that a therapy session could again produce more change than she is ready for. The result is a rather narrow focus that does not, at least initially, provide the same kind of opportunity for exploration and deepening of the session as was the case with Louise.

Paul:	Right, right. Okay.
Melissa:	Yeah.
Paul:	Right.
Melissa:	So . . .
Paul:	So, the divorce was more your decision?

* * * * *

In making this comment here, I am trying to pull us back to the topic I had begun exploring, the meaning and impact of the divorce. I am also highlighting Melissa as an active agent in her life.

Melissa:	Uh-huh . . .
Paul:	Uh-huh . . . uh-huh . . .
Melissa:	I initiated it, but in the end it was mutual.
Paul:	Uh-huh . . . and how are you feeling about the divorce at this point?

* * * * *

An obvious but nonetheless important question.

Melissa: I question a lot of things, you know, there's a lot of "what if's. What if we would have . . . ?" And that's part of the reason why I continue talking to Diana, 'cause she was trying to refer me a therapist in Chicago.

Paul: Uh-huh . . .

Melissa: And I thought what if we would have found a third party to commit to help us, you know. Could things have been different between us? So there's a lot of that. What stinks about the whole situation is that there was never, there was never any closure. You know, it was like I said in November, that's when I came to him and told him I wanted to get a divorce, and then we continued to live together until we sold our house in April.

Paul: Uh-huh . . .

Melissa: April 1. We both had doubts and we stayed in the house. You know, he didn't move and go anywhere, so that's what was really hard. And people would say, "Oh, you know, so what's it like to still be living together knowing you're getting divorced?" and then I'd say, "Kind of strange, it's almost like we're not getting divorced." You know, it was really bizarre.

* * * * *

Apropos my comments earlier, the divorce is clearly still a source of some conflict and uncertainty for her, not a "slam dunk" good decision. So it is natural that she would be a bit hesitant about making another decision at this point that, if less momentous, is still of considerable import.

Paul: Uh-huh . . . what were your feelings at the time you were thinking about the divorce?

Melissa: I just felt like I was unhappy. If I would stay, I'd feel like I was in a relationship where I was never gonna be accepted for who I was and what I did, you know, was never gonna be good enough. So, there was a lot of that in there, you know.

Paul: So part of it wasn't just that he wasn't interesting or exciting enough. He also wasn't taking care of you very well, being attentive or responsive to you.

* * * * *

As I read over this part of the session, I am reminded of my comments earlier regarding the critical inner voice. The experience of "never being good enough" is both an experience of an external criticism and, most likely, an experience that activates the *inner* voice as well, raising the specter of her implicitly colluding with or agreeing with the critical voice from her husband.

Melissa: Uh-huh . . . yeah. There was—it was just, it's, I had said I think even to Diana that it was—it's one of the, I'd say it's probably the most emotionally unavailable relationship I've ever been in.

Paul: Uh-huh . . .

Melissa: That's how it was. It was really—you know it's like, and it's so strange 'cause it's like there are so many levels where, you know, I can connect with him and, you know, we can just, kind of do nothing or you know, even just sitting together or watching TV that was fine. But there's a lot of other levels that we just, you know, there was a lot of just butting heads. Too much of that all the time, you know and it's like, stupid stuff too.

Paul: What—can you give me an example, so I have some feeling for what it was like?

Melissa: You know, there were issues with parenting, like . . . I have a 3-year-old.

Paul: Uh-huh . . .

Melissa: And you know, we just butt heads on that. Like he'd say, like anytime Dakota would whine or cry or, you know, it's like the minute I would walk into the room, you know, she . . . he would have her all day and let's say, I work on a weekend and then I come home and he'd say, "You know, when you walk into the house, it's like a tornado. Because Dakota hasn't cried and she hasn't whined all day, but the minute mom walks indoors suddenly we're crying and we're whining."

Paul: Uh-huh . . .

Melissa: And it's like, there was no tolerance of that, and what she would do when I was around, and there was no patience and he resented that stuff.

Paul: And did you feel criticized by him?

Melissa: Oh, yeah, yeah. I was definitely.

Paul: Yeah.

Melissa: You know, I felt very criticized by him and just—but even with my daughter, it's like there was a competition there and, you know, we can—it's like we were competitive on a lot of levels, but—yeah, I mean that was just something that, that was just annoying. It's like, so what. She's gonna cry, she's gonna whine. She obviously is—feels comfortable with me to do those things, you know, to be emotional with me, you know.

Paul: So, there were ways in which he wasn't in a sense being nice to you, he wasn't understanding you, he was blaming you. But there was a whole other part of it. It sounds like that was more about he's not connecting with you.

Melissa: Uh-huh . . .

Paul: Tell me about that part.

Melissa: I just don't feel that he was very accepting of a lot of things. I look at him as . . . I see him as, and he knows it. He is a very critical, judgmental person and very opinionated and, you know, I'm the opposite of that, you know. It's like, you know, he'll get mad because—I even talked to Diana about this. He'll get mad because, you know, and he is a very black-and-white person. I live in the world where there is a lot of gray. And so, you know, he'd get mad when I wouldn't choose one or the other and I wouldn't take a stand one way or another, you know. That always bugs him.

* * * * *

Here, apropos the presenting issue that Melissa brought in, it appears that making decisions is a more *general* issue for her, that she is someone who has a hard time making up her mind. This makes the very rapid decision to divorce, and the apparent impact of the session with Diana, even more note-worthy. At the same time, as I read it now, it suggests that the interim period, when they continued to live together and it was "almost like we're not get-ting divorced" is an experience it would be useful to explore further.

Paul: So, he'd be really angry if you were in the situation you are right now about work.

Melissa: He'd be angry about that?

Paul: Well, you're saying that he gets mad when you can't make up your mind.

Melissa: Oh! In that way, okay. Oh, yeah, that's definitely something that he would tell me about too. He'd say, "You know what, you have a bachelor's. You have a bachelor's degree. You could go out and get a job. There's something you can do and make decent money." Really? Okay. Well, you talk to all the people here at Governor's State that have a Bachelor's in psychology and ask any one of them what they've done, what types of job they've done with the social service field, ask them what their pay is. But he thinks you have a degree, you are educated, and you should be able to go out and get a good job. And you shouldn't be waitressing anymore and you don't need to do that.

Paul: Uh-huh . . .

Melissa: Yeah, he is right, I don't need to do that, but financially speaking, that's why I do it.

Paul: So, it must feel almost like a luxury to be able to be undecided and not have somebody criticize you for it, right now.

* * * * *

Here I am trying to join her, to offer support and affirmation for her taking her time to make up her mind. In the sense that the attitude I am expressing differs from the one she experienced from her husband, this could be viewed as a kind of corrective emotional experience (Alexander & French, 1946). It could also be understood in terms of the concept of "joining the resistance" as it is used in paradigmatic, family systems, and narrative approaches, for example. Melissa has been very self-critical regarding her difficulties in making this choice, and I am here trying to create some breathing room for her by reframing the indecision as a luxury rather than a character flaw.

Melissa: Oh, yeah. Right now it's like he's off my back, you know, but I did tell him the other day, I said that, that I was gonna be switching from marriage and family and that I was gonna be going into school counseling and he's like, oh that's so good. Like, he was really happy to hear that because he had said to me before, "You know, why don't you just go get a bachelor's or a master's in school psych." And you know, his mom had a friend that said, "If you had a master's in school psychology, I'll hire you right now, starting mid-50s." And all he thinks about are the numbers. I said, that's great, sounds like a nice number, you know, it's a good salary. However, how am I gonna pay for myself to get an education in that field? You don't just wing it in school psychology, you just don't. It's like, I'm sorry, but I don't support that.

Paul: Right.

* * * * *

Here, as in many places in the three transcripts, "right" is not a comment on the correctness or incorrectness of what she is saying but is just a term of acknowledgment that I have heard what she said, not very different from "uh-huh." This is important for the reader to keep clear because in reading a transcript, in contrast to seeing a video, the tone is not as clear, and it can seem like I am making a judgment.

> *Melissa:* So, you know, but to him it was about the numbers and that doesn't seem right to me. I was like, are you kidding me. First of all I'm not gonna pay for a master's degree in something that I'm just gonna—you don't just go into the mental health profession just winging it. I don't support that. You know, and that's kind of how he was. I was like, you gotta be kidding me.
>
> *Paul:* It seems a lot of things you really, you value, you know in yourself . . .
>
> *Melissa:* Right.
>
> *Paul:* And you don't wanna be pushed around about those things.

* * * * *

Here again, I am trying to stand beside her and be a supportive presence. There is also clearly an attributional dimension to this comment. In the sense that I have discussed attributional comments in earlier chapters, by attributing to her the attitude that she will not permit herself to be pushed around, I am attempting to stimulate and bolster that attitude on her part.

> *Melissa:* No. There are certain things I just . . .
>
> *Paul:* Not about what you really want, what you really feel.
>
> *Melissa:* Uh-huh . . . well, then he would say, "You know, my back hurts and I don't wanna be a carpenter forever either, but sometimes, you know, you just suck it up and you just do a job." I was like, okay, but you didn't pay to have an education. You didn't get a master's in carpentry. You didn't have . . . that to me does just not make sense to most people I talk to. It doesn't make sense to go pay for a master's degree in the field that you're just gonna wing it in for the salary.

* * * * *

We are seeing here some of the impact of class, a crucial variable for so much of life in our and other societies, but one which our field so often ignores. There is a clash here that is only partly personal. Her husband is expressing the attitude that work is inherently a "cost," something one does only because one is getting *paid* to do it and to be measured or valued only in terms of the money it brings in. Melissa is viewing her work as something to be evaluated as well in terms of its meaningfulness

I do not mean here to suggest that working-class values do not include pride in one's work or preference for work that feels satisfying rather than just whatever pays better. Especially in the realm of skilled labor, such as carpentry, many working-class individuals take as much pride in their work, and value the quality of their work life, as highly educated professionals. In that sense, Melissa's husband is expressing a *personal* rather than a class attitude. Conversely, one of the tragedies in our society, at least from the point of view of my own values, is how pervasive is the very attitude that Melissa's husband is expressing among the most elite upper middle class and upper class individuals. The percentage of intellectually gifted graduates of Ivy League colleges who choose to go into investment banking and managing hedge funds rather than such endeavors as cancer research or public service reflects a similar attitude, and to my mind it is a misallocation of intellectual resources of the highest order.

Nonetheless, it is a *neglectful* rejection of stereotyping to ignore the class dimension of the conflict between Melissa and her husband. Melissa seems to be a woman who is on the boundary of two different class identities, and that is part of her individual struggle and part of the matrix of misunderstanding between her and her husband.

Paul: Uh-huh . . . so, were you . . . ?

Melissa: . . . just so, this is crazy to me.

Paul: Right, right. So, when you're here at this point in your life and you're trying to make decisions, and you are thinking about, "Well, there's the disadvantage to staying waitressing for a while, there's a disadvantage to doing that," and you're conflicted about it and there are in essence . . . you know, whenever we're conflicted about things it's partly to do with voices in our head that are pushing us in different ways. Is one of those voices "you have to suck it up"?

* * * * *

I am here introducing an aspect of the idea of internal voices that I mentioned in an earlier interpolated comment. In this case, of course, it is the voice of her husband, but I am also preparing the soil, as it were, for other comments that address parental voices and voices representing *conflicting* internal imperatives. Apropos a theme I have been addressing throughout my comments on this session, there is certainly more to Melissa's conflict than the identifications and internalizations of others' attitudes. But I am not any more capable of helping her sort out "total future projected earnings" than any other noneconomist or nonfinancial consultant. I *am* more capable, however, of helping her to sort out the kinds of issues and considerations I have been trying to introduce to our dialogue, issues and considerations that may be contributing more significantly than she realizes to making it difficult for her to make a decision.

Melissa: When I think about switching jobs? No.

Paul: Uh-huh . . .

Melissa: No.

Paul: Uh-huh . . . so, his voice is not part of this.

Melissa: No. I don't think at all to myself, you know, "I'll just have to quit waitressing and I'll just suck it up whenever that take out might be."

Paul: Right.

Melissa: No.

Paul: Right. So, you're liberated from that.

Melissa: Yeah, oh yeah, that's not a thought as mine at all.

Paul: Yeah. When you were living with him, would that have sort of intruded into your head more?

* * * * *

I am here engaging in a kind of "testing the limits." As the reader can probably tell, I am still not convinced that the direction I am pursuing is totally irrelevant. I am trying to offer a framing of it to which she might be more receptive. At moments like this in the therapeutic work, I usually adopt a kind of wait-and-see attitude. That is, I certainly don't assume that my interpretations are correct regardless of what the patient says, that she is just defending against awareness of what I am pointing out. At the same time, there *are* ways in which people struggle against awareness or acknowledgment of various aspects of their psychological dynamics, and to *just* take the attitude that "if the patient says no right at the moment, then the matter is closed" is equally problematic. One must chart a more complex course, neither pushing a hobbyhorse on a "resisting" patient nor engaging in wholesale rejection of one's hypotheses if the patient is not immediately receptive. One can keep an idea in mind to be tried again later, when the patient may be able to view it from a different angle, and one can do so without perseverating or browbeating the patient. (One must also, of course, be able eventually to relinquish the hypothesis if confirmation remains unforthcoming.)

Melissa: I don't think so, because I didn't quit my job, because I could stay home with my daughter for 9 1/2 months after I had her. And then I went back to work just like 2 days a week, even 3 days, and I would pick up more days here and there. So, I mean the job was great, and he knew that. It was good, quick, easy cash, so it was like, you know, it was fine at the time, you know. There wasn't a push for me to get out there and get a real job with my bachelor's degree. There wasn't a real push for that because I was staying at home with her all the time, you know, and we didn't want her in day care and all that stuff. But, yeah, he's, you know, even at the time of living with him, you know, I never even pushed to get a full-time job, you know, I would pick up extra days here and there, but I wasn't about just going to anything either, you know.

Paul: Now, these feelings you have now, and actually, let me share with you, I have, I'm of two minds about what I hear. I'm a little unclear.

Melissa: Okay.

Paul: Because I'm hearing, I think, two things. I'm hearing one thing that's "I can't make up my mind what I wanna do and it's bothering me and that's why I'm coming for help" . . .

Melissa: Uh-huh . . .

Paul: . . . and then I'm hearing, "There's something nice about not having anybody push me to make up my mind, and it feels sort of comfortable and it feels like where I ought to be right now. And I *have* made up my mind. I have made up my mind not to make up my mind yet."

* * * * *

Several things are going on in this comment. For one, I am engaging in the kind of sharing of my thought processes, and even my dilemma, that Renik (e.g., 1995, 1999) has depicted particularly well from a two-person point of view. I am also attempting to articulate a bit more for Melissa the element of *conflict* and to sharpen the issue in a psychological way. Moreover, I am trying to point out that in some way Melissa *has* made a decision, but that it is one she is feeling uncomfortable with, and I am trying to open up an exploration of what that discomfort is about (including whether some of it may be a function of the internalized voice of her husband—and possibly earlier internal voices with which it resonates).

Melissa: Uh-huh . . .

Paul: Is that . . . ?

Melissa: The comfort is there to know that I don't have him, you know, pushing me to go and get a job. I mean, even though it's been a couple of months that we've been divorced now, you know, he'll still even say, "You know, you can get still get a job in your field." You know, or "because you're educated." It's like I still hear him say that, but I guess the other push would be that I just got a letter in the mail saying that my insurance . . . I took a major medical plan out during the school. So, I'm covered with all that stuff, but I've got a month left before it expires, and now it's a matter do I wanna renew it for 3 more months.

Paul: Uh-huh . . .

Melissa: And it's like, that could be my push to say, all right, let's get some resumes out, let's, you know, look into a job change. But, I think part of me is just going to stay.

Paul: All right.

Melissa: It sounds so bad but, and I know I need the switch, but it's like there's that comfort there.

Paul: What do you mean it sounds so bad?

* * * * *

Here again I am trying to pick up on the self-critical dimension as a prelude to helping her to liberate herself from that.

Melissa: You know, it's like . . .

Paul: Tell me about that. Why does it sound so bad?

Melissa: It's only because it's like—it's like it's . . . you know, I said a year ago I would quit my job. I—when I started my program. I had met with one teacher, who I didn't know, but I had heard about her, and one of my friends said, you know, go see her. She would know about, you know, what you should go into. And I went to her last summer and she told me some things that she did along the way and I still didn't quit.

Paul: Uh-huh . . .

Melissa: I still didn't quit my job, and I don't know if it's just a comfort thing, I mean, I just say it's bad. That's like I know that I say it's bad because I know that I need to get just some regular insurance and not just major medical. But I think that part of me is just like, oh well, I have major medical covered at least, and what, I made good money in the restaurant, so screw it. Make a few more bucks for the next, you know, couple of months, and then maybe decide from there.

Paul: Uh-huh . . .

Melissa: You know.

Paul:	Uh-huh . . .
Melissa:	I don't know.
Paul:	Well, you spent, it sounds like, several years feeling sort of pushed around.
Melissa:	Yeah.
Paul:	All right. One thing I'm wondering about, that experience of being pushed around, which you are now saying, "I don't wanna be pushed around anymore . . . "
Melissa:	Uh-huh . . .
Paul:	"I wanna make up my own mind in my own good time about what I wanna do," and I'm wondering about that experience of being pushed around, was that unique to this relationship, or is that a familiar experience from earlier in your life?

* * * * *

In these comments, I am in essence trying to state for her what I hear as one of the conflicted and at times submerged parts of her experience, to put it out there, make it acceptable, give it words. Then she can look at it in a way that might make it more possible for her to begin to resolve the conflict. I also open up here the issue of whether this difficulty in according legitimacy to her wishes for comfort and her desire to resist and challenge being pushed around has deeper roots and has been a more long-standing and more general issue in her life.

Melissa:	When you say that, that I was being pushed around, this is a very controlling person and in some levels, it's like okay, you know, it didn't bother me 'cause I don't feel that I'm a very dominating person in a relationship . . .
Paul:	Uh-huh . . .
Melissa:	You know, and so, in some way it didn't bother me, but in other areas it did.
Paul:	Uh-huh . . .
Melissa:	But as for—tell me again, you had asked if this was connected to an earlier experience?
Paul:	Well, I was thinking that part of what you're experiencing now, you know, part of this confusion I was having about hearing two things, they both can be there. I mean, it's not like it has to be one or the other.
Melissa:	Uh-huh . . .

Paul: But, you know, the feeling of, "I should make up my mind, my problem is I can't decide," and then the feeling of, "I really *have* decided, I'm just not doing what *they* want me to," but that you're doing what *you* want, like what you're doing right now? That felt to me like it was partly a, kind of part of the liberation that came with not living with someone who was telling you all the time what you should do, whether you go along with it or not.

* * * * *

Here again, I am emphasizing the feeling of *liberation* that is associated with doing what she wants, including simply not making a decision right away—or not making the "responsible" decision but rather what feels good right now.

I notice, however, as I read the transcript, that I have not followed through on my question regarding whether the feeling of being pushed around was familiar from earlier in her life, and relatedly, I have not really answered the question she just asked, "Tell me again, you had asked if this was connected to an earlier experience?"

Melissa: Right.

Paul: It's irritating to have to live with that all the time.

* * * * *

Here is an attributional comment that, like most attributional comments, is both a straightforward empathic acknowledgment of something that the patient is already feeling and at the same time a "predictive" statement that puts into words a feeling that the patient has *not yet* fully articulated for herself or fully endorsed.

Melissa: Uh-huh . . .

Paul: And I was wondering, that feeling of being told what to do, being told to suck it up, being told you should do this and so on. Is that something that felt like, "How did I get into this relationship? I've never experienced this before"? Or is it something that sort of, if you think about it, happened a lot in your life before that?

* * * * *

Here I do get back to the question of whether this is an experience that she had earlier in her life as well. The question is first framed in a way that endorses the more "isolated instance" version of the experience ("I've never experienced this before"). This has two purposes. First, it lets her know that if that *is* her experience I am prepared to hear it; that is, it makes it acceptable to view it that way, it doesn't force the alternative on her. At the same time, it also frames things in a way that puts it into stark relief ("I've *never* experienced this before") so that it might call to her attention that that way of thinking about it might misrepresent the reality of her life, and it does so in a way that enables her to hear or notice this without it being "interpreted" as a denial or minimization. Then, by offering her the "or" statement ("Or is it something that has happened a lot in your life before that?")the comment goes on to articulate a broader possibility that opens the door to examine it as a pattern in her life that can be worked on.

Melissa: I don't know how it would or if it would connect with something that I've experienced a lot in my life. There are other relationships or even family members, but what's funny is that it's like everyone in my family is even saying, you know you can't waitress forever. It's like, oh yeah, no kidding?

Paul: Uh-huh . . . uh-huh . . .

Melissa: You know, but I don't know. Yeah, it seems like—actually, it seems like in my family that everyone is on the streak of you go to school, you go to college and you get your education and you go out and you get a real job. And everyone has a career in my family.

Paul: Uh-huh . . .

Melissa: Except for my one brother, but everyone's pretty much like set, whereas I'm still kind of dangling like that, hoping I'm in the process of my master's, so, you know . . . and that's not where I wanna be just yet. But it doesn't bother me. I don't think it really bothers me to be doing what I'm doing right now. I mean, on some levels, yes, because of what I need, like the insurance and stuff, but—I don't know, I mean, it's like, so . . . a couple of them, like my dad or, you know, or like my stepmother, whoever, have just said, you know, you can't waitress forever, and I'd go like, I know. But, so maybe it's not that kind of, it's not that they're on me all the time [*several words inaudible here*] mentioned especially once I was coming closer to getting my divorce finalized. And they're like, what are you going to do? What are you going to do for a job? So, they don't know what I make at the restaurant. And so, you know, to them it's like—they probably think I'm making peanuts and I know that they're concerned and they're looking out for me. But it's only been then that they've really said anything, but they've mentioned it. They're not like calling me every week like, you're putting your resume out there. So, I mean they push me a little bit, but . . .

Paul:	And how do you feel when they do that?
Melissa:	Kind of like, lay off my back.

* * * * *

She has been trying to minimize the irritation and the pressure ("they push me 'a little bit'"), but then a strong feeling does come through. This stronger expression of her wish for them to lay off her may be in part a product of the therapeutic interaction up to this point.

We may also note that the foregoing does confirm that the experience she has had with her husband of feeling pushed *is not* an isolated instance, and *has* happened before in her life.

Paul:	Uh-huh . . .
Melissa:	Like, I'm almost 30 years old, and I know what I need to do. And maybe *to them* it doesn't seem very responsible of me that I'm still waitressing, but I seem to be getting by okay.
Paul:	Uh-huh . . .
Melissa:	So, you know, maybe that tires them too.
Paul:	And that's something you're proud of, you know. That's something that you're . . .
Melissa:	Because I'm making it. I'm not relying on any of them for any help.
Paul:	Yeah.
Melissa:	I'm not calling them saying I need money or whatever.
Paul:	Yeah.

* * * * *

I have highlighted the feeling of pride, a feeling she does not generally let herself experience, and I think it is my having done that that enables her to then elaborate on it further and further articulate it for herself that she is not relying on any of them for help or asking them for money. Part of what I think is illustrated here is how the therapeutic dialogue, when engaged in from the point of view I have been advocating, offers the patient the security and encouragement to make room for some of the feelings she has not been able to permit herself much before. The expectation is that then, *having* said to herself, and said out loud, that yes, there is something to be proud of, that she has managed rather successfully on her own, that she has shown a strength and independence that she does not usually attribute to herself so readily, she is then just a bit more likely to think such thoughts again and to assimilate this perspective more into her sense of herself.

Melissa:	Yeah. So, I think that part of it to them is, I mean, maybe that's what it is. I don't know.
Paul:	Is there something—I'm hearing that pride, and I'm seeing that you're . . . you know, when you talk about it, there is a certain, almost a glow. There's something that feels *good*, but . . .
Melissa:	Probably because I'm not being told what to do.
Paul:	Yeah.
Melissa:	I mean, I'm not letting anybody else tell me, you know.
Paul:	Yeah.
Melissa:	Yeah.
Paul:	And that's really *important* to you.

* * * * *

In these last comments, I am further highlighting and affirming the pride and determination and feeling good about herself, and she is further responding by elaborating still more on it. Of course, this is not a permanent, once-and-for-all change resulting from these interventions; but it is a part—an important part, I think—of the process whereby, with repetition, changes do become more permanent and more integrated into the patient's sense of self.

For this to happen, though, more is needed than just the "internalization" that is emphasized by many dynamic therapists or the "cognitive restructuring" that is emphasized by many cognitive therapists. Both of these processes do contribute, very substantially in fact, but they are part of a larger process in which changed *behavior* is also essential. As I have discussed in a number of places (e.g., P. L. Wachtel, 1993, 1997, 2008 [especially Chapter 12], 2009), for change to be enduring and reasonably pervasive, the patterns in the patient's actual interactions with others need to change. Those patterns are not determined solely by the internal processes within the patient but are part of a continuing, reciprocal set of transactions with others, in which the actions of each party feed back to change both the actions *and,* at least to some degree, the internal processes of the other.

Melissa:	Yeah. I mean, I will make the final decision because I *wanna* do it, not because of somebody else, you know.
Paul:	So, everybody in your family, you were saying, sort of is on a track, you know, sort of from the beginning, and is going along in a direction, not supposed to veer off. And you've chosen differently.

* * * * *

I'm emphasizing here her having made a *choice*. That is, she has not failed in pursuing their course; she has chosen a *different* course. And implicitly I am framing her choice as a courageous one rather than a foolish one. This is done very incidentally, however, more in the manner of an implicit attributional comment.

Melissa: Uh-huh . . .

Paul: Were you different in the family all along? Did you have a different role in the family? How did that happen that you were able to do this?

* * * * *

Here I am doing two different things. One is to examine the pattern from a historical or developmental perspective. The other is to continue with the positive attributional dimension—how were you able to do such a difficult (and, implicitly, impressive, daring) thing?

Melissa: Yeah, I'd say I was a little bit different from the rest of them. There's four others, and the eldest two, well, the eldest two and then the one above me. They all have their careers, you know, and then my brother Dave works at a pizza place, but he's a little bit slower anyway. So, and he never went to college like that, you know, but—but yes, I don't think that—I don't really think that they were surprised that it's, you know, maybe that I am where I'm at today. And I guess I would describe it as I'm just taking a later start on things, you know, because they all have their careers by now. You know, but I'm just taking a little longer to get there.

Paul: And when you were growing up, did you *enjoy* being different from them or was it *hard* for you to be different from them?

* * * * *

Framing the question in this way makes it easier for her to embrace either side (or both sides) without there being a "right" and a "wrong" answer.

Melissa: I don't think it's really hard to be different from them. Like none of them—like I know I'm different, like everyone—I mean, it's a good family. I mean, everyone's got their issues, but it's like none of them like partied in high school, none of them smoked or, you know, drank till they puked, you know. I did that. It was me that did that, you know, and so . . . so, in that way, yeah, I'm very different from them. Like none of them did a—they're all just more conservative people and, you know, that's fine, that's good, you know. Nobody's into drugs. None of them do any of that, not that I am either, but you know—so, again, it was like myself . . . or when I got my ear pierced up here, you know. It's like, yeah, that would be Melissa that would do that. Or I would be the one to get a tattoo. Or I would be the one to have another piercing of some kind—they know that that's a Melissa thing.

Paul: Uh-huh . . .

Melissa: You know, like none of the others would do that kind of a thing. So, it didn't bother me to be that way.

Paul: And was there a feeling of they were really not having a lot of fun, that you didn't wanna live like them because it wouldn't be fun?

Melissa: I don't think so. I just think that they are who they are, and that's their personality and, you know, I'm just a little bit different from them.

Paul: So, let me ask you something. I mean, the more you're talking about it, the more—and I know it might just be off—but the more it's sounding to me like right now at least, you're feeling good about the choice you've made. So, what's the part of it that I'm not hearing or seeing?

* * * * *

Here I'm doing two things—on the one hand, continuing to affirm the choice she has made, to help her to feel that her choices have been legitimate, but on the other hand, also opening up again the question of what part of her choice she is *not* so comfortable with, what is the conflict that brought her into the session with me.

In part I am thinking in terms of this second (conflictual) dimension because throughout the session thus far, Melissa has had a hard time staying with it, and I am trying to enable her to explore it. I am also doing so because I don't want my own affirmation to close a door on that exploration, to leave her no room for her doubts and concerns. In a sense, this is an illustration of what I think is very frequently the case when the therapy is proceeding in a useful manner—one works the gas and the brakes at the same time. That is not very good for a car, but it is actually a fine strategy for therapy.

Melissa: The choice I've made with staying at the restaurant right now?

Paul: Yeah. Because that's what you said is the problem that's bringing you in.

Melissa: Yeah, yeah. You know, maybe it's just a matter of it's what I'm supposed to do. I'm *supposed* to quit my job at this point.

Paul: Uh-huh . . .

Melissa: You know. I mean, I'm fine with staying there for now, but maybe there's that part of me that's like, it's not what you should be doing.

Paul: Uh-huh . . .

Melissa: You should really quit your job, you should really get going, just take the pay cut and, you know, get the insurance that you need. You know maybe it's just that part of me that . . . [*inaudible*]

Paul: And you so much don't like to hear that "should" that it makes you almost not wanna even think about the insurance or anything like that.

Melissa: Yeah.

Paul: There's really something really aversive about having to deal with that "should."

* * * * *

I am approaching Melissa's conflict from a vantage point within her own subjective experience. She is accustomed to being told her experience and her choices are wrong, and I am attempting to affirm and to explicate how things look through her eyes. At the same time, I am, one might say, amplifying or "purifying" her experience—highlighting that the "shoulds" are aversive. This stance may well have contributed to Melissa's taking a stronger position in affirming her own inclinations as the session proceeded from this point.

Melissa: Uh-huh . . . I don't know.

Paul: What just went through your head? There was just sort of a smile on your face.

* * * * *

It is important for the therapist to be attentive to nonverbal affective cues. That kind of smile, seemingly coming out of nowhere, is often a particularly valuable kind of cue for the therapist to attend to. I give very high priority to attending to such cues, although I do not always comment on them or ask about them as I did here. Whether I do or not depends on whether I judge, from what I know about the patient, that she will experience my doing so as friendly and responsive or as watching her in a hypervigilant fashion or "catching" her at something. In the latter circumstances, I simply note to myself that something important is going on. For an interesting example of an instance when I merely noted to myself what had happened but did not bring it up with the patient, see P. L. Wachtel (2010b).

Melissa:	I just don't care.
Paul:	Uh-huh . . .
Melissa:	I mean, I just, like there for instance, I don't care that I'm waitressing, you know. I mean, there's this part of me that just I'm fine with that for now, you know.
Paul:	Uh-huh . . .
Melissa:	But then it's like, okay, maybe that perspective from my parents, where it's like oh well, you really should have quit waitressing, you know. You really need to get a job, a real job.
Paul:	Uh-huh . . .
Melissa:	So, then, you know, you're sure that . . . and I think that's what it is, but it's like, you know, but then again, it's just me. It's like everyone else would have, you know, probably done something different, but, you know, this kind of path I like for now.
Paul:	Right. So, you wanna do it the Melissa way.
Melissa:	Right.
Paul:	All right, and what they're asking you to do doesn't feel like the Melissa way.
Melissa:	Uh-huh . . .
Paul:	So, what's the Melissa way? If we make room for, put all the "shoulds" out of the picture and we just say, okay, we wanna look at if you are really paying attention to your own gut.

* * * * *

Referring to "the Melissa way" picks up on her reference to herself in the third person a minute before ("they know that that's a Melissa thing"), resonating with her personal style. This is a small but important way therapists build rapport or the alliance and also create a path for the therapist's words to reach inside the patient on an emotional level. In addition, this way of putting it affirms Melissa's uniqueness. There is most people's way and there is the Melissa way.

Melissa:	Uh-huh . . .
Paul:	What does the life trajectory, the scenario, the picture, look like without anybody telling you what you should do and when you should do it?
Melissa:	[*pause*] I just, I don't know that I have a picture or a time frame, but it's like I just know I'll get there when I get there.

You know, and I don't know, I mean, I have some deadlines for myself, but you know, I know we know when I make—need to make things done. So, I guess maybe there's that part of me that's, which is thinking you're—I'll quit waitressing when it's *time* for me to quit.

Paul: Uh-huh . . .

Melissa: You know, I mean I don't wanna do it 2 months before I graduate with my master's, but, and maybe for just right now, after, you know, a couple of months of how it has been with the divorce and everything, maybe for now, I'm like screw it, I just wanna stay where I'm at.

Paul: So, we know for sure I think, pretty close to sure, that the Melissa way of doing it isn't to say, "On September 26 at 2 p.m., I'm gonna do this," okay.

Melissa: Right.

Paul: And my question almost felt like that a little bit, like you were feeling that now I was pressuring you, that, you know, I would say, "What's the Melissa way?" but it still felt like I was a, you know, watching you . . .

Melissa: When's it gonna be? Yeah.

Paul: Right, right. So, it's very easy to experience that the other person's doing that.

Melissa: Uh-huh . . . I mean, I don't know why. I don't know when it would, when it would be or what it would look like, what my way would be, but I don't know, I just, I'll get there, I guess.

Paul: Uh-huh . . . uh-huh . . . well, that's part of the answer to what [*inaudible*].

Melissa: It's hard to say, you know. Yeah, yeah.

Paul: The answer you're giving me that feels like it's important for me to hear it is, "I don't wanna think about it in terms of when am I gonna do what, or where am I heading?", that you want, that you like where you are. You have confidence you'll move along it anyway, and that feels appropriate.

Melissa: Uh-huh . . .

Paul: And the problem in a sense isn't so much that you really doubt the decisions you're making. The problem is that those nagging voices of "you should do it differently" are still there, and you're still feeling you'll finally get there.

Melissa:	Uh-huh . . . yeah, I mean, I guess I do feel confident that I'll get on the path I need to get on when the time is right for me, you know. Yeah.
Paul:	Uh-huh . . . do you have trouble saying that to other people, to your parents, to your ex-husband?
Melissa:	I've never said that to them. I know to my ex-husband he would just—you see, again to him it's like that's just—see, I'm not in a black or white world.
Paul:	Uh-huh . . .
Melissa:	So, it's like, I don't have a deadline of when I'm gonna quit the job or when I'm gonna start a new one and, you know, where I'm like, it will come, you know. When the time is right I'll quit. And you know, that's like, for him that's really hard to just see it my way.
Paul:	And it's hard for you to say that, you just don't know how.
Melissa:	I never said to him, I never said to my family, you know, when the time is right, I'll quit, you know. I've never said that to them either.
Paul:	What would you like to say to them?
Melissa:	They would probably just say like, she's nuts.

* * * * *

Here I was attempting to help Melissa begin to articulate for herself not just how she feels subjectively but how she might *state it to others*. The aim here is to enable her to be more effective in *expressing* and *defending* her point of view so that she does not get caught in situations where she retreats from her own experience because she does not feel equipped to represent and defend her position. A problematic omission in much therapy that is focused on helping the patient to be more in touch with her subjective experience is that it assumes that once the patient understands, she will readily be able to express it to others or to take the actions needed to create harmonious and satisfying interactions with others. That, however, is not necessarily the case; often it is essential to attend not just to the patient's subjective experience but to the ways she expresses it in verbal exchanges and interactions with others (P. L. Wachtel, 1993, 1997, 2008, 2009).

It seems to me worth noticing in this regard that in response to my question about what she would like to say to members of her family, Melissa speaks about what *they* would say. This suggests a focus on and concern about other people's reactions—notwithstanding her view of herself as a kind of individualist rebel or free spirit—that leaves her often unable to effectively or comfortably give voice to her own experiences and desires.

> *Paul:* Uh-huh . . . uh-huh . . .
>
> *Melissa:* Like how could she just live like that?
>
> *Paul:* Right.
>
> *Melissa:* How could she just be fine with that, having a job with [no] insurance. I'm sure that's like what my dad or my stepmom might think. At least my dad, you know.
>
> *Paul:* Uh-huh . . .
>
> *Melissa:* Definitely.
>
> *Paul:* And would they also envy you at all?

* * * * *

Here I am again introducing a quite different, and more positive, perspective on Melissa's choices. I raise it just as a question, not as something I am explicitly suggesting is the case. But even to raise it—to raise this "peculiar" question sort of out of the blue—is to introduce an idea that Melissa has not consciously thought, an idea, moreover, that casts her in an "enviable" light, that implies that in at least certain ways, she is freer to pay attention to her own experience and to what pleases her, and that they are constrained by a dogged pursuit of the straight and narrow and might secretly wish to be more like her.

Here again, apropos my earlier "gas and brake" comment, my affirmation of Melissa's choices needs to be coupled with attention to the side of Melissa that really does worry about her choices, that worries from within her own gut and her own frame of reference, not just as the reflection of the internalized voices of her parents.

> *Melissa:* I don't know. I kind of think not.
>
> *Paul:* Not at all?
>
> *Melissa:* I don't know.
>
> *Paul:* I mean, because the message you would get from them, and I assume that must be the message you got while growing up, was the things you were doing, that's nuts.
>
> *Melissa:* No, I wouldn't—it's not like, it's not like a lot of things I'm doing or a lot of the decisions I've made are nuts. I don't know, I guess it's probably just it's not as conservative or, you know, it's not what they would do.
>
> *Paul:* Uh-huh . . .

Melissa:	I don't know that they would be envious of that.
Paul:	Uh-huh . . .
Melissa:	Perhaps. You know, maybe, one or two of them think, "I wish I could just do that. I wish I could have that kind of an attitude," that, you know . . .
Paul:	But, I'm sort of wondering, it's like *you* became the person in the family who could express more of that freedom, more of that living out of your own real self, and they couldn't do that. And they couldn't *let* themselves do that, or even maybe let themselves know that they enjoy *your* doing that. But somebody in the family was living that way.
Melissa:	Uh-huh . . .
Paul:	Was that?
Melissa:	[*pause*] I'm sure there's my one sister. I'm sure that she looks at me like, you know, "That's great, I wish I could do that."
Paul:	Uh-huh . . .
Melissa:	I think she did, or she—maybe not right now, maybe she doesn't now, but maybe when I was younger, you know. I think she might have.
Paul:	Uh-huh . . . so you sort of carry the freedom for all of them?
Melissa:	Yeah, 'cause none of them were just, you know, kinda did whatever, you know. None of them would be, you know, too adventurous or . . . not that I'm like—I'm not that crazy either in that way, but, they're just conservative, you know, it's like the best way to describe them, I guess.
Paul:	Let me ask you about another sort of a link I'm curious about, that may—*link* isn't the right word exactly, but a parallel that may or may not be the same. One way in which you and your parents were alike is they got divorced and you got divorced.

* * * * *

As I read through the transcript here, I am a bit puzzled why I raised this question at this point. It seems to divert us from what we were talking about. There must have been something that elicited this question, some thought or link that I can no longer reconstruct or something I was picking up in the unspoken affective experience in the session. But if I were to view this comment as a "supervisor," I would be inquiring into why the therapist introduced what seems like a non sequitur.

Melissa: Uh-huh . . .

Paul: Was their divorce like yours, different from yours?

Melissa: Nothing like mine. It was nasty, angry, bitter breakup.

Paul: Uh-huh . . .

Melissa: Took almost 3 years to finalize.

Paul: How old were you?

Melissa: I think I was 3 or 4 when they separated.

Paul: Uh-huh . . .

Melissa: So, which is exactly the age of my daughter, she is 3, except we finalized in a month and a half.

Paul: Uh-huh . . .

Melissa: I was probably like 6 or 7 when they were done with it.

Paul: What was it like for you?

Melissa: It's really strange, but it's like I remember standing on my drive-way with this girl from school and I remember her saying to me, she's like, "So, how do you feel about your parents being divorced or getting divorced?" or something. And for as young as I was, I had said, "If that's what they need to do to get along, then that's okay." And it's like, and I looked back that it's like it's just something that I'll never forget me saying, and it's like I don't remember like talking to a counselor at school or my mom about anything that was going on, or a neighbor or a friend, but I don't know why I had such a mature response about it at such a young age, but I mean, I was probably 6, you know. And I just felt at that time I was very accepting of that.

Paul: Uh-huh . . .

Melissa: There's a lot I don't remember with my parents still being married and living in the house together, I mean other than, you know, there was mom was always upstairs and dad was always downstairs.

Paul: Uh-huh . . .

Melissa: And then they would fight. But I don't remember a lot of that. But maybe at that time, I mean, I knew they weren't getting along and I just for some reason that around 6 or maybe 7, I don't even know, but maybe at that time I just felt, well, maybe they're better off. I don't know how I came to that, but, so I mean, it didn't bother me, like I never looked at my parents like, "God, why couldn't they make it work?" I look at the two of them like, "God, how did it *ever* work?"

Paul: Uh-huh . . .

Melissa: When I looked at who each of [*inaudible*]. And I've had a step-mom for 20 years. So, my dad remarried, my mom never did. And I love my stepmom dearly. She's been such a good role model in my life, you know. So, I never looked at them like why didn't they work out. You know, how come they couldn't make it work.

Paul: Uh-huh . . . so, you developed . . .

Melissa: So, it's weird.

Paul: . . . this ability to, sort of let things roll off your back, like [*inaudible*].

Melissa: Yeah, maybe. Yeah, it's weird, like I don't even think today like, gosh it's too bad mom and dad didn't work out.

Paul: Uh-huh . . .

Melissa: I don't have those thoughts, you know. I have the opposite of, I don't even know how they had five kids together, you know.

Paul: Yeah. Uh-huh . . .

Melissa: That's different.

Paul: Uh-huh . . . we're gonna have to stop shortly.

Melissa: Yeah.

Paul: I'm wondering, if you think about the different things we've talked about so far, does any one sort of stand out for you or seem like a useful thing to think further about?

Melissa: I think the fact that I am confident with kind of not knowing where I might go with my career, but . . . or my job for now, but that, you know, when the time is right, I'll get there.

Paul: Uh-huh . . .

Melissa: And I kind of like, I'm just the kind of person that likes to be unknown in some areas, you know.

Paul: Uh-huh . . .

Melissa: That certain things I need to know.

Paul: Uh-huh . . .

Melissa:	So, that's something to me that it's like, yeah, I guess. If I was terribly stressed out or had, you know, a lot of anxiety over my job I would have done something about it.
Paul:	Uh-huh . . .
Melissa:	But I have comfort there, and I think that it will follow where it needs to be.
Paul:	Uh-huh . . .
Melissa:	So, that's something to me that, you know maybe makes me feel a bit more relaxed in a way. It will happen.
Paul:	Yeah. Yeah, it certainly sounds to me like there's a lot about the decision that you're making—'cause you're making the decision . . .
Melissa:	Uh-huh . . .
Paul:	It's not like you're not making the decision.
Melissa:	Right.
Paul:	You're making the decision.

* * * * *

In this sequence what I am doing is clearly to highlight Melissa's activity, to underline, and affirm, that she *is* deciding.

Melissa:	Right.
Paul:	And in many ways, it's a decision that feels like the way that will really be true to yourself right now. The only thing I would be concerned about with it is, do you also have the freedom to *make* the change? Do you have the freedom to not be the one who carries all the fun for the family, 'cause that's a burden in its own right. Let them have their own fun!

* * * * *

Here I am, on the one hand, affirming the choice she seems to be making, to stay in the waitress job for now, underlining that that is a choice that feels like it is truest to her own experience and what she feels will work best for her. But I am also introducing a question about whether the choice might not have been quite as free and rooted in her own gut as it is feeling.

One possibility is that she is making the choice reactively—that is, "They want to push me to quit the job, so I will automatically say no so as not to be pushed around (whether it really feels like what I will eventually feel best having done or not)." A second is that the choice might also reflect a form of covert *obedience*; that is, Melissa's responding in a way that continues to play her old role in the family (again, somewhat independently of whether it is what is best for her). In this second possibility, what is being highlighted is that most of the family always takes the conservative, straight-and-narrow path and that Melissa, in contrast, has been cast as the one who takes the more fun direction, who is playful and rebellious. Even Melissa's *excesses* in this direction (e.g., drinking until she throws up) might reflect, from this vantage point, her implicit role as the "designated funster" of the family.

Viewed from this angle, there is a possibility that although the family is urging Melissa to quit the waitressing job and move along the conventional career path, there is another, more subtle and less conscious, pressure for Melissa to have the fun that they do not permit themselves but that they enjoy vicariously by identifying with Melissa. It seems clear that for Melissa, the waitressing, whatever its *long-term* implications are for her, *feels* better in the short run. Is she in part playing out a script that was written in the family system, a script that requires her to be the fun-loving, "irresponsible" one so that the rest of the family can, in turn, be sober and responsible, and is she *trapped* in this script, in that it is difficult to moderate this role to accommodate the complexities of her own quite varied needs?

It is certainly not my contention that any of these speculations are, at this point, *anything more than* speculations. But these are questions that the psychotherapist, familiar with the many intricate ways in which people and families work out their conflicting needs, can serve the patient or client by raising. The job here, as in much else that I have been emphasizing, is to make room for exploration, to open the door to possibilities, but to do so without pushing one's own hobbyhorse.

Melissa: Uh-huh . . .

Paul: You shouldn't have to get squeezed into being the fun person any more than you have to get squeezed into being the one who makes the decision.

Melissa: Uh-huh . . .

Paul: That would be my only concern about it at this point.

Melissa: Uh-huh . . .

Paul: But, I also think you'll be the best judge of that.

Melissa: Yeah, yeah.

Paul: [*inaudible*]

Melissa: Yeah.

Paul: I think this was a useful talk we've had.

Melissa: Yeah. It was nice talking to you.

Paul:	Yeah, good.
Melissa:	Thank you.
Paul:	Pleased to meet you.
Melissa:	Uh-huh . . . you too.
Paul:	'Bye.

* * * * *

Viewing the session as a whole, it is apparent that the process of making a real connection with Melissa and of forming a therapeutic alliance based on a shared understanding of our aims was a significant challenge. With Louise, an alliance was evident almost from the first moment of the session, and it grew or was maintained throughout our contact.[4] With Melissa, this was not the case; much of the session was taken up, in essence, with the task of forming and developing some degree of alliance. Here, as I have already discussed in the comments interpolated throughout the transcript, both the format of our contact and Melissa's previous experience with Diana Fosha played a very significant role. But it is important to note that what also contributed was my own initial attitude and mode of participation. *I* had in mind a particular image of what it meant to be a "psychotherapist," and this image, and the aims and practices associated with it, contributed both to what was difficult in the first part of the session *and*, I think, to what went well later in the session.

Turning first to the factors present in the room at the very moment Melissa entered (even before I uttered a word), the fact that this was to be a one-session contact influenced Melissa in a number of ways. In one sense, the nature of the problem she chose to address was, I think, chosen by her very appropriately for the single-session nature of our contact. Although, as I shall discuss further momentarily, I had some difficulty with the way that Melissa framed her focus for the session, it was in fact a very apt choice. She chose, in essence, something that *could* be discussed in a single session, that did *not* necessarily require an extended therapeutic contact. But at the same time, by the very way that she framed her goal in a manner appropriate to a one-session therapeutic encounter, she also made it more difficult for the session to be rep-

---

[4]Of course, the therapeutic alliance is not something that is created and maintained "once and for all." The nature of the mutual experience of the two parties in the room will inevitably vary considerably over the course of their time together as new perceptions and experiences are introduced and as mutual *mis*perceptions and misunderstandings unavoidably arise. Indeed, the examination of those variations—and of the disruptions and crises (or, as one hopes, *mini*crises) that inevitably ensue—is, over time, a critical part of what is therapeutic about psychotherapy (Ruiz-Cordell & Safran, 2007; Safran & Muran, 2000; Safran, Muran, & Proskurov, 2009).

resentative of what happens in a more extended *set* of therapeutic contacts, which is, after all, the norm.[5]

The fact that our encounter was arranged in advance to be but a single session interacted with the fact that Melissa had had a previous one-session encounter with Diana Fosha. Melissa was not only aware that this would be our only contact, a contextual factor that would have relevance in any event; she also had in mind, even if only implicitly, a *previous experience* with such a format, and it was an experience that was literally life-altering. One may wonder how much the single session with Diana actually contributed to Melissa's decision to divorce her husband; she was, after all, already contemplating this course when she began the session with Diana, and she might well have reached the same conclusion had the session never occurred. But there can be little doubt that Melissa *thought* and *felt* that the session with Diana played a powerful role. Given the difficulty she has still been having in coming to terms with this decision now that the divorce is a fact, and even the practical difficulties she has encountered as a single mother—the very difficulties that did become the focus of our session—it is more than understandable that Melissa would enter the session with a determination, whether consciously articulated or not, not to let this session reach her in the same powerfully wrenching way. Even given that the session with Diana had felt to her like a very valuable contribution to her ultimate well-being, it is easy to understand a feeling of "enough is enough for now" and of "I know what just one session can potentially do to turn my life upside down, and I am not going to let that happen again."

Turning to my own role and my conception of what good psychotherapy entails, we see both a further source of some of the difficulties Melissa and I encountered at the beginning and some of the ways in which being a psychotherapist almost inevitably introduces one to contradictions and paradoxes. As a therapist, I am committed to two central goals or ideals that, among others, form the core of my therapeutic practice and my therapeutic philosophy: (a) listening to the patient in a way that is respectful and validating, in contrast to the approach that seeks to "unmask," "uncover," "interpret defenses," and so on (P. L. Wachtel, 1993, 2008; see also Wile, 1984); and (b) seeking to address the patient on a deep affective level and to make room for the experiences that the patient has, out of fear, guilt, or shame, cast out

---

[5]It is interesting that Louise *did* choose a therapeutic focus that was of a sort suited for a more extended therapeutic process. In that respect, the degree of progress we made in the session in working on the issue she presented might be viewed as surprising. To be sure, what we achieved was only an *initial* step in the process of Louise's working through the issues with Ken's family. They were very complicated and related to many aspects of her earlier history that also need to be worked through. But nonetheless, the session did seem to me to open up and clarify a number of important issues that, if properly followed up, can be very helpful to Louise. As a result, our time together more closely resembled a longer course of therapy than did the time I spent with Melissa.

of awareness and excluded from her sense of self (again, see P. L. Wachtel, 1993, 2008). Usually these two aims work hand in glove, each enhancing the other in the process of therapeutic collaboration. In the session with Melissa, however, they seemed for extended periods of the session to be at odds, and much of the challenge I experienced in the session can be seen as due to the difficulty in reconciling them. As I just noted, Melissa's limiting her focus very largely to practical matters made a good deal of sense and deserved respect and validation. At the same time, at least as the session proceeded in its early stages, this focus also prevented me from addressing the larger issues that had given shape to Melissa's sense of impasse and the deeper levels of experiencing I had hoped to help her contact and assimilate. This contrasted, for example, with the sessions with Louise, in which I mostly experienced the validation of her experience and the expansion and deepening of her experience as proceeding apace and in mutually facilitative fashion.

As the session proceeded, I kept trying to expand the frame of our discussion to discover *what else* Melissa wanted to explore but perhaps was rather hesitant to. In this interface, we floundered together for a while. My aims and hers did not seem to be consonant. To some degree, I was too impatient to turn the session in a direction that felt to me more like "psychotherapy" and less like career counseling. I was having a hard time doing what a good therapist should do—attend to what *the patient* is interested in and wants to do without imposing one's own agenda. It is likely that this difficulty on my part was related to the knowledge that this would be my only session with Melissa and hence my wanting to do as much for her as I could (leading me to want to do *too* much, to be racing ahead of where she was). Very importantly, it was also probably related to the unusual circumstance that was in the background (maybe even closer to the foreground than I was comfortable acknowledging to myself)—that the session was being videotaped and that the video might potentially be shown, warts and all, to thousands of students and colleagues around the country. As it turned out, as the reader will probably readily understand, I chose to have the session with Louise released for the APA video series rather than this one. But at the time I was in the session with Melissa, I had not yet had my session with Louise, and there may well have been a slightly panicked background sense of, "Is *this* the session that will represent to the public the way I work? Nothing of what I usually do is happening!"

The experience of the session began to change as we started discussing Melissa's divorce and her relationship with her husband both before and after the divorce. This led to a clarification of the experience of pressure and coercion that Melissa has experienced, both from him and from her parents and siblings, whom she describes as rather cautious, conservative, straight arrows for whom the path toward career and professionalism did not seem to run through a job as a waitress. We saw that Melissa was the rebel in her family, the one who did not take the straight path but ventured along the way to parties and tattoo parlors and "the Melissa thing." And I speculated with Melissa that perhaps she had been the "designated funster" in the family and that perhaps she was caught in a puzzling crossfire between rebelling against their overt expectations that she "straighten up and fly right" and simultaneously having had to meet their additional, far less conscious, wish that she keep on being the fun-loving rebel who, vicariously, introduced some color into their gray, doggedly purposeful lives. Caught between these conflicting expectations and demands, one more or less overt and up front, the other inaccessible to awareness for any of them, she found herself having great difficulty in resolving a dilemma that she was framing as a purely practical issue.

As I noted in my interpolated comments in the transcript, I am by no means confident that my specific speculations about the additional dimensions of Melissa's dilemma and indecision were correct. The view of her playing a role in the family that introduced some life and adventure and earthiness with which they could covertly identify provides one possible way of understanding why Melissa was having a hard enough time deciding on her immediate course that she wanted a consultation with a psychotherapist, but it could easily turn out to be a false lead. I am far *more* confident in the general assumption that there was more to the story than medical benefits, as important as they genuinely are. As the session evolved, I experienced more and more strongly a sense that Melissa seemed, in her heart of hearts, to be leaning much more toward staying in the waitress job for now. And it is interesting that it was in the very process of pointing to this and supporting her in this choice (including by reframing her statements to highlight the ways in which doing so represented doing things "the Melissa way") that I found myself gaining a more articulated sense of the possible dynamic of her having been the member of the family who carried their more rebellious and pleasure-seeking impulses for them, expressing them in the world and providing a model from whom to gain vicarious participation in aspects of living they had closed off for themselves.

Put differently—and bearing in mind again that the specific content of this speculation may or may not be on the mark—in the very process of supporting Melissa in what appeared to be the direction she most wanted to move, my enduring interest in the central role of *conflict* in psychological life led me to look more closely at the other side of her experience. Few of us, if any, are single-minded, even when we appear to be. Multiple ways of thinking, experiencing, and behaving, varying from one context to another or in the degree to which they are conscious at any given moment, have been emphasized by thinkers in orientations as diverse as social learning theory (Mischel, 1968; see also Wachtel, 1973b, 1977a) and relational psychoanalysis (Bromberg, 1998a; Mitchell, 1993). The degree to which this diversity is a source of richness and flexibility in living or a painful, wrenching, dissociative way of life can vary enormously from person to person. But we all, I believe, are far less "simple" and "consistent" than we may appear.

Finally, the session with Melissa reminds us how important the *social* factor is. Had the United States had a different health care system than it did at the time of this session, Melissa would have experienced the decision she had to make quite differently. Perhaps some of the other issues that came up later in the session might have been explored more, and there would then have been more time to examine, refine, revise, or further explore them. But the level on which Melissa introduced her dilemma was one that was all too appropriate for America in 2009. Our psychological experience and psychological dynamics are a function not only of the internalized residues of our earliest experiences and the present systemic realities of our more intimate relationships but also of the broader realities of race, class, culture, and society. The economy is not some "additional" or "external" variable that *interacts* with our personality and subjectivity; it is an intricate and intrinsic part of how we experience ourselves and our lives (P. L. Wachtel, 2003). When we distinguish between the psychological and the social, we end up with an impoverished understanding of both.

III

REFLECTIONS

6

THE SESSIONS IN RETROSPECT

The three sessions just presented provide an opportunity to reflect not just on the sessions per se but also on the perspective they offer regarding the theoretical assumptions and principles of therapeutic technique described in Part I of this volume. In what ways do these sessions reflect or represent those principles? In what ways do they seem to depart from them? What are the specific needs and challenges, varying to some degree with every patient and every session, that necessitate some refinement or rethinking of the general principles? How do they require us to reframe the general principles as a version of "in general do X, but sometimes it is better to do Y," and how do we understand just *when* that time to do Y is? Relatedly, how do the specifics of any given case lead to an understanding that even when *in general* it is useful to do X, in this particular case, or at this particular point in the therapeutic process, there is *not much opportunity* to do X? That is, sometimes to follow the general principle is wrong in a specific case or session; but sometimes it is not necessarily wrong but simply irrelevant, not what the session is providing an opportunity for or calling for.

In reflecting on these questions, it is essential again to remind ourselves that these sessions were not part of an ongoing therapeutic relationship but were scheduled as one-session demonstration sessions. There is sufficient similarity between the interactions and the therapeutic process in these sessions and those occurring in a more extended therapy that much can be learned from them. But there clearly also are differences, and those differences too must be taken into account if we are to draw the most useful conclusions from what is presented here. Put differently, when I view these sessions, I see a great deal that feels very familiar, that feels like what happens in just about any session of my "ordinary" clinical work. Yet at the same time, there are inevitably ways in which the work reflects its special provenance, and these too must be considered in achieving the kind of contextualized understanding that I believe is essential for *all* therapeutic work and all efforts to understand personality development and dynamics.

As discussed in the previous chapter, the impact of the particular framework of these sessions was especially obvious in the session with Melissa. It is difficult to predict precisely how the session would have differed had it been the first of a projected *series* of sessions, whether of brief or long-term therapy. But it is not very difficult to discern at least some of the ways in which the fact that it was the *only* session contributed to how it proceeded. Issues of trust, of how Melissa defined the problem she wished to focus on, of how I responded to that problem choice and chose to follow up or not follow up all were clearly related to the single-session format (further complicated, as I noted, by Melissa's prior experience with such a format in her session a year before with Diana Fosha).

The single-session format had its impact in different ways with Louise. With Louise, there was not so much indication of constraint per se. Louise opened herself, it seemed to me, at least as much as patients usually do in first sessions. Perhaps she did so even more, knowing that this would be our only opportunity to work together. (We did, of course, have a second session, but we did not know we would until the first session was already completed.) For someone who has undergone such significant trauma in her life, Louise was surprisingly trusting. I did not feel the tug of war I did at the beginning with Melissa. There were certainly places where Louise initially warded off perception or understanding of the complexities of her life experience (as in her initial presentation of the other children at school as jealous of her close, happy family, or in her account of her family as the "individualistic" family that didn't get together for holidays but was "always there for each other"). But it did not take an inordinate amount of work for her to reach a point where she could begin to take in an alternate perspective or even to spontaneously generate the memories and new material that gave substance to that new perspective (e.g., her not inviting Ken's family to their wedding; her father's stroke; her mother's abandonment of them in Paris). Indeed, these three major revelations, all coming in the course of one initial session, gave the session a narrative thrust for which a film director or film editor would be justly praised. And each of these three major revelations not only enabled me to see things significantly differently and to gain new insights into Louise's struggles, they also led to exchanges between us in which *Louise* seemed to gain important insights.

The point here is not that once Louise had achieved these "insights" her problem was "resolved." I have commented throughout this book about the importance of working through, and the necessity of not being lured by the "fool's gold" of apparent insights to conclude that the therapeutic goals have been achieved. Insights come and go, appear and then are submerged again, and their solid incorporation will depend on their being expressed in daily life in ways that change the feedback patterns that maintain the patient's difficulties (see P. L. Wachtel, 2008, Chapter 12). But what is noteworthy regarding the difference between the ways that Louise and Melissa experienced the one-session format is that Louise seemed receptive to *reexamining* how she viewed her experience to a much greater degree than Melissa did. She was, in that sense, more open and trusting in the session. Perhaps most important to notice is simply that two different patients responded to the single-session format in quite different ways, as different people *always* respond in their individual fashion to a context or situation that an outside observer might label as "the same."

THE THERAPEUTIC ALLIANCE

Part of what is implicated in the differences I have been pointing to between Melissa and Louise is the dimension of the therapeutic alliance. There is accumulating evidence that—as much as or perhaps even more than "technique" or theoretical orientation as these are usually defined—the quality of the therapeutic alliance is a highly significant factor contributing to the success or failure of the therapeutic effort (Duncan, Miller, Wampold, & Hubble, 2009; Norcross, 2002; Ruiz-Cordell, & Safran, 2007; Safran, Muran, & Proskurov, 2009; Wampold, 2001). It is my strong guess that most readers would judge that the alliance was stronger with Louise than with Melissa. But here is also an opportunity to see once again, and perhaps still more clearly, how the lens of a two-person perspective enables us to see how the quality of the alliance, like everything else that transpires in the session, is *co-constructed* (Aron, 1996).

In my discussions of the session with Melissa thus far, I have highlighted her hesitancy to open herself up to the kind of destabilizing (if also in important respects very positive) experience that she had with Diana Fosha and her resolute focus on a narrow question pursued within a narrow framework. But that behavior in the session is not simply a quality of Melissa's "personality." As I have noted, there are ways in which the different ways that I responded to and interacted with Louise and Melissa contributed to the different ways that they participated in the session. Within the very first minute of my session with Louise, I actively went out of my way to ally myself with her hurt feelings regarding the way Ken's family responded to her father's death. She was mentioning that Ken's sister Denise, in halfheartedly apologizing for not calling right away when Louise's father died, had said that she "didn't have time to call." I immediately said, even interrupting Louise's narrative to do so, "As if it was a trivial event, rather than something so centrally important." In doing this, I was, right at the beginning of the session, signaling that I was on Louise's side and, implicitly, that I would not treat her like Denise had. This early—and actively and explicitly inserted—bit of alliance building did not have an equivalent in the session with Melissa, especially at the beginning. Thus, right from the start, the degree to which the patient felt I was attuned to her and on her side was different for Louise and for Melissa—and not just for reasons having to do with their already existing internal states or predispositions but for reasons having to do with my own behavior.

My point here is not simply to shift responsibility for what transpired from Louise or Melissa to me. If the reader has been following me throughout the book, it should be clear that I do not view things as that simple or dichotomous. The point of a two-person perspective, after all, is not to create a different *one*-person view, with the focus merely shifted from the acontextualized behavior of the patient to the acontextualized behavior of the therapist. The point, clearly, of a two-person point of view is that *both* parties contribute to what transpires between them and, moreover, that that contribution is a continuously evolving one, as each responds from moment to moment to what the other is doing. From that vantage point, one can point, for example, to the vulnerability I sensed in Louise as part of *why* I actively offered her my strong sympathetic alignment so early in the session.

Correspondingly, part of why I was *less* actively supportive in the beginning of the session with Melissa is that without it necessarily having been a conscious perception or conscious choice at the time, I was responding to the sense that Melissa was warding me off, that she would not be easy to reach, and that the meshing of our aims and modes of proceeding would be a more difficult process. Thus, my different behavior toward Louise and Melissa could be seen as a response to differences in them. But at the same time, I *did* behave differently with each of them, and my own behavior, in turn, partially *created* (and at the very least maintained) the differences in their behavior toward me over the course of the session. There is no clear chicken or egg here. Everything is scrambled.[1]

---

[1] It is sometimes mistakenly thought that attending to this co-constructed nature of what is observed in the therapy room implies a denial that the patient has any preexisting personality traits or inclinations at all. This is a serious misunderstanding of the relational or two-person point of view (see P. L. Wachtel, 2008).

MAKING ROOM FOR THE PATIENT'S FEELINGS

Central to the therapeutic approach illustrated in these transcripts is a set of ideas and procedures that intersect and overlap substantially enough that they are not fully separable but rather constitute different takes or perspectives on a single process viewed from different angles. These different, complementary takes include (a) attending to the anxiety, guilt, or shame that have led the person to defend against or cast aside certain thoughts, feelings, wishes, and experiences of self and other, rather than viewing these defensive efforts primarily from the vantage point of resistance or evasion; (b) helping the patient to overcome that anxiety, often through methods that combine the behavioral concept of exposure with empathic identification and articulation of the rejected self-experiences (overlapping considerably with what is often referred to as interpretation, but approached in a different spirit); (c) affirmation and validation of the experiences that the patient has felt were unacceptable; and (d) enabling the person to make room for and reappropriate feelings that have been cast out or cast aside as dangerous or objectionable. In what follows, I use these ways of viewing the therapeutic process extensively in discussing the sessions and what transpired, but the reader should bear in mind that these are not four separate conceptualizations but alternative, and largely overlapping, ways of talking about much the same process and much the same attitude.

As I noted in Part I of this volume, the ways in which Freud's revised theory of anxiety implied a substantially different attitude toward the patient and the therapeutic process were not sufficiently attended to in the mainstream of psychoanalytic practice. Taken seriously, this important theoretical revision points to a much more supportive and compassionate view of the patient's struggles than inhered in the more austere and frequently adversarial view of the patient's resistance, self-deception, and manipulative efforts to wring improper gratifications from the analyst, and they imply a quite different approach to the process of interpretation (P. L. Wachtel, 1993; Weiss & Sampson, 1986; Wile, 1984). It points as well, as the field of psychotherapy has continued to evolve, to a convergence between the interpretative approach of psychoanalysis and the behavioral focus on exposure, enabling a more *experiential* version of interpretation to emerge.

Although it is obvious to any attentive observer that neither psychodynamic nor cognitive–behavioral therapies are by any stretch of the imagination monolithically reliant on a single type or category of intervention, it is nonetheless not difficult to identify the most prominent and prototypical interventions in each approach. For psychodynamic therapists, the quintessential intervention would clearly be interpretation (see, e.g., Bibring, 1954; Friedman, 2002; Laplanche & Pontalis, 1974). For cognitive–behavioral therapists, with just a bit more ambiguity, I would suggest it is exposure, in all of its varied forms (e.g., Barlow, Allen, & Basden, 2007; Foa & Kozak, 1986; Foa, Rothbaum & Furr, 2003; Moscovitch, Antony, & Swinson, 2009). What would seem to be a radical difference between an interpretation-based therapy and an exposure-based approach is close to the heart of the gulf that is assumed by many in our field to lie between psychodynamic and cognitive–behavioral therapies.

From the vantage point of the integrative approach that underlies the work presented in this book, however, interpretation and exposure are not so radically different. In fact, they are but two sides of the same coin: The most effective interpretations are those that promote the patient's concrete and experiential *exposure* to the thoughts, feelings, and desires that he has warded off or marginalized in his awareness; the most effective exposure is, in many cases, exposure to the stimuli associated with the person's own thoughts and feelings, an understanding of the therapeutic process from a learning theory vantage point that predates the development of behavior therapy and cognitive–behavioral therapy (Dollard & Miller, 1950). In the model upon which the therapeutic work presented in this book is based, a central aim is determining the ways that anxiety, guilt, or shame have led the patient to retreat from noticing important aspects of his psychological life or from permitting them to gain expression in his overt behavior. The apprehension that the patient has developed toward his own thoughts, feelings, and perceptions leads to defensive efforts to reject, avoid, mislabel, or constrict these experiences. These defensive efforts go on in an automatic and largely unnoticed fashion. They are called into play not by the high level of distress that would ensue if the defensive actions were not to occur—a level of distress that would at least alert the person that something noteworthy is going on—but by *minute increments* in anxiety that are sufficient to elicit their execution and to enable them to be strongly reinforced when the increment in anxiety is diminished.[2] Put differently, they are maintained by the short-term comfort they yield when they prevent us from moving further into a threatening affective or behavioral configuration, but they yield a variety of consequences that lead to continuing psychological distress; dysfunctional social interaction; or feelings of dullness, emptiness, or lack of vitality.

To feel more secure, grounded, and enlivened, the patient needs to become more familiar and more comfortable with the affects and inclinations that he has cast out of his experienced sense of self, and a central aim of the therapy is to help him to reappropriate these cast-off aspects of vital and authentic (if at times frightening) self-experience, to *make room for them* in the person's life and in his structure of self and subjective experience. Much of what is illustrated in the

---

[2]Freud (1926/1959) called these minute increments *signal anxiety*. Both Sullivan (1953) and Dollard and Miller (1950), from different theoretical frameworks, referred to them in terms of an anxiety *gradient* in which even very small increases in anxiety can powerfully initiate defensive efforts.

sessions presented in this book is an effort to accomplish this aim, and much of what I discuss further in this chapter is the difference between approaching the therapeutic task with this aim in mind and approaching it from the vantage point of "interpreting" or unmasking what the patient has hidden from himself.

When an individual banishes important parts of himself from awareness or from the experienced sense of self, they do not necessarily disappear or cease to influence his behavior. But the role they play in shaping his behavior is obscured, and it becomes difficult for him to fine-tune his behavior effectively. This is especially the case because it is often particularly the affective meanings that are banished from awareness, and the affective tone associated with the person's behavior is often both the most crucial element in eliciting different responses from others and the most difficult for the person to control, especially if it is denied or not noticed. Thus, the cast-off experiences or inclinations may continue to be expressed in the person's life but in a fashion that is largely out of awareness and hence in which it is difficult to anticipate the reactions of others, which often seem to blindside the patient.[3]

Louise, for example, seems to have been very largely taken by surprise by Ken's family's reaction to her not inviting them to their wedding, and it is likely that much of the difficulty she had with being bullied as a child was similarly rooted in a difficulty anticipating and understanding how her actions and communicated emotions were perceived by the other children. In both instances, and in other aspects of Louise's struggles as well, this vulnerability may be understood as a consequence of the ways in which anxiety, shame, and guilt have kept her from experiencing her perceptions and her affective reactions and inclinations as safe or acceptable. It was difficult for Louise to integrate the feelings of terror, shame, and abandonment that resulted from her father's stroke and its impact on her family life. Even up to the time of our first session, she needed to portray her family as "there for each other" in a way that seems not very consonant with the facts of their family life, and her feelings about her mother's not permitting her to come to Sweden when her father was dying, or even her feelings about the terrifying events in Paris when Louise was 14, had little place in the life narrative she struggled to maintain. The virtual demonizing of Ken's family seems to have been a way of maintaining the fragile image of her own mother and own family as benign, caring, and attentive to her needs.

In helping Louise—or any patient—to move beyond this state of affairs, it is essential not to approach it from a "diagnostic" vantage point or to center one's communications on showing how the person is deceiving herself,

---

[3]This formulation is consistent with the accumulating research on brain processes, from which it has become clear that the brain engages in parallel processing, with many organizing processes going on at once and combining in complex ways to yield the final behavior and subjective experience that can be observed. Contemporary cognitive and affective neuroscience also makes it clear that many of these organizing processes are not conscious and are difficult to make conscious.

confronting her with "the truth" she has avoided, and so on. From my exchanges with colleagues over the years and experiences with supervising young therapists, it is clear to me that this approach to clinical work is still troublingly common (see Wile, 1984, for an examination of how it is evident even among highly experienced and respected therapists). In the sessions with Louise, I attempted instead to help her with these conflicted and difficult-to-assimilate feelings through comments that highlighted that some aspects of what she felt and thought had been more familiar and comfortable to experience whereas other important aspects of her own experience had not yet found a voice. Thus, the message was not that she had deceived herself, that she thought she was feeling one thing and "really" she was feeling something else. Rather, it was that there was great complexity to her experience, and it was important to give full voice to all parts of it. Implicitly it was also that the less familiar feelings, the ones that had been cast aside, were legitimate and worthy of respect, not shameful or bad.

Implicit in this way of approaching the clinical work is the combination of interpretation and exposure referred to earlier. Interpretation is not primarily engaged in for the purpose of promoting insight (though of course insight is valued and welcomed) but rather as a means of evoking or *calling forth* the thoughts, feelings, or perceptions that have been cast out of the experienced self. The defensive processes that anxiety drives people to engage in render aspects of their psychological life hazy or even invisible, and in the process they impede the very exposure that is so essential to their overcoming that anxiety. From this vantage point, the therapist's comments are designed not only to point to or articulate the warded-off experience but also to evoke the actual occurrence of the forbidden thought or feeling since only then can the patient be exposed to it and have the opportunity that such exposure offers for the anxiety to be diminished.

Thus, in my sessions with both Louise and Melissa, my comments were not concerned as much with getting them to *see* or *acknowledge* what they had been denying to themselves as with promoting their *experiencing* the affects, desires, and other aspects of themselves that they had retreated from out of anxiety and with doing so in a way that enabled the previously avoided experience to feel safe and capable of being assimilated into a larger and more encompassing sense of self. The degree to which this could be achieved in a single session, of course, was limited. But the *process* was very much the same as I would engage in in a more long-term therapeutic effort. My aim was to *encourage* them to feel the forbidden feeling or think the forbidden thought; to create internal *permission* for this to happen; to *invite* the feeling or wish rather than unearthing, unmasking, or confronting it. Put differently, it was to *make room for* the experience.

With Louise, one of the aspects of herself I was trying to liberate and make room for was the wish for greater closeness to Ken's family, a wish that was being submerged and obscured by her fear that such closeness would lead to her being engulfed by them and by her guilty concern that to acknowledge her longings for greater closeness with them would betray her mother. This latter concern was heightened, it seemed to me, by a fear that such acknowledgment of the positive qualities in Ken's family would release feelings of anger and disappointment toward her mother that were being kept at bay in good part by the very way that she perceptually rendered Ken's family as the one—the only one—that was injurious and unresponsive to her needs. As Louise initially presented it, time spent with Ken's family was a distasteful obligation that she would consider only to keep Ken happy. As the session proceeded, I increasingly sensed that Louise might be more conflicted about connection with them than she had permitted herself to recognize. Although it was clear that she felt very real grievances and had very real worries about the ways that opening the door even a little might lead to her getting sucked into a black hole from which she would never emerge, I increasingly began to wonder if she *also* felt some *desire* to be a part of this large, enveloping family that, for all the negatives, offered something that her own small and affectively restricted family did not.

In addressing this idea, I did not offer an interpretation designed to confront her with how she had been deceiving herself. Nor did I try to demonstrate to her that what she thought she felt or wanted was not her "real" feeling. Rather, I inquired into whether she was also feeling something additional, something that did not invalidate or render false what she thought she was feeling, but that *expanded* the picture of what she felt and expanded as well the range of what it might feel *permissible* to feel. This is what I mean by "making room for" the warded-off experiences.

I certainly did feel that in some ways the "surface" attitude had a defensive element, that it was contributing to keeping submerged the attitudes with which she was less comfortable. But I approached Louise with the view that the parts of her experience with which she was more familiar, the "surface" attitudes, were *also* valid and real (even if they played a role in preventing her from seeing *another* equally valid side of herself). Put differently, my aim here was not to persuade Louise that although she thought she wanted to keep Ken's family at bay, she "really" wanted to get closer to them—that is, that she was simply engaged in self-deception and did not really know what she wanted. Rather, it was to make room for *other* things that she *also* wanted and to help her to find a way to reconcile these competing desires, something that could not be done until there was both awareness of and room for the side that had been submerged.

In many of the moments in the sessions when I attempted to address an aspect of Louise's or Melissa's experience that they had had difficulty in acknowledging, I approached it by highlighting the *conflict* that they were experiencing or the ways in which there was potential discomfort or danger in giving the thus far unacknowledged feeling greater access. Thus, in attempting to bring into the open the aspect of Louise's experience that includes a wish to be closer to Ken's family, I approach it by first acknowledging the other side of the experience and making clear that I understand it and respect it. I state explicitly that she feels "a pull from them that you feel the need to resist, and that creates conflict, because they want to pull you in, and you want to keep some boundary." But then I wonder out loud whether there is *another side* to her feelings toward them. I note that she grew up in a very small family, where she was the only child, and then add that "in a certain sense the family was even smaller because your father wasn't fully there, either." And I then ask "whether there's something about this large enveloping family that's in some way appealing and attractive." And then, when she has acknowledged this, I kind of circle back to highlight the other side of the conflict: "But maybe feels a little too . . . sort of almost like *threateningly* appealing." Thus, I return to acknowledge that there is something very *uncomfortable* about feeling drawn to them, that experiencing that attraction to them puts her in conflict.

PROVISIONAL HYPOTHESES AND THERAPIST–PATIENT COLLABORATION

It is also worth noting that an important part of how I approached exploring this issue with Louise, as well as how I approached most of the issues I raised with both Louise and Melissa, is that it was not an instance of my testing or communicating a fully formed hypothesis, of my "already knowing" what the issue was and working to help *her* to know it too. Addressing a related theme, Renik (1993) has commented,

> The term *interpretation* dates from a conception of the psychoanalytic process that is now generally criticized, a conception in which the analyst decodes the patient's thoughts to reveal the unconscious, decides what hidden meanings lie beneath the manifest content of the patient's verbalizations—like the well-traveled railway conductor of Freud's famous analogy who tells the ignorant passenger where he is. (p. 560)

Renik notes that one serious problem with this approach to the work is that "the interpreter is always better informed than the recipient of the interpretation" (p. 560). Or, as the fictional therapist Paul Weston says in the HBO series *In Treatment*, in psychotherapy the customer is always wrong.

In my work with Louise, I did not regard her as the ignorant passenger, nor did I view myself as knowing all the routes that we would travel. I had hunches, intuitions, but they evolved and took clearer shape in collaboration with Louise and in response to her responses to my initial attempts to formulate what I was at first dimly perceiving. In first introducing the idea that Louise might actually have a desire for greater closeness with Ken's family, I presented it in the following way:

> One thing I'm wondering about is . . . I, one thing I understand clearly, and that you've described, and I, it makes sense to me, that there's a way in which there's this pull from them that you feel the need to resist and that creates conflict, because they want to pull you in, and you want to keep some boundary. But I'm also wondering, is there another part of it that is, that there's something about—after all you grew up in a very small family; you were the only child, and in a certain sense the family was even smaller because your father wasn't fully there, either—whether there's something about this large enveloping family that's in some way appealing and attractive.

The provisional nature of my formulation, the sense that, far from offering an already printed route map to an ignorant passenger, I am myself searching for a destination that I am only beginning to envisage, is evident in the very way the comment is presented, with broken sentences and changes of direction as it gropes toward its purpose and articulation. I am struggling to formulate and express something that is occurring to me right then and there. And when I say I am "wondering" if there is another set of feelings that is harder to get at, this is one place where I really mean it. Therapists sometimes cloak rather assertive formulations, offered with great confidence and conviction, in the sheep's clothing of "I wonder" ("I wonder if you are really very angry at me right now"). This was very different. I was certainly drawn to this idea, intrigued by it; otherwise, it would not have been worth stating. But in contrast to the times when I myself say "I wonder if" and really mean (if I am honest with myself) "I am sure that"—with maybe the only element of real wondering being wondering if the patient will "see" the truth I am offering—in this instance it *really was* a wondering, a very provisional idea that I would hold more strongly or let go of depending on how Louise responded.

A good example of how the patient's response shapes the degree to which I have more or less conviction about the ideas I very provisionally offer occurred in response to my exploration of whether Louise was not quite as sanguine about her mother's support and responsiveness to her needs as she had initially indicated. After hearing about her not inviting Ken's family to the wedding, I had been exploring the sources of that decision on her part, and picked up on her saying, "I'm not getting married to make other people happy. I'm getting married to make me happy." Hearing this, I wondered out loud shortly afterward, "The importance of being able to take a stand that this is for me, this is not to make other people happy, that sounds like there must have been pulls in your life before that to make other people happy." Louise then says that she's a big people-pleaser and is now determined to change that. In elaborating on this theme, she presents her mother as encouraging her to do things the way *she* wants to. I had had glimpses and hunches in what had gone before that suggested to me that her mother had not been quite as supportive and reliably on Louise's side as this comment implied.[4] I therefore inquired about this by first underlining what *Louise* had said, and only then inquiring for the other side:

> Paul: Now that sounds like your, your mom was really supporting you and what you wanted.
>
> Louise: Uh-huh.
>
> Paul: The experience growing up of being bullied by the other kids, were there any ways in your own family, where your mom and dad, where you were a people-pleaser with them too?

An indication that this inquiry opened up something important for Louise is that almost immediately afterward she began to discuss, for the first time, the traumatic experience of her father's stroke and, not long after, her mother's abandonment of her in Paris. Had Louise simply said, as she first did, "Absolutely, yeah," that would have been scant affirmation, even if Louise was agreeing. She was, after all, a people-pleaser, and affirming what I had suggested fit the profile. But here she offers not just an affirmation but an elaboration that brings in new, emotionally meaningful material (and that, indeed, as the session proceeds, points to still further new perspectives to be introduced and worked on in a similar fashion, building on each other's input).

In the work with Melissa, this process of enabling her to reappropriate feelings and perceptions that had been cast aside was more limited. I suspect that these warded-off feelings included more grief and ambivalence regarding the divorce than she is presently able to acknowledge; but it is certainly very understandable that Melissa would, in essence, choose to put her head down and plunge ahead in her new life rather than letting herself get caught in a tangle of ambivalence and regrets. We were more successful in our work together in making more room for a different set of Melissa's feelings—her feeling of *wanting* to remain undecided for a while, or of *wanting* to stay at the waitress job. Here again, I approached the topic by speaking to it through *Melissa's own* frame of reference, taking as my point of departure how she sees and experiences things rather than challenging that way of seeing things in any direct way. At one point I say to her, "So it must feel like a luxury to be able to be undecided and not have somebody criticize your for it, right now," and then, a minute or two later, after some further dialogue, I say,

---

[4]As discussed in a moment, at the time in the session I am referring to here, I had not yet heard about her father's stroke or the abandonment in Paris.

Because I'm hearing, I think, two things. I'm hearing one thing that's "I can't make up my mind what I wanna do and it's bothering me and that's why I'm coming for help," . . . and then I'm hearing "there's something nice about not having anybody push me to make up my mind, and it feels sort of comfortable and it feels like where I ought to be right now. And I *have* made up my mind. I have made up my mind not to make up my mind yet."

In Melissa's case, what needed to be taken out from behind the veil and supported was the affirmative aspect of her indecision, the wish to not have to make a "career" decision yet, and the desire to say to her ex-husband and her family some version of, "Back off! I'll make up my mind about the future when I'm ready. Meanwhile this feels good." It seemed that Melissa's distress arose because she had a hard time feeling this was a legitimate attitude to have. As a consequence, it was difficult for her to stand behind it, and hence she felt vulnerable to being pushed around by the other key people in her life.[5]

In exploring this topic as she is experiencing it now, I raise the question—certainly a common one for therapists to consider—of whether there are earlier roots to this pattern. I do so, however, in a fashion that offers her the choice of affirming that there is a long-standing pattern or indicating that this is a relatively unusual circumstance in her life:

I was wondering, that feeling of being told what to do, being told suck it up, being told you should do this and so on. Is that something that felt like, "How did I get into this relationship? I've never experienced this before"? Or is it something that sort of, if you think about it, happened a lot in your life before that?

I certainly am very explicitly introducing the idea that what she is experiencing has earlier roots and am clearly interested in exploring whether there is a familial context for the state of conflict she is presently in. But by putting the alternative into clear, vivid, first-person language—"How did I get into this relationship? I've never experienced this before"—I am attempting to give her more freedom to respond on the basis of her own experience and not some implicit pressure from me to affirm a strongly suggestive inquiry. Until I began to see videos of my therapy sessions, I was not aware that I did this, even though I now realize that this style of offering an alternative that enables even a probing inquiry not to be a "leading question" is a regular part of my style as a therapist. It was not something I did self-consciously; rather, it seemed to happen

---

[5]To be sure, she was also rebellious, as I discuss shortly. But what we are seeing here suggests that at least some of that rebelliousness is reactive. That is, although she is very committed in certain ways to doing "the Melissa thing," she is not fully comfortable with this way of being and struggles with the sense that she is doing things the wrong way. As she puts it, in her family "everyone is on the streak of you go to school, you go to college and you get your education and you go out and you get a real job. And everyone has a career in my family." It is not easy to swim against that stream.

almost automatically. But it seems consistent with my overall therapeutic style and with my strong concern with affirming the patient's experience and making room for whatever facet of that experience is most heartfelt at any given moment.

BUILDING ON THE PATIENT'S STRENGTHS

A related feature of the way I work entails an emphasis on approaching the patient from the vantage point of her strengths and avoiding pathologizing. It is unfortunately the case that there are strong tendencies in our field to view people through the lens of pathology and often, particularly for students when they are learning to become members of the profession, rewards for their perspicacity if they see "beneath" the patient's surface adaptations and discern their borderline, narcissistic, and so on, features. At one time, behavioral and cognitive–behavioral therapists were less prone to do this because early in their history they were strong opponents of the medical model. However, these days it is often cognitive–behavioral therapists who most strongly endorse a medical model, emphasizing specific "treatments" for specific "disorders" and insisting on *DSM* diagnoses as intrinsic to the task of providing empirical support for the work we do as therapists (see P. L. Wachtel, 2010a).

In my own work, I find diagnostic categories of limited value most of the time (there are, of course, exceptions, especially when medication is at issue). But I am concerned not simply with avoiding diagnostic *categories* (which in themselves shape and filter our perceptions in often unproductive ways—the *DSM* is a remarkably blunt instrument). I am concerned as well with avoiding the pathologizing *attitude* that searches for disorders and often in the process either misses or devalues the aspect of the same behavior that can be seen as a person's meaningful (if not always successful) effort to deal with the circumstances and challenges his or her life presents.

Within my approach to the work, a central feature of the skillfulness of the really good therapist is the capacity to address the difficult and painful issues in the patient's life in a fashion that is clear-eyed and unflinching while at the same time approaching the patient in a way that attends to, and even highlights, his strengths. At times, this aspect of the work entails simply *noticing*—and, in many instances, underlining—those strengths. Thus, one of the important moments in the first session with Louise occurred when we were discussing her friendships and I observed to her that she had actually achieved her goals with regard to friendships, and Louise broke out into a delighted smile, and I commented that she looked surprised when I said that. I made the first observation (that she had achieved her goals) in part to call her attention to the fact that this process was not just going to be one in which her "problems" were examined but one as well in which her strengths and achievements would be noticed and acknowledged. I noted her surprise at my saying this in order to underline the observation. I did this because, as I noted in my comments in Chapter 3, all too often in therapy, patients see something differently but *do not notice* that their perceptions have changed, and as a consequence, the change may be more short-lived than it might have been. This limitation in the change achieved occurs because the kinds of new behaviors that could consolidate the changed perception and weave them into the fabric of the patient's life—creating changes in the feedback loops that have been maintaining the problematic patterns—do not occur.

DISSOCIATION, UNFORMULATED EXPERIENCE, AND THE CHANGING UNDERSTANDING OF THE UNCONSCIOUS

Much of what I have been discussing thus far, of course, can be understood in terms of the mode of psychological functioning that psychoanalytic theory refers to as *unconscious*. In my own thinking, I have found that greater clarity is introduced by viewing many of the phenomena encountered in clinical work through the lens of what D. B. Stern (1997) called "unformulated experience." As I noted in Chapter 2 of this volume, even Freud (1914/1959) acknowledged that psychoanalysis only rarely unearthed memories and experiences that had been completely inaccessible to awareness prior to analysis. Most often, what we see clinically are not fully elaborated desires or fully articulated fantasies that have simply been buried or disguised and must be unearthed and revealed as what they really are; rather, we see a complex amalgam of different degrees of awareness and articulation and different *kinds* of awareness and articulation. Thus, the most important question is usually not whether something "is" or "is not" conscious but *in what way* is it conscious—how complete, focal, and articulated is the awareness; to what degree is awareness of thoughts or ideas linked to *feelings* that might be expected to accompany them; to what degree is that awareness linked to related *actions*; to what degree do the actions display the same degree of nuance and differentiation as the ideation; and so forth.

Many different configurations of these psychological qualities may be observed in the course of the work, and abstract concepts like "making the unconscious conscious" do not sufficiently address the complexity and subtlety of what is observed. Often it is the very activity of consciously articulating some aspect of experience that contributes to the absence of articulation of another, and these figure–ground dynamics may shift frequently in the course of a single session. This is part of why concepts such as dissociation and multiple self-states have come increasingly to be used by psychoanalytic thinkers to complement, and to some degree to replace, the older concept of a permanently buried, inaccessible, repressed unconscious (e.g., Bromberg, 1998a; Davies, 1998; Harris, 1996; Slavin, 1996; D. B. Stern, 1997).

Louise, for example, in response to my comment that Ken's family lives the way she did growing up, responds enthusiastically—"Yeah, I never thought about that. That's a great way of putting it"—and goes on to further endorse the comment and even say that seeing that similarity enables her to be more empathic toward them. Yet barely a minute later, discussing basically the same issue, she says, "That is so foreign to me." It does not seem she "did not understand" my comment and so said something contradictory shortly after agreeing to it. Rather, it seems that in one state of mind that point of view made a great deal of sense to her and in another, fed probably by the same need to cordon off the realm of "good" for her own family, she puts aside the understanding she had just achieved to return to her old mode of seeing things. Through the rest of the session, these two ways of experiencing alternate, as Louise works to make room for both her grievances toward Ken's family and her longing to be closer to them and to make room as well for similarly mixed (and even harder to own) feelings toward her mother.

Relatedly, Melissa, at several points in the session is able to articulate fairly clearly that it makes sense to her to stay in her present job for a while and that she feels unfairly pressured by her family and her ex-husband, yet those articulated perceptions alternate with feelings that she "should" pursue a more career-oriented direction. In one sense, this can be described quite adequately under the rubric of conflict. But the understanding of why the conflict is so difficult to resolve is aided by attention to the phenomenon of dissociation, of alternating experiences that run on parallel tracks, as it were, rather than being integrated.

A glimpse of how these dissociations begin to be resolved is evident in the course of the work with Louise. In the second session, she spontaneously refers back to our exchange in the first session, when after her reverting to seeing Ken's family's ways as "foreign," I said, "so foreign, and at the same time so central." In my putting it this way, rather than "interpreting" the view of Ken's family as foreign as a "defense" or distortion, I was attending evenhandedly and integratively to *both* sides of her experience. In part, this reflects the spirit of the work I have already discussed—not dismissing one part of the patient's experience as a false facade hiding a "deeper" experience that is more "real" or "true." But it addresses the process of dissociation as well by weaving the two sides of her experience, previously kept determinedly apart, into a understanding of her experience that embraces both sides and *brings them together* in a more unified, less dissociated whole. As the two sessions proceeded, and she used them to begin to work through these issues, she spontaneously came back several times to my "so foreign and yet so central" comment and made it more her own. An indication that she had done some real therapeutic work—and was not merely continuing in a dissociated alternation of perspectives—was her opening up of her feelings about her own family in a way that was hard for her to access earlier. To do so, she begins by focusing on Ken's family—an approach that contributes to making it "safe" to reconsider her own—but then she does go on to reflect on her own family as well:

> I've always felt like yeah, family is important, but, you know, these people [Ken's family] are going to the extreme. But still . . . you know, *my* family went to the extreme too. I mean, we never see each other. We never get together, it's all phone conversations and stuff like that, but yeah, there was, you know, "Don't tell other people about our problems."[6]

ATTENDING TO DAILY LIFE: PROMOTING
CHANGE OUTSIDE THE SESSIONS

Ultimately, the aim of the work going on in the session is to contribute to change in the patient's life *outside* the session. This is, of course, an obvious point, and yet it is one that is sometimes overlooked or cast to the margins in the therapist's focus on what is happening in the room. In certain ways, this tendency to "forget" this important point is especially prevalent in one of the realms of clinical thought that has been an especially central element in my own integrative therapeutic approach, namely, relational psychoanalysis (see P. L. Wachtel, 2008, especially Chapter 12, for a more detailed discussion of this issue). The relational point of view has made enormously important contributions to renewing psychoanalytic thought and, as I discussed in Part I, it has provided a more congenial foundation for integrating psychoanalytic theory and practice with ideas from other therapeutic orientations and with the findings of empirical research. But one of its major contributions—clarifying the therapeutic impact of the relationship and the therapeutic interaction in their own right—has also at times contributed to a problematic inattention to the patient's daily life. As I have discussed elsewhere (P. L. Wachtel, 2008), relational analysts often are so focused on understanding what is happening in the room between the two parties that the events of the patient's daily life become rather secondary.

Such an attitude is not intrinsic to the relational point of view; indeed, my own relational approach is *very centrally* concerned with the patient's daily life outside the consulting room, as I alluded to in Part I and further elaborate

---

[6]In referring to this sequence as providing a glimpse of how dissociations or conflicts are resolved, it is important to be clear that I am referring to small steps in what needs to be an ongoing process, not to a once-and-for-all "insight" that puts the matter to rest.

here. But for precisely the reason that the relational point of view does contribute so significantly to my overall clinical approach, it is important for me to clarify here how my own work differs in this regard from that of many other proponents of relational theory and practice.

In a related vein, it is useful to clarify as well the implications of the accumulating research findings that highlight the powerful role of the therapeutic alliance and the therapeutic relationship in contributing to therapeutic gains (e.g., Norcross, 2002, 2009). Here again, it is important not to let our focus on developing and facilitating the alliance distract us from the equally important role played by attention to the events of the patient's life outside the session. The therapeutic alliance contributes to therapeutic change in at least two different (though complementary) ways. First, much as emphasized by relational analysts, the quality of the relationship itself, as a model of a facilitative human relationship that is likely to differ in at least some important respects from that experienced when the patient was growing up, may have a direct effect on the patient's experience of self and others and on the problematic feelings and experiences that brought him to therapy. It offers a direct experience in which new ways of interacting and of experiencing oneself and others can be nurtured, modeled, and facilitated. In the process, it becomes a laboratory or workshop in which, based on the experience in the room itself, the patient learns new behaviors, develops new modes of affect regulation, and reworks his schemas and representations.

But there is a second important dimension to the contribution of the therapeutic alliance, a second reason why therapeutic gains are significantly correlated with a strong and positive alliance. A good working alliance facilitates *all the other work* that is done in a successful experience of psychotherapy. When there is a cooperative, collaborative quality to the interaction between patient and therapist, when the patient trusts and values the therapist and experiences her as understanding and respecting him, he is likely to engage in the process more fully and productively. That fuller and more productive participation includes engaging in a wide range of processes and experiences (often discussed in terms of therapeutic technique or specific interventions) that cannot be reduced to the quality or nature of the relationship alone. To acknowledge this—that is, to acknowledge that the impact of the alliance needs to be understood very largely in terms of its impact on *other* aspects of the therapeutic process, which are often the more proximate cause of change—is not a minimization of the value of the alliance; it is an elaboration of *how the alliance works*, of how it contributes to and enables therapeutic change. Put differently, the therapeutic alliance contributes to the work not only in its direct effect (as a new relational experience that has an impact on the patient's experience of himself and the world in its own right) but also as a *catalyst*, a contributing factor to facilitating *other* processes. The impact of those other processes is separate from that of the alliance per se, but that impact is diminished if there is not a strong and facilitative therapeutic alliance.

In understanding those other processes, it is important to remind ourselves again that much of the value of what happens in the therapy room derives from what it brings about *outside* the therapy room. The more obvious part of what I mean by this is simply that the ultimate *criterion* for whether the therapy has been successful is whether the patient's daily life has changed. Therapists are sometimes overly sanguine about the effectiveness of their work because they see with their own eyes that the patient has changed significantly in the way that he relates *to the therapist*. The patient who came in affectively restricted begins to relate to the therapist in a more feelingful and engaged way, the patient who came in hostile and argumentative becomes more cooperative, the patient who came in suspicious and withdrawn becomes more trusting. These changes can be dramatic, and they have a powerful impact on the therapist's judgment of the success of the work. But unfortunately, it is not infrequently the case that such changes in the therapy room are not paralleled by changes in the patient's daily life.

The therapy relationship is a very special kind of relationship. That is part of its potential for promoting change but also one of the reasons that therapists can sometimes be misled. The therapist is likely to be more understanding than others in the patient's life of the reasons for the bumps in the road between them and more tolerant of the patient's foibles as he struggles toward a more effective version of himself. Consequently, the patient may find that when he applies the lessons, as it were, of the therapeutic experience to the experiences of his daily life outside the therapy room, others are not as understanding or tolerant. The new ways of being and the new experience of self and other that evolve in the therapy room do not always hold up outside. The patient may not consciously articulate to himself that this is happening or even that he is applying the lessons of the therapy room to his daily interactions outside. But he may nonetheless be learning powerful discriminations that in effect come down to "*In here*, I can be myself, express dissatisfaction if I am dissatisfied, express need if I feel needy, dare to reveal both the weak and the strong sides of myself. But *out there* I cannot."

Even more important, but not so clearly understood by many therapists, is that the process of change—like the processes that maintain the patient's difficulties—is one in which the person's internal state and the events of the person's life are not separate realms but thoroughly intertwined. The events in our lives that account for experiences of affection, hostility, affirmation, embarrassment, understanding, misconnection, and so forth—that is, the kinds of experiences that are usually most central to how we view ourselves and our lives and that are central as well to what brings most people into therapy—are not "external" events like a thunderstorm or a nationwide economic recession. They are very largely events that we have contributed significantly to bringing about through our actions and interactions and the affective tone that accompanies them.

In one sense, and from the primary vantage point of some therapists, those actions and affective inclinations, especially when they are repeated frequently in the person's life, reflect long-standing characterological attributes—characteristic configurations of thought, desire, affect, and representation that lead the person to interact in certain ways and that need to be the target of the therapeutic effort. But, as I highlighted in Part I of this volume, this understanding needs to be complemented by an understanding that these long-standing psychological inclinations do not reflect the influence of a separate "inner" world hermetically sealed off from the events of the person's current life. As much as the inner state is the cause of the way the interactions with others repeatedly go, so too is the repetitive interactional pattern with others the cause of the inner state. It is the continuous back and forth between the two thoroughly intertwined dimensions of personhood and experience that lies at the root of both enduring personality characteristics and most of the complaints that bring people to therapy (see, e.g., P. L. Wachtel, 1977a, 1980, 1993, 1994, 1997, 2008). And it is in the effort to intervene in the repetitive recycling of this bidirectional pattern, to break the vicious circles in which the patient is caught, that therapy has its most powerful leverage to bring about enduring change. Without attention to how the patterns in the patient's life are repeatedly confirmed and maintained in his daily interactions with others, changes that occur as a result of a good experience in the therapy room are likely either to be short-lived or to be *limited* to the therapy room by the processes of discrimination discussed above ("Here it's safe to be different; there it's not").

Thus, from this understanding of the dynamics of personality and of psychological difficulty, the therapeutic effort must include keen attention to the subtleties of the patient's state of mind *and* equally keen attention to the daily interactions and experiences that both reflect his subjective experience of the world and maintain it. Attention to the patient's daily interactions and to the tangles he or she gets caught in is thus, far from being "superficial" (Boston Change Process Study Group, 2007; P. L. Wachtel, 2003), an essential part of understanding the person in depth and promoting change that is both extensive and enduring.

This approach to and way of understanding the therapeutic process was more evident in the work with Louise than it was with Melissa. Melissa's focus on salary, benefits, and so on clearly reflected important and meaningful concerns, but it did not permit much access to or work on broader aspects of her life experience (though there were more opportunities to begin to explore her dilemmas more complexly in the second half of the session). With Louise, in contrast, approaching her concerns through simultaneous attention to her subjective experience and long-standing psychological structures and inclinations on the one hand and her actual behavior in relation to others and the cyclical processes it contributed to perpetuating on the other was a prominent feature of the work we did. A central aim of the work with Louise was to help her to find a way to reconnect with Ken's family and to do so in a way that did not leave her feeling that she had submerged her own needs in a compliant, people-pleasing way that ultimately left her feeling frustrated and angry.[7] Part of this effort entailed helping her to *see* the patterns between them more clearly and to understand better the consequences of some of the ways she has interacted with them. But the work was also aimed at enabling her to actually *behave* differently, to interact with Ken's family in a way that would break the repetitive cycle in which they were all caught, in which each of them brought out in the other the very behaviors they most wished were different. (For a discussion of how similar patterns of bringing out the very behavior one complains about are perpetuated on the larger canvas of racial and ethnic mistrust and stereotyping, see P. L. Wachtel, 1999.)

In pursuing these interlocking aims, a significant part of the bridge to new action was constructed via comments that in some way had the structure of what are often called *interpretations*, but interpretations that were action oriented—that is, comments aimed at identifying, empathizing with, clarifying, and articulating what Louise was wanting and experiencing but stated in a way that framed it in terms of things she'd like to *say or do* ("It sounds like what you'd like to say to them is . . ."). There is an element in such comments not only of interpretation or empathy but of modeling, suggestion, and even implicit behavior rehearsal. Akin, perhaps, to what occurs when mirror neurons are fired, I assume that hearing me say, *as Louise,* something she could say to Ken's family serves as a kind of virtual experience of saying it herself, potentially enabling her to become a little more desensitized to saying such things. It potentially promotes as well a kind of implicit practicing in which she can, to the degree that what I said was consistent with her experience, internalize and rework my words to make them her own.

The commitment to giving serious attention to the dimension of action in daily life was manifested in a different way later in the session. After Louise had achieved some useful new perspectives on Ken's family and her relation to them, she says, "Yeah, I need to face it. I just don't know . . . again, it's just working on how." In saying this, she is at once conveying that, indeed, she *does not* know how to deal with it but also that she, implicitly, doesn't think

---

[7]Were she to do the latter—achieving a kind of "pseudo-resolution" by ignoring her own needs and desires—she would likely, as a consequence, end up relating to them in a way that sabotaged the very attempt to connect.

it is appropriate for her get any help from me on this. "It's just working on how" in some sense takes *too much* responsibility onto herself. If it's "just working on how," she probably *will not* work on how, because it is daunting to work on how when one has spent so much of one's life avoiding the very thing one is now needing to work on. The "default position" (P. L. Wachtel, 2008) from which many therapists implicitly operate entails not picking up on such highly indirect and essentially self-negating requests for help. Louise states things in a way that makes it feel natural to just leave her with the sense that she has to "work on how" by herself. But I do not leave her with this. I say to her, "Let's *think together* about how," and then I follow this up with explicit prompts to *help* her to think about it: "How would you *like* to approach them? What would you *like* to say to them?"

Thus, I do try to elicit Louise's active participation, and I do let the process emerge as much as possible from her own inclinations, preferences, style, and capacities. But I convey to her in a number of ways that she has a *partner* in this effort. I do this, first of all, by the very fact that I pick up on what she has, in effect, volunteered to do on her own (but would probably be unable to). I do it as well by saying let's think *together*. I am emphasizing a cooperative, collaborative process, not a process of self-exploration in which I am merely an observer. The very fact that Louise is caught in a cycle in which her behavior and Ken's family's behavior have repeatedly aggravated each other's wounds makes it extremely difficult to break that cycle. Without *active assistance* in breaking it, it is likely to remain self-perpetuating in a way that will render any insights attained fragile and unable to yield real change.

Clearly I do value the insights and changes in internal state that enable the patient to become more aware of and to be more accepting toward her thoughts, feelings, and desires. This is why I have placed such great emphasis throughout this book on *making room for the patient's feelings*. But this change in "internal" state cannot be reliably maintained without a change in the "external" transactions with other people that make up the person's life (or, put differently, and more accurately, without an understanding that the distinction between "internal" and "external" is very largely an artificial one). For many therapists, if we promote insight or bring about modifications in the patient's "inner world," behavior change will follow in due course. I am skeptical that this happens very often.

It is not, I hope it is clear from what I have already said, that I endorse the *opposite* of this unidimensional, linear view—that is, that I view the direction of causality as flowing exclusively from manifest transactions with others to the patient's internal state. Rather, I see the process of change as one in which causality is reciprocal and continuous, in which change in one aspect of the person's living (whether it be the patient's state of mind or his overt interactions with others) not only leads to change in the other but also can only be *maintained by* change in the other.

CONCLUDING COMMENTS

Louise and Melissa were both struggling with life dilemmas that were rendered difficult to resolve because of strong discomfort with some of the feelings, thoughts, and perceptions stirred in them as they attempted to address their concerns. For Louise, among the warded-off or threatening experiences were awareness of the ways in which her family had been a painful place growing up; the ways in which it was "different" from the families of the other kids she grew up with; the feelings of shame and of anger and disappointment she felt about that; the recognition of the ways in which her mother was unreliable and troubled and the ways she abandoned her; the lack of connection in the family that was covered over by the idea that when they really needed each other they were there for each other; and the longings to be closer to Ken's family, which felt to her like a betrayal of her own mother, whose flaws were pushed to the margins of consciousness by Louise's focus on the flaws in Ken's family.

In the work with Melissa, the exploration of her conflicted feelings and perceptions was more limited. Louise engaged more in the therapeutic process than Melissa did, and I got to know Louise better, even if still in what was of course only a preliminary way.[8] But for Melissa too there were indications of some of the experiences that she had difficulty accepting and integrating into her sense of herself and her place in the world. Melissa seemed quite conflicted, for example, regarding whether to value and affirm her rebellious, fun-loving, live-in-the-moment side or whether to view herself as needing to be more serious and to conform to the family's ideals about education, career advancement, and responsible behavior. Although the first set of feelings certainly found expression in her life and was part of her sense of self and of what felt to her like "the Melissa thing" or "the Melissa way," there were also indications that she was not so comfortable accepting these aspects of herself. They were not "repressed" or "unconscious" in the older (and in some ways more simplistic) understanding of that term, but they seemed clearly to be experiences of herself and her inclinations that were difficult for her to experience in a fully affirmatory way. It was in good part this difficulty in affirming her own experience and her own perceptions and desires, I believe, that made it difficult for her to resolve the conflict about whether to stay in her present job.

---

[8] I say this not because I had a second session with Louise but on the basis of the difference in the initial sessions with both.

In thinking about my sessions with Louise and with Melissa and comparing them with the way I usually work, I see many ways in which the sessions were representative of the way I generally work and a few ways in which they differed. Most clearly representative of my way of working was the focus on conflictual or not fully accepted feelings and inclinations and the effort to *make room for* those feelings and inclinations in the patient's psychological organization and experience of self. Equally representative was the effort to do so not by "interpretations" that demonstrate to the patient that she has been deceiving herself or harbors infantile feelings and desires but via comments that *expand on* her experience, respecting the ways of seeing herself with which she is more familiar while attempting to make room for other feelings and inclinations that have not yet found a place in her sense of who she is or who she feels she is *supposed to* be.

Evident in the sessions as well is another element typical of the way I work—the use of what I call *attributional* comments or interpretations. This emphasis on attributional comments evolved for me over a number of years before I became explicitly aware of it and before I had yet given it a name or begun to further elaborate on the concept in writing my book on effective therapeutic communication (P. L. Wachtel, 1993, in press). At this point I think of a considerable range of comments as fitting the label of *attributional* (a term I use in a somewhat different sense than is used in the social psychological literature on "attribution theory" [e.g., Heider, 1958; Jones et al., 1972; Weiner, 1986]). One common feature of the interventions to which I give this label—and one of the qualities that led me to use the term *attributional* to describe them— is that these comments *attribute* a range of therapeutic achievements to the patient to a significantly greater degree than is common in much therapeutic discourse. In part, this proceeds by the therapist's phrasing her comments in a way that has the structure of acknowledging what the patient has already seen ("If I'm understanding you properly, what you're saying is . . . ") rather than a structure of imparting insight to the patient who has not yet attained it (cf. Renik, 1993). In other instances, the attributional dimension consists of focusing on the ways that the patient has *already* taken steps toward greater clarity or more effective behavior. Here attributional comments build on the point of view discussed above under the rubric of building on the patient's strengths, reflecting the assumption that one of the best ways to promote the patient's taking new action in the world is to help the patient to sense that the seeds or buds of that new action are already in his repertoire. In discussing a rather similar therapeutic approach, my wife, Ellen Wachtel, has referred to "the language of becoming" (E. F. Wachtel, 2001), and this term captures well much of the spirit of what I am here calling attributional.

Thus, the attributional element sometimes lies in the degree to which insights and therapeutic gains are ascribed to the patient rather than the therapist (i.e., in playing down the therapist's contribution and emphasizing the patient's) and sometimes in depicting these gains as further along than they might seem to most observers, and in doing so, *enabling* them to be further along (see P. L. Wachtel, 1993, for a fuller discussion of this theme). In my interpolated comments accompanying the transcripts, I pointed out some of these attributional qualities on a number of occasions.

Another way in which the sessions reflected my usual way of working is that they were characterized, as my work usually is, by considerable attention to the patient's daily interactions with others and by efforts to directly work on how she acts in the world and on the consequences of those actions. This interest in the world of manifest events in everyday life—proceeding hand in hand with the interest in the "inner world" that is more typical of practitioners guided by psychoanalytic premises—derives from my central concern with the vicious circles that so pervasively characterize the difficulties that bring people to psychotherapy and with the way that, as a consequence of those largely self-perpetuating patterns, the "inner" world and the "outer" world of manifest transactions with others continually replicate and maintain each other. The focus on manifest relationship events—in the broader body of my work not just with regard to family but with other relationships as well, such as those at work, with friends, and so forth—reflects the expansion of my earlier integrative efforts to include as well the contributions of systems thinking and systemic therapeutic approaches in the evolving integrative model (E. F. Wachtel & P. L. Wachtel, 1986; P. L. Wachtel, 1997). People are not isolated monads; we live immersed in a range of social and psychological *systems,* and the behavior and experience of each person in the system can be understood as the complex product of the mutual interactions of each participant. The interactions between Louise and Ken's family represent a good example of a systemic pattern that needs to be understood not just in terms of the characteristics of each individual but also in terms of the system itself, the emergent pattern that, over time, takes on a life of its own and must be addressed in its own right.

The final of the four large therapeutic streams that contributed to the integrative approach I use is the experiential. The term *experiential* refers to a wide range of theoretical and clinical approaches (e.g., Elliott, Greenberg, & Lietaer, 2004; Fosha, Paivio, Gleiser, & Ford, 2009; L. S. Greenberg & Pascual-Leone, 2006), and at this point I am least clear about exactly where the different perspectives that are part of this therapeutic tradition intersect with my own way of thinking. But I have become increasingly drawn to the literature of the experiential point of view as I have become even clearer that the initial impetus for my integrative efforts, even many years ago, lay in dissatisfactions with what seemed to me the overly verbal and intellectualized quality of then-standard psychoanalytic practice. Certain behavioral methods, such as behavior rehearsal or the various forms of exposure, seemed to me to offer a more directly experiential confrontation with the objects of patients' fears and the challenging situations they came to therapy to work on, and this opportunity for direct experience seemed to me to provide a useful complement to the more verbal and reflective emphasis of the psychoanalytic tradition. As my work has continued to evolve, it has selectively drawn from each of the traditions in ways determined particularly by the wish to make the work more experiential. Thus, as I discussed in Chapter 1, I am more drawn to the versions of cognitive–behavioral therapy that highlight acceptance of and attention to affect than to those that try to persuade people that their affective experiences are "irrational"; and I am similarly drawn, in the psychoanalytic realm, to the relational emphasis on *participation* (cf. K. A. Frank, 1999) and the impact of direct relational experience more than to the stance of "neutrally interpreting" the patient's experience from a vantage point outside the interactive field.

In the sessions discussed in this book, the directly experiential dimension of the work was probably less evident than it is in the ordinary course of my work, in part because these were initial sessions; but this dimension was not completely absent. The effort, for example, essentially to *invite in* the inclinations and affective experiences that Louise and Melissa had largely cast out of their permissible selves rather than to "interpret" them was a feature of the sessions at numerous points. There were other ways, however, in which common aspects of my work were absent to a greater degree. I usually spend a good deal of time examining and discussing with the patient what is going on between us or our mutual experiences of each other. This attention to what is happening in the room complements the attention to what is happening in daily life, with each illuminating the other in a continuous back and forth that deepens the understanding of both. In these sessions, however, in large measure because they were not only initial sessions but initial sessions that were not intended or anticipated to be part of a longer, ongoing therapeutic effort, the same attention to the relationship was not evident. I did certainly *think* about this dimension while in the room with both Louise and Melissa, but there was little discussion of it, and so in this respect, the sessions differed from the way that many of my sessions proceed.

At the same time, it may be noted that it is by no means the case that in my work every single session is devoted to a focus on what is transpiring in the room. As I noted earlier, there are some relational therapists and analysts who set for themselves an ideal in which the examination of the subtleties of emotional connection and disconnection in the room is the center of the therapeutic process and who view attention to the details of the patient's daily life as relatively superficial. In my own work that is not the case. My attention to the events and dilemmas in Louise's and Melissa's daily living reflects a focus that is always a central one for me. What was absent in these sessions was something that *only sometimes* happens in my sessions but that happens often enough and is an important enough part of the overall therapeutic process and approach that its absence is worth noting, even if the particular sessions presented here did not depart dramatically from what many of my sessions tend to look like. Put differently, what was different about these sessions is that because an ongoing collaborative relationship had not already been established over time and in a secure way, I was less inclined to introduce this focus into the session than I might have been in a therapy that was expected to proceed through time.

Paralleling the absence of much discussion of the relationship, there was also little if any of what is usually called *self-disclosure* in the sessions. Or, to be more accurate, there was little if any *considered and intentional* self-disclosure; inadvertent or unintended self-disclosure—that is, self-disclosure that is simply a product of the therapist being a human being with a specific age, height, appearance, gender, voice, office location, fee structure, mode of speaking, and so on—occurs whether one intends it or not (K. A. Frank, 1997; Renik, 1995, 1999). Sharing with the patient some of my thoughts and feelings in the room, and at times even sharing accounts of events or experiences in my life outside the room or even in my own childhood, occurs with some regularity in my work (P. L. Wachtel, 1993, 2008). It is not something that happens in every session, to be sure, and so again, the sessions presented here are not dramatically atypical of how I usually work. But as with discussions of transference or countertransference phenomena, it is important to note that the very structure of the interaction (a contact scheduled to be for a single session and videotaped for potential scrutiny by large numbers of other therapists and therapists in training) made the absence have a somewhat different meaning than it would as a simple matter of course in an ongoing therapy in which it occurred in some sessions and not in others.

All in all, I believe these sessions offer a fair representation of what I do as a therapist. In reviewing them, they also seem, to a quite substantial degree, to reflect the theoretical considerations that I presented in the introductory chapters as guiding my therapeutic work. But, as I continue to reflect on the sessions with Louise and Melissa, it is my hope that they will also contribute—in ways of which I may still be unaware—to the further evolution of that theoretical understanding. Good theory is not theory that is fixed and venerated. It is theory that is responsive to the new observations that continually accrue from both clinical experience and attention to the ongoing flow of new empirical research.

I do not belong to that subset of therapists who believe that most therapy should be manualized or that a single research paradigm is appropriate for evaluating whether a therapeutic approach is "empirically supported" (P. L. Wachtel, 2010a). But I do believe it is important that we root our thinking in the evidence from empirical observations (both clinical observations and observations deriving from systematic research) and that doing so is essential to keep our theories alive and useful. Precisely what it means for a therapeutic approach to be "evidence based" is in fact a topic that is much more complex and controversial than some might have it (see, e.g., Norcross, Beutler & Levant, 2006; Shedler, 2010; P. L. Wachtel, 2010a). A range of respected researchers have argued that it is a sounder empirical strategy to pursue an understanding of the fundamental processes, principles, and mediating variables that account for therapeutic success than to attempt to validate or give a seal of approval to particular "packages" or "brand names" to place on a list of "empirically supported treatments" (e.g., Castonguay & Beutler, 2003; Goldfried & Eubanks-Carter, 2004; Kazdin, 2007, 2008; Kazdin & Nock, 2003; Pachankis & Goldfried, 2007; Rosen & Davison, 2003; see also P. L. Wachtel, 2010a for further discussion of how such a focus on principles better contributes to *improving* our effectiveness as therapists, not merely evaluating the effectiveness of the approaches we have developed thus far).

The approach depicted in this book is largely guided by this process-centered view of the relevant research base for therapeutic practice. There is considerable empirical support for the basic principles—deriving from research conducted from cognitive–behavioral, psychodynamic, systemic, and experiential vantage points—on which the integrative approach presented in this book is grounded (see, e.g., reviews of this evidence in P. L. Wachtel, 1994, 1997; P. L. Wachtel, Kruk, & McKinney, 2005; see also Andersen & Saribay, 2005; Andersen, Thorpe, & Kooij, 2007; Bargh, 2006; Elliot, Lietaer, & Greenberg, 2004; Greenberg & Pascual-Leone, 2006; Hofman & Weinberger, 2007; Norcross, 2002; Shedler, 2010; Wampold, 2001; Westen, 1998; Wilson, 2002). But in contrast to the "empirically supported treatment" (EST) approach to empirical validation (e.g., Chambless & Ollendick, 2001), the work depicted here examines the relevant research not for fixed, manualized therapeutic "packages" but for a broad understanding of psychological change principles that can be brought to bear in any particular case. The preponderant reliance on manuals and randomized controlled trials on the part of the "EST" movement reflects an ideologically driven approach to science that, in its methodological tunnel vision, impedes the grounding of clinical practice in the broadest foundation of scientific method and ignores an enormous body of sound and relevant data (P. L. Wachtel, 2010a).

In pointing this out, I am by no means advocating a blanket dismissal of the use of randomized controlled trials to test specific treatments for specific psychological problems. The appropriateness of such an approach depends on the nature of the therapy being evaluated and the clinical problems to which it is addressed. The treatment of certain problems is similar enough from patient to patient that such an approach can have considerable value if pursued as part of a larger research enterprise. But in many other instances, the premises of the "EST" approach entail a range of unwarranted and empirically questionable assumptions that impede rather than enhance the progress of a meaningful and sophisticated clinical science in our field (P. L. Wachtel, 2010a; Westen, Novotny, & Thompson-Brenner, 2004)

Attention to basic principles that have received support from systematic empirical research has modified my clinical practice a good deal over the years (see, e.g., P. L. Wachtel, 1997; P. L. Wachtel et al., 2005). But the approach presented in this book has not been manualized and tested as a "package" in a randomized controlled trial. In part, this is because to do so would actually violate some of its implicit premises, which include careful individualized attention to the patient's experience and the ways that that experience changes from moment to moment in response to the reciprocally interactive events of the session. It is also because although some sophisticated manuals have been created that do include as part of their instruction set guidelines for responding to the constantly changing contingencies that the therapeutic interaction creates, the very nature of those more flexible and clinically responsive manuals stretches the meaning of the term *manual* itself to a point where it serves more a political than a scientific purpose (P. L. Wachtel, 2010a).

Many of the ways that empirical validation of therapeutic outcome is presently approached reflect an inappropriate application of a methodology that is useful for testing drug treatments in medical settings but often reflects a rather maladroit, mechanical approach to science when employed to address the significantly different investigative challenges presented in studying the process and outcome of psychotherapy.[9] The "EST" methodology, for example, fails to consider the central importance in the drug research it emulates of conducting the study on a double-blind basis and the severe threats to internal validity if the double-blind status of the research is not maintained. In psychotherapy research, of course, it is virtually impossible to keep both patient and therapist unaware of what treatment is being administered (see P. L. Wachtel, 2010a, for further discussion of this and related issues).

---

[9]Ironically, this mimicking of the methodology of drug trials (and related insistence on restricting outcome research to studies of specific psychiatric diagnoses) has often been especially strongly emphasized by advocates of the very approaches that long criticized therapeutic approaches that purportedly adhered to a "medical model."

There is a large and productive realm between slavish adherence to narrow, and often ideologically driven, rules for "empirical validation" or "empirical support" on the one hand and the veneration of uncontrolled "clinical intuition" on the other. It is in this broad, fertile domain that the seeds of the approach described in this book have been planted. The quality of those seeds and their value for those who consume their fruits must be continually and responsibly monitored. But the process of monitoring and evaluating must not be one that destroys the very seeds and fruits being monitored. It is in the continuing close examination of the intersection between the human qualities of patient and therapist and the background of knowledge provided by ongoing research that our patients are best served and our field best advanced.

REFERENCES

Alexander, F., & French, T. M. (1946). *Psychoanalytic therapy: Principles and applications*. New York, NY: Ronald Press.

Allen, L. B., McHugh, R. K., & Barlow, D. H. (2008). Emotional disorders: A unified protocol. In D. H. Barlow (Ed.), *Clinical handbook of psychological disorders: A step-by-step treatment manual* (4th ed., pp. 216–249). New York, NY: Guilford Press.

American Psychological Association. (Producer). (2007). *Integrative relational psychotherapy* [DVD]. Available from http://www.apa.org/pubs/videos/

Andersen, S. M., & Chen, S. (2002). The relational self: An interpersonal social–cognitive theory. *Psychological Review, 109*(4), 619–645. doi:10.1037/0033-295X.109.4.619

Andersen, S. M., & Saribay, S. A. (2005). The relational self and transference: Evoking motives, self-regulation, and emotions through activation of mental representations of significant others. In M. W. Baldwin (Ed.), *Interpersonal cognition* (pp. 1–32). New York, NY: Guilford Press.

Andersen, S. M., Saribay, S. A., Kooij, C. S (2008). Contextual variability in personality: The case of the relational self and the process of transference. In F. Rhodewalt (Ed.), *Personality and social behavior: Frontiers of social psychology* (pp. 79–116). New York, NY: Psychology Press.

Andersen, S. M., Thorpe, J. S., & Kooij, C. S. (2007). Character in context: The relational self and transference. In Y. Shoda, D. Cervone, & G. Downey (Eds.), *Persons in context: Building a science of the individual* (pp. 169–200). New York, NY: Guilford Press.

Angus, L. E. & McLeod, J. (2003). *The handbook of narrative and psychotherapy: Practice, theory and research*. Thousand Oaks, CA: Sage.

Apfelbaum, B. (2005). Interpretive neutrality. *Journal of the American Psychoanalytic Association, 53*, 917–943. doi:10.1177/00030651050530030101

Aron, L. (1990). One person and two person psychologies and the method of psychoanalysis. *Psychoanalytic Psychology, 7*, 475–485. doi:10.1037/0736-9735.7.4.475

Aron, L. (1991). Working through the past, working toward the future. *Contemporary Psychoanalysis, 27*, 81–109.

Aron, L. (1996). *A meeting of minds: Mutuality in psychoanalysis*. Hillsdale, NJ: The Analytic Press.

Aron, L. (2006). Analytic impasse and the third: Clinical implications of intersubjectivity theory. *The International Journal of Psychoanalysis, 87*, 349–368. doi:10.1516/15EL-284Y-7Y26-DHRK

Balint, M. (1950). Changing therapeutical aims and techniques in psycho-analysis. *The International Journal of Psychoanalysis, 31*, 117–124.

Bargh, J. (2006). *Social psychology and the unconscious: The automaticity of higher mental processes*. New York, NY: Psychology Press.

Barlow, D.H. (2002). *Anxiety and its disorders: The nature and treatment of anxiety and panic* (2nd ed.). New York, NY: Guilford Press.

Barlow, D. H., Allen, L. B., & Basden, S. L. (2007). Psychological treatments for panic disorders, phobias, and generalized anxiety disorder. In P. E. Nathan & J. M. Gorman (Eds.), *A guide to treatments that work* (3rd ed., pp. 351–394). New York, NY: Oxford University Press.

Barlow, D. H., Allen, L. B., & Choate, M. L. (2004). Toward a unified treatment for emotional disorders. *Behavior Therapy, 35,* 205–230. doi:10.1016/S0005-7894(04)80036-4

Bass, A. (2003). "E" enactments in psychoanalysis: Another medium, another message. *Psychoanalytic Dialogues, 13,* 657–675. doi:10.1080/10481881309348762

Beebe, B., & Lachmann, F. (2002). *Infant research and adult treatment: Co-constructing interactions.* Hillsdale, NJ: The Analytic Press.

Beebe, B., & Lachmann, F. (2003). The relational turn in psychoanalysis: A dyadic systems view from infant research. *Contemporary Psychoanalysis, 39,* 379–409.

Benjamin, J. (2004). Beyond doer and done to: An intersubjective view of thirdness. *The Psychoanalytic Quarterly, 73,* 5–46.

Berman, E. (1981). Multiple personality: Psychoanalytic perspectives. *The International Journal of Psychoanalysis, 62,* 283–300.

Bibring, E. (1954). Psychoanalysis and the dynamic psychotherapies. *Journal of the American Psychoanalytic Association, 2,* 745–770. doi:10.1177/000306515400200412

Bornstein, R. (1988). Psychoanalysis in the undergraduate curriculum: The treatment of psychoanalytic theory in abnormal psychology texts. *Psychoanalytic Psychology, 5,* 83–93. doi:10.1037/h0085122

Boston Change Process Study Group. (2007). The foundational level of psychodynamic meaning: Implicit process in relation to conflict, defense and the dynamic unconscious. *The International Journal of Psychoanalysis, 88,* 843–860. doi:10.1516/ijpa.2007.843

Bowers, K. S. (1973). Situationism in psychology: An analysis and a critique. *Psychological Review, 80,* 307–336. doi:10.1037/h0035592

Bowlby, J. (1969). *Attachment and loss: Vol. 1. Attachment.* New York, NY: Basic Books.

Bowlby, J. (1973). *Attachment and loss: Vol. 2. Separation.* New York, NY: Basic Books.

Bowlby, J. (1980). *Attachment and loss: Vol. 3. Loss.* New York, NY: Basic Books.

Bowlby, J. (1988). *A secure base: Parent–child attachment and healthy human development.* New York, NY: Basic Books.

Brenner, C. (1979). Working alliance, therapeutic alliance, and transference. *Journal of the American Psychoanalytic Association, 27,* 137–157.

Bromberg, P. M. (1996). Hysteria, dissociation, and cure: Emmy von N revisited. *Psychoanalytic Dialogues, 6,* 55–71. doi:10.1080/10481889609539106

Bromberg, P. M. (1998a). *Standing in the spaces: Essays on clinical process, trauma, and dissociation.* Hillsdale, NJ: The Analytic Press.

Bromberg, P. M. (1998b). Staying the same while changing: Reflections on clinical judgment. *Psychoanalytic Dialogues, 8,* 225–236. doi:10.1080/10481889809539244

Bromberg, P. M. (2003). Something wicked this way comes: Trauma, dissociation, and conflict: the space where psychoanalysis, cognitive science, and neuroscience overlap. *Psychoanalytic Psychology, 20,* 558–574. doi:10.1037/0736-9735.20.3.558

Burton, N. (2005). Finding the lost girls: Multiplicity and dissociation in the treatment of addictions. *Psychoanalytic Dialogues, 15,* 587–612. doi:10.1080/10481881509348852

Cacioppo, J. T., & Berntson, G. G. (1992). Social psychological contributions to the decade of the brain: Doctrine of multilevel analysis. *American Psychologist, 47,* 1019–1028. doi:10.1037/0003-066X.47.8.1019

Cacioppo, J. T., Berntson, G. G., Sheridan, J. F., & McClintock, M. K. (2000). Multilevel integrative analyses of human behavior: *Psychological Bulletin, 126,* 829–843. doi:10.1037/0033-2909.126.6.829

Castonguay, L. G., & Beutler, L. E. (Eds.). (2003). *Empirically supported principles of therapeutic change.* New York, NY: Oxford University Press.

Chambless, D. L., & Ollendick, T. H. (2001). Empirically supported psychological interventions: Controversies and evidence. *Annual Review of Psychology, 52,* 685–716. doi:10.1146/annurev.psych.52.1.685

Cohen, J., & Tronick, E. (1988). Mother–infant face-to-face interaction: Influence is bidirectional and unrelated to periodic cycles in either partner's behavior. *Developmental Psychology, 24,* 386–392.

Cortina, M., & Marrone, M. (2003). *Attachment theory and the psychoanalytic process.* London, England: Whurr.

Craske, M. G., & Barlow, D. H. (2008). Panic disorder and agoraphobia. In D. H. Barlow (Ed.), *Clinical handbook of psychological disorders* (4th ed., pp. 1–64). New York, NY: Guilford Press.

Craske, M. G., & Mystkowski, J. (2006). Exposure therapy and extinction: Clinical studies. In M. G. Craske, D. Hermans, & D. Vansteenwegen (Eds.), *Fear and learning: Basic science to clinical application* (pp. 217–233). Washington, DC: American Psychological Association. doi:10.1037/11474-011

Crastnopol, M. (2001). On the importance of being (earnestly) hybrid—Or, qualms of a qu. *Psychoanalytic Dialogues, 11,* 253–267. doi:10.1080/10481881109348610

Crastnopol, M. (2007). The multiplicity of self-worth. *Contemporary Psychoanalysis, 43,* 1–16.

Davies, J. M. (1996). Linking the "pre-analytic" with the postclassical: Integration, dissociation, and the multiplicity of unconscious process. *Contemporary Psychoanalysis, 32,* 553–576.

Davies, J. M. (1998). Multiple perspectives on multiplicity. *Psychoanalytic Dialogues, 8,* 195–206. doi:10.1080/10481889809539241

Deacon, B. J., & Abromowitz, J. S. (2004). Cognitive and behavioral treatments for anxiety disorders: A review of meta-analytic findings. *Journal of Clinical Psychology, 60,* 429–441. doi:10.1002/jclp.10255 de Shazer, S., Dolan, Y., Korman, H., McCollum, E., Trepper, T., & Berg, I. K. (2007). *More than miracles: The state of the art of solution focused brief therapy.* New York, NY: Haworth Press.

Dimen, M. (2004). The return of the dissociated [Discussion]. *Psychoanalytic Dialogues, 14,* 859–865. doi:10.1080/10481880409353132

Dollard, J., & Miller, N. E. (1950). *Personality and psychotherapy.* New York, NY: McGraw-Hill.

Duncan, B. L., Miller, S. D., Wampold, B. E., and Hubble, M. A. (Eds.). (2009). *The heart and soul of change, second edition: Delivering what works in therapy.* Washington, DC: American Psychological Association.

Eccles, J. S. (2004). *Contextual influences on life span/life course.* Hillsdale, NJ: Erlbaum.

Ehrenreich, J. T., Buzzella, B. A., & Barlow, D. H. (2007). General principles of the treatment of emotional disorders across the lifespan. In S. G. Hoffman & J. Weinberger (Eds.), *The art and science of psychotherapy* (pp. 191–210). New York, NY: Routledge.

Elliott, R., Lietaer, G., & Greenberg, L. S. (2004). Research on experiential psychotherapies. In M. J. Lambert (Ed.), *Bergin and Garfield's handbook of psychotherapy and behavior change* (5th ed., pp. 493–540). New York, NY: Wiley.

Erickson, M. H. (1982). *My voice will go with you: The teaching tales of Milton H. Erickson.* New York, NY: Norton.

Erickson, M. H., & Lankton, S. R. (1987). *Central themes and principles of Ericksonian therapy.* New York, NY: Brunner/Mazel.

Erikson, E. H. (1950). *Childhood and society.* New York, NY: Norton.

Erikson, E. H. (1980). *Identity and the life cycle.* New York, NY: Norton.

Fairbairn, W. R. D. (1952). *An object relations theory of the personality.* New York, NY: Basic Books.

Fairbairn, W. D. (1958). On the nature and aims of psycho-analytical treatment. *International Journal of Psychoanalysis, 39,* 374–385.

Ferenczi, S. (1926). *Further contributions to the theory and technique of psychoanalysis.* London, England: Hogarth Press & the Institute of Psychoanalysis.

Foa, E. B., Huppert, J. D., Cahill, S. P., & Rothbaum, B. O. (Eds.). (2006). *Emotional processing theory: An update.* New York, NY: Guilford Press.

Foa, E. B., & Kozak, M. J. (1986). Emotional processing of fear: Exposure to corrective information. *Psychological Bulletin, 99,* 20–35. doi:10.1037/0033-2909.99.1.20

Foa, E. B., & Meadows, E. A. (1997). Psychosocial treatments for posttraumatic stress disorder: A critical review. *Annual Review of Psychology, 48,* 449–480. doi:10.1146/annurev.psych.48.1.449

Foa, E. B., Rothbaum, B. O., & Furr, J. M. (2003). Augmenting exposure therapy with other CBT procedures. *Psychiatric Annals, 33,* 47–53.

Fonagy, P. (2001). *Attachment theory and psychoanalysis.* New York, NY: Other Press.

Fosha, D. (2000). *The transforming power of affect: A model for accelerated change*. New York, NY: Basic Books.

Fosha, D., Paivio, S. C., Gleiser, K., & Ford, J. D. (2009). Experiential and emotion-focused therapy. In Courtois, C. A. & Ford, J. D. (Eds.), *Treating complex traumatic stress disorders: An evidence-based guide*. (pp. 286–311). New York, NY: Guilford Press.

Fosha, D., & Yeung, D. (2006). Accelerated experiential–dynamic psychotherapy: The seamless integration of emotional transformation and dyadic relatedness at work. In G. Stricker & J. Gold (Eds.), *A casebook of psychotherapy integration* (pp. 165–184). Washington, DC: American Psychological Association. doi:10.1037/11436-013

Frank, J. D. (1973). *Persuasion and healing: A comparative study of psychotherapy* (Rev. ed.). Baltimore, MD: Johns Hopkins University Press.

Frank, K. A. (1997). The role of the analyst's inadvertent self-revelations. *Psychoanalytic dialogues, 7*, 281–314.

Frank, K. A. (1999). *Psychoanalytic participation: Action, interaction and integration*. Hillsdale, NJ: Analytic Press.

Frank, K. A. (2002). The "ins" and "outs" of enactment. *Journal of Psychotherapy Integration, 12*, 267–286. doi:10.1037/1053-0479.12.3.267

Freud, A. (1936). *The ego and the mechanisms of defense*. New York, NY: International Universities Press.

Freud, S. (1957). Remembering, repeating and working through In J. Strachey (Ed. & Trans.), *The standard edition of the complete psychological works of Sigmund Freud* (Vol., 12, pp. 145–156). London, England: Hogarth Press. (Original work published 1914)

Freud, S. (1959). The neuro-psychoses of defence. In J. Strachey (Ed. & Trans.), *The standard edition of the complete psychological works of Sigmund Freud* (Vol. 3, pp. 41–61). London, England: Hogarth Press. (Original work published 1894)

Freud, S. (1959). Further remarks on the neuro-psychoses of defence. In J. Strachey (Ed. & Trans.), *The standard edition of the complete psychological works of Sigmund Freud* (Vol. 3, pp. 157 –185). London, England: Hogarth Press. (Original work published 1896)

Freud, S. (1959). On the history of the psychoanalytic movement. In J. Strachey (Ed. & Trans.), *The standard edition of the complete psychological works of Sigmund Freud* (Vol. 14, pp. 7–66.). London, England: Hogarth Press. (Original work published 1914)

Freud, S. (1959). Repression. In J. Strachey (Ed. & Trans.), *The standard edition of the complete psychological works of Sigmund Freud* (Vol. 14, pp. 141–158). London, England: Hogarth Press. (Original work published 1915)

Freud, S. (1959). Inhibitions, symptoms, and anxiety. In J. Strachey (Ed. & Trans.), *The standard edition of the complete psychological works of Sigmund Freud* (Vol. 20, pp. 87–172). London, England: Hogarth Press. (Original work published 1926)

Freud, S. (1959). New introductory lectures on psycho analysis. In J. Strachey (Ed. & Trans.), *The standard edition of the complete psychological works of Sigmund Freud* (Vol. 22, pp. 1–182). London, England: Hogarth Press. (Original work published 1933)

Friedman, L. (2002). What lies beyond interpretation, and is that the right question? *Psychoanalytic Psychology, 19,* 540–551. doi:10.1037/0736-9735.19.3.540

Ghent, E. (1989). Credo—The dialectics of one-person and two-person psychologies. *Contemporary Psychoanalysis, 25,* 169–211.

Gill, M. M. (1954). Psychoanalysis and exploratory psychotherapy. *Journal of the American Psychoanalytic Association, 2,* 771–797.

Gill, M. M. (1979). The analysis of the transference. *Journal of the American Psychoanalytic Association, 27*(Suppl.), 263–288.

Gill, M. M. (1982). *Analysis of transference.* New York, NY: International Universities Press.

Gill, M. M. (1984). Psychoanalysis and psychotherapy: A revision. *The International Review of Psychoanalysis, 11,* 161–179.

Goldfried, M. R., & Eubanks-Carter, C. (2004). On the need for a new psychotherapy research paradigm. *Psychological Bulletin, 130,* 669–673. doi:10.1037/0033-2909.130.4.669

Greenberg, J. R., & Mitchell, S. A. (1983). *Object relations in psychoanalytic theory.* Cambridge, MA: Harvard University Press.

Greenberg, L. S. (2002). *Emotion-focused therapy: Coaching clients to work through their feelings.* Washington, DC: American Psychological Association.

Greenberg, L. S., & Pascual-Leone, A. (2006). Emotion in psychotherapy: A practice-friendly research review. *Journal of Clinical Psychology, 62,* 611–630.

Harris, A. (1996). The conceptual power of multiplicity. *Contemporary Psychoanalysis, 32,* 537–552.

Havens, L. (1986). *Making contact: Uses of language in psychotherapy.* Cambridge, MA: Harvard University Press.

Hayes, S. C., Follette, V. M., & Linehan, M. M. (Eds.). (2004). *Mindfulness and acceptance: Expanding the cognitive–behavioral tradition.* New York, NY: Guilford Press.

Hayes, S. C., Luoma, J., Bond, F., Masuda, A., & Lillis, J. (2006). Acceptance and commitment therapy: Model, processes, and outcomes. *Behaviour Research and Therapy, 44,* 1–25. doi:10.1016/j.brat.2005.06.006

Hayes, S. C., Strosahl, K. D., & Wilson, K. G. (1999). *Acceptance and commitment therapy: An experiential approach to behavior change.* New York, NY: Guilford Press.

Heider, F. (1958). *The psychology of interpersonal relations.* New York, NY: Wiley.

Hoffman, I. Z. (1998). *Ritual and spontaneity in psychoanalysis: A dialectical–constructivist view.* Hillsdale, NJ: The Analytic Press.

Hofman, S. G., & Weinberger, J. L. (Eds.). (2007). *The art and science of psychotherapy.* New York, NY: Routledge.

Howell, E. (2006). *The dissociative mind.* Hillsdale, NJ: The Analytic Press.

Jaffe, J., Beebe, B., Feldstein, S., Crown, C. L., & Jasnow, M. (2001). Rhythms of dialogue in infancy: Coordinated timing in development. *Monographs of the Society for Research in Child Development, 66*(2), vi–131.

Johnson, S. M. (2004). *The practice of emotionally focused couple therapy: Creating connection* (2nd ed.). New York, NY: Routledge.

Jones, E. (1961). *The life and work of Sigmund Freud.* New York, NY: Basic Books.

Jones, E. E., Kannouse, D. E., Kelley, H. H., Nisbett, R. E. ,Valins, S. & Weiner, B. (Eds.). (1972). *Attribution: Perceiving the causes of behavior.* Morristown, NJ: General Learning Press.

Kazdin, A. E. (2007). Mediators and mechanisms of change in psychotherapy research. *Annual Review of Clinical Psychology, 3*, 1–27. doi:10.1146/annurev.clinpsy.3.022806.091432

Kazdin, A. E. (2008). Evidence-based treatment and practice: New opportunities to bridge clinical research and practice, enhance the knowledge base, and improve patient care. *American Psychologist, 63*, 146–159. doi:10.1037/0003-066X.63.3.146

Kazdin, A. E., & Nock, M. K. (2003). Delineating mechanisms of change in child and adolescent therapy: Methodological issues and research recommendations. *Journal of Child Psychology and Psychiatry, and Allied Disciplines, 44*, 1116–1129. doi:10.1111/1469-7610.00195

Keane, T. M. (1995). The role of exposure therapy in the psychological treatment of PTSD. *National Center for PTSD Clinical Quarterly, 5*, 1–6.

Keane, T. M. (1998). Psychological and behavioral treatments of posttraumatic stress disorder. In P. E. Nathan & J. M. Gorman (Eds.), *A guide to treatments that work* (pp. 398–407). New York, NY: Oxford University Press.

Kernberg, O. F. (1976). *Object relations theory and clinical psychoanalysis.* New York, NY: Jason Aronson.

Klein, M. (1952). *Developments in psycho-analysis* (J. Riviere, Ed.). London, England: Hogarth Press.

Klein, M. (1957). *Envy and gratitude; a study of unconscious sources.* London, England: Tavistock.

Klein, M. (1961). *Narrative of a child analysis; the conduct of the psychoanalysis of children as seen in the treatment of a ten year old boy.* New York, NY: Basic Books.

Klein, M. (1984). *Love, guilt, and reparation, and other works, 1921–1945.* New York, NY: Free Press.

Kohut, H. (1984). *How does analysis cure?* Chicago, IL: University of Chicago Press.

Leichsenring, F., & Rabung, S. (2008). Effectiveness of long-term psychodynamic psychotherapy: A meta-analysis. *JAMA, 300*, 1551–1565. doi:10.1001/jama.300.13.1551

Levy, R. A., & Ablon, J. S. (Eds.). *Handbook of evidence-based psychodynamic psychotherapy: Bridging the gap between science and practice.* Totowa, NJ: Humana Press.

Linehan, M. M. (1993). *Cognitive–behavioral treatment of borderline personality disorder*. New York, NY: Guilford Press.

Linehan, M. M., & Dexter-Mazza, E. T. (2008). Dialectical behavior therapy for borderline personality disorder. In D. H. Barlow (Ed.), *Clinical handbook of psychological disorders: A step-by-step treatment manual* (4th ed., pp. 365–420). New York, NY: Guilford Press.

Loewald, H. W. (1960). On the therapeutic action of psycho-analysis. *The International Journal of Psychoanalysis, 41*, 16–33.

Loewenstein, R. J., & Ross, D. R. (1992). Multiple personality and psychoanalysis: An introduction. *Psychoanalytic Inquiry, 12*, 3–48. doi:10.1080/07351699209533881

Lyons-Ruth, K. (1998). Implicit relational knowing: Its role in development and psychoanalytic treatment. *Infant Mental Health Journal, 19*, 282–289. doi:10.1002/(SICI)1097-0355(199823)19:3<282::AID-IMHJ3>3.0.CO;2-O

Magnusson, D., & Endler, N. (Eds.). (1977). *Personality at the crossroads: Issues in interactional psychology*. Hillsdale, NJ: Erlbaum.

Mahoney, M. J. (1995). *Cognitive and constructive psychotherapies: Theory, research, and practice*. New York, NY: Springer.

Mahoney, M. J. (2003). *Constructive psychotherapy: A practical guide*. New York, NY: Guilford Press.

Mancini, J. A. (Ed.). (2009). *Pathways of human development: Explorations of change*. Lanham, MD: Lexington Books.

Maroda, K. J. (1999). *Seduction, surrender, and transformation: Emotional engagement in the analytic process*. Mahwah, NJ: The Analytic Press.

Mayes, L., Fonagy, P., & Target, M. (2007). *Developmental science and psychoanalysis: Integration and innovation*. New York, NY: Karnac.

McCullough, L. (2003). *Treating affect phobia: A manual for short-term dynamic psychotherapy*. New York, NY: Guilford Press.

McNeilly, R. B. (2000). *Healing the whole person: A solution-focused approach to using empowering language, emotions, and actions in therapy*. New York, NY: Wiley.

McWilliams, N. (2004). *Psychoanalytic psychotherapy: A practitioner's guide*. New York, NY: Guilford Press.

Messer, S. B. (2000). Applying the visions of reality to a case of brief psychotherapy. *Journal of Psychotherapy Integration, 10*, 55–70. doi:10.1023/A:1009470427889

Miller, S. D., Hubble, M. A., & Duncan, B. L. (Eds.). (1996). *Handbook of solution-focused brief therapy*. San Francisco, CA: Jossey-Bass.

Minuchin, S. (1974). *Families and family therapy*. Cambridge, MA: Harvard University Press.

Mischel, W. (1968). *Personality and assessment*. New York, NY: Wiley.

Mischel, W., & Shoda, Y. (1998). Reconciling processing dynamics and personality dispositions. *Annual Review of Psychology, 49*, 229–258.

Mitchell, S. A. (1988). *Relational concepts in psychoanalysis*. Cambridge, MA: Harvard University Press.

Mitchell, S. A. (1993). *Hope and dread in psychoanalysis*. New York, NY: Basic Books.

Mitchell, S. A. (1995). Interaction in the Kleinian and interpersonal traditions. *Contemporary Psychoanalysis, 31*, 65–91.

Modell, A. H. (1984). *Psychoanalysis in a new context*. New York, NY: International Universities Press.

Molnar, A., & de Shazer, S. (1987). Solution focused therapy: Toward the identification of therapeutic tasks. *Journal of Marital and Family Therapy, 13*, 349–358.

Moscovitch, D. A., Antony, M. M., & Swinson, R. P. (2009). Exposure-based treatments for anxiety disorders: Theory and process. In M. M. Antony & M. B. Stein (Eds.), *Oxford handbook of anxiety and related disorders* (pp. 461–475). New York, NY: Oxford University Press.

Moses, E. B., & Barlow, D. H. (2006). A new unified treatment approach for emotional disorders based on emotion science. *Current Directions in Psychological Science, 15*, 146–150. doi:10.1111/j.0963-7214.2006.00425.x

Neimeyer, R. (2009). *Constructivist psychotherapy: Distinctive features*. New York, NY: Routledge.

Neimeyer, R. A., & Mahoney, M. M. (Eds.). (1995). *Constructivism in psychotherapy*. Washington, DC: American Psychological Association. doi:10.1037/10170-000

Norcross, J. (Ed.). (2002). *Psychotherapy relationships that work: Therapist contributions and responsiveness to patients*. New York, NY: Oxford University Press.

Norcross, J. C. (2009). The therapeutic relationship. In B. L. Duncan, S. D. Miller, B. E. Wampold, & M. A. Hubble (Eds.), *The heart and soul of change, second edition: Delivering what works in therapy* (pp. 113–142). Washington, DC: American Psychological Association.

Norcross, J. C., Beutler, L. E., & Levant, R. F. (Eds.). (2006). *Evidence-based practices in mental health: Debate and dialogue on the fundamental questions*. Washington, DC: American Psychological Association.

O'Hanlon, B., & Weiner-Davis, M. (1989). *In search of solutions: A new direction in psychotherapy*. New York, NY: Norton.

Ogden, T. H. (1994). The analytic third: Working with intersubjective clinical facts. *The International Journal of Psychoanalysis, 75*, 3–19.

Ogden, T. H. (2004). The analytic third: Implications for psychoanalytic theory and technique. *The Psychoanalytic Quarterly, 73*, 167–195.

Orange, D. M., Atwood, G. E., & Stolorow, R. D (1997). *Working intersubjectively: Contextualism in psychoanalytic practice*. Mahwah, NJ: Analytic Press.

Pachankis, J. E., & Goldfried, M. R. (2007). An integrative, principle-based approach to psychotherapy. In S. G. Hoffman & J. Weinberger (Eds.), *The art and science of psychotherapy* (pp. 49–68). New York, NY: Routledge.

Pizer, S. A. (1996). The distributed self: Introduction to symposium on "The Multiplicity of Self and Analytic Technique" *Contemporary Psychoanalysis, 32,* 499–507.

Polanyi, M. (1958). *Personal knowledge: Towards a post-critical philosophy.* Chicago, IL: University of Chicago Press.

Polanyi, M. (1967). *The tacit dimension.* Chicago, IL: University of Chicago Press.

Pos, A. E., Greenberg, L. S., & Elliott, R. (2008). Experiential therapy. In J. L. Lebow (Ed.), *Twenty-first century psychotherapies: Contemporary approaches to theory and practice* (pp. 80–122). Hoboken, NJ: Wiley.

Psychological & Educational Films. (Producer). (1989). *Integrative psychotherapy, Part 4: A demonstration with Dr. Paul Wachtel.* Available from http://www.psychedfilms.com/index.html

Redmond, J., & Schulman, M. (2008). Access to psychoanalytic ideas in American undergraduate institutions. *Journal of the American Psychoanalytic Association, 56,* 391–408. doi:10.1177/0003065108318639

Renik, O. (1993). Analytic interaction: Conceptualizing technique in light of the analyst's irreducible subjectivity. *The Psychoanalytic Quarterly, 62,* 553–571.

Renik, O. (1995). The ideal of the anonymous analyst and the problem of self-disclosure. *The Psychoanalytic Quarterly, 64,* 466–495.

Renik, O. (1999). Playing one's cards face up in analysis: An approach to the problem of self-disclosure. *The Psychoanalytic Quarterly, 68,* 521–530.

Rhodewalt, F. (Ed.).(2008). *Personality and social behavior: Frontiers of social psychology.* New York, NY: Psychology Press.

Rickman, J. (1957). *Selected contributions to psycho-analysis.* Oxford, England: Basic Books.

Ricoeur, P. (1970). *Freud and philosophy: An essay in interpretation* (D. Savage, Trans.). New Haven, CT: Yale University Press.

Rosen, G. M., & Davison, G. R. (2003). Psychology should list empirically supported principles of change (ESPs) and not credential trademarked therapies or other treatment packages. *Behavior Modification, 27,* 300–312. doi:10.1177/0145445503027003003

Ruiz-Cordell, K., & Safran, J. D. (2007). Alliance ruptures: Theory, research, and practice. In S. G. Hoffman & J. Weinberger (Eds.), *The art and science of psychotherapy* (pp. 155–170). New York, NY: Routledge.

Safran, J. D., & Muran, J. C. (2000). *Negotiating the therapeutic alliance: A relational treatment guide.* New York, NY: Guilford Press.

Safran, J. D., Muran, J. C., & Proskurov, B. (2009). Alliance, negotiation, and rupture resolution. In R. A. Levy & J. S. Ablon (Eds.), *Handbook of evidence-based psychodynamic psychotherapy: Bridging the gap between science and practice* (pp. 201–225). Totowa, NJ: Humana Press. doi:10.1007/978-1-59745-444-5_9

Schafer, R. (1983). *The analytic attitude.* New York, NY: Basic Books.

Schafer, R. (1992). *Retelling a life: Narration and dialogue in psychoanalysis*. New York, NY: Basic Books.

Schafer, R. (1997). *The contemporary Kleinians of London*. Madison, CT: International Universities Press.

Schore, A. N. (2003). *Affect regulation and the repair of the self*. New York, NY: Norton.

Shapiro, D. (1965). *Neurotic styles*. New York, NY: Basic Books.

Shawver, L. (1983). Harnessing the power of interpretive language. *Psychotherapy: Theory, Research and Practice, 20*, 3–11.

Shedler, J. (2010). The efficacy of psychodynamic psychotherapy. *American Psychologist, 65*, 98–109.

Shoda, Y., Cervone, D., & Downey, G. (Eds.). (2007). *Persons in context: Building a science of the individual*. New York, NY: Guilford Press.

Slavin, M. O. (1996). Is one self enough? Multiplicity in self-organization and the capacity to negotiate relational conflict. *Contemporary Psychoanalysis, 32*, 615–625.

Spence, D. P. (1982). *Narrative truth and historical truth*. New York, NY: Norton.

Spence, D. P. (1983). Narrative persuasion. *Psychoanalysis and Contemporary Thought, 6*, 457–481.

Spezzano, C. (1996). The three faces of two-person psychology: Development, ontology, and epistemology. *Psychoanalytic Dialogues, 6*, 599–622. doi:10.1080/10481889609539141

Stern, D. B. (1997). *Unformulated experience: From dissociation to imagination in psychoanalysis*. Hillsdale, NJ: The Analytic Press.

Stern, D. B. (2003). The fusion of horizons: Dissociation, enactment, and understanding. *Psychoanalytic Dialogues, 13*, 843–873. doi:10.1080/10481881309348770

Stern, D. B. (2004). The eye sees itself: Dissociation, enactment, and the achievement of conflict. *Contemporary Psychoanalysis, 40*, 197–237.

Stern, D. N. (1985). *The interpersonal world of the infant: A view from psychoanalysis and developmental psychology*. New York, NY: Basic Books.

Stern, D. N. (2004). *The present moment in psychotherapy and everyday life*. New York, NY: Norton.

Stern, D. N., Sander, L. W., Nahum, J. P., Harrison, A. M., Lyons-Ruth, K., Morgan, A. C., . . . Tronick, E. Z. (1998). Non-interpretive mechanisms in psychoanalytic therapy: The "something more" than interpretation. *International Journal of Psycho-Analysis, 79*, 903–921.

Stolorow, R. D. (1997a). Dynamic, dyadic, intersubjective systems. *Psychoanalytic Psychology, 14*, 337–346. doi:10.1037/h0079729

Stolorow, R. D. (1997b). Principles of dynamic systems, intersubjectivity, and the obsolete distinction between one-person and two-person psychologies. *Psychoanalytic Dialogues, 7*, 859–868. doi:10.1080/10481889709539224

Stolorow, R. D., & Atwood, G. E. (1992). *Contexts of being: The intersubjective foundations of psychological life*. Hillsdale, NJ: Analytic Press.

Stolorow, R. D., Atwood, G. E. & Orange, D. M. (1999). Kohut and contextualism: Toward a post-Cartesian psychoanalytic theory. *Psychoanalytic Psychology, 16*, 380–388.

Stolorow, R. D., Brandchaft, B., & Atwood, G. E. (2000). *Psychoanalytic treatment: An intersubjective approach*. Hillsdale, NJ: The Analytic Press.

Stone, L. (1961). *The psychoanalytic situation*. New York, NY: International Universities Press.

Strachey, J. (1934). The nature of the therapeutic action of psychoanalysis. *The International Journal of Psychoanalysis, 15*, 127–159.

Sullivan, H. S. (1947). *Conceptions of modern psychiatry*. New York, NY: Norton.

Sullivan, H. S. (1950). The illusion of personal individuality. *Psychiatry, 13*, 317–332.

Sullivan, H. S. (1953). *The interpersonal theory of psychiatry*. New York, NY: Norton.

Swales, M. A., & Heard, H. L. (2009). *Dialectical behaviour therapy*. New York, NY: Routledge.

Tenzer, A. (1984). Piaget and psychoanalysis: II. The problem of working through. *Contemporary Psychoanalysis, 20*, 421–436.

Tronick, E. (1989). Emotions and emotional communication in infants. *American Psychologist, 44*, 112–119.

Wachtel, E. F. (2001). The language of becoming: Helping children change how they think about themselves. *Family Process, 40*, 369–384. doi:10.1111/j.1545-5300.2001.4040100369.x

Wachtel, E. F., & Wachtel, P. L. (1986). *Family dynamics in individual psychotherapy*. New York, NY: Guilford Press.

Wachtel, P. L. (1973a). On fact, hunch, and stereotype: A reply to Mischel. *Journal of Abnormal Psychology, 82*, 537–540. doi:10.1037/h0035375

Wachtel, P. L. (1973b). Psychodynamics, behavior therapy, and the implacable experimenter: An inquiry into the consistency of personality. *Journal of Abnormal Psychology, 82* 324–334.

Wachtel, P. L. (1977a). Interaction cycles, unconscious processes, and the person situation issue. In D. Magnusson & N. Endler (Eds.), *Personality at the crossroads: Issues in interactional psychology* (pp. 317–331). Hillsdale, NJ: Erlbaum.

Wachtel, P. L. (1977b). *Psychoanalysis and behavior therapy: Toward an integration*. New York, NY: Basic Books.

Wachtel, P. L. (1980). Transference, schema, and assimilation: The relevance of Piaget to the psychoanalytic theory of transference. *The Annual of Psychoanalysis, 8*, 59–76.

Wachtel, P. L. (1983). *The poverty of affluence*. New York, NY: Free Press.

Wachtel, P. L. (1987). *Action and insight*. New York, NY: Guilford Press.

Wachtel, P. L. (1991). The role of accomplices in preventing and facilitating change. In R. Curtis & G. Stricker (Eds.), *How people change: Inside and outside therapy* (pp. 21–28). New York, NY: Plenum Press.

Wachtel, P. L. (1993). *Therapeutic communication: Principles and effective practice.* New York, NY: Guilford Press.

Wachtel, P. L. (1994). Cyclical processes in psychopathology. *Journal of Abnormal Psychology, 103,* 51–54. doi:10.1037/0021-843X.103.1.51

Wachtel, P. L. (1995). The contextual self. In C. Strozier & M. Flynn (Eds.), *Trauma and self* (pp. 45–56). London, England: Rowman & Littlefield.

Wachtel, P. L. (1997). *Psychoanalysis, behavior therapy, and the relational world.* Washington, DC: American Psychological Association. doi:10.1037/10383-000

Wachtel, P. L. (1999). *Race in the mind of America: Breaking the vicious circle between Blacks and Whites.* New York, NY: Routledge.

Wachtel, P. L. (2003). Full pockets, empty lives: A psychoanalytic exploration of the contemporary culture of greed. *American Journal of Psychoanalysis, 63,* 103–122. doi:10.1023/A:1024037330427

Wachtel, P. L. (2005). Anxiety, consciousness, and self-acceptance: Placing the idea of making the unconscious conscious in an integrative framework. *Journal of Psychotherapy Integration, 15,* 243–253. doi:10.1037/1053-0479.15.3.243

Wachtel, P. L. (2008). *Relational theory and the practice of psychotherapy.* New York, NY: Guilford Press.

Wachtel, P. L. (2009). Knowing oneself from the inside out, knowing oneself from the outside in: The "inner" and "outer" worlds and their link through action. *Psychoanalytic Psychology, 26,* 158–170.

Wachtel, P. L. (2010a). Beyond "ESTs": Problematic assumptions in the pursuit of evidence-based practice. *Psychoanalytic Psychology, 27,* 251–272.

Wachtel, P. L. (2010b). One-person and two-person conceptions of attachment and their implications for psychoanalytic thought. *International Journal of Psychoanalysis, 91,* 561–581.

Wachtel, P. L. (in press). *Therapeutic communication* (2nd ed.). New York, NY: Guilford Press.

Wachtel, P. L., Kruk, J., & McKinney, M. (2005). Cyclical psychodynamics and integrative relational psychotherapy. In J. Norcross & M. Goldfried (Eds.), *Handbook of psychotherapy integration* (2nd ed., pp. 172–195). New York, NY: Oxford University Press.

Wallerstein, R. S. (1989). The psychotherapy research project of the Menninger Foundation: An overview. *Journal of Consulting and Clinical Psychology, 57,* 195–205. doi:10.1037/0022-006X.57.2.195

Wallin, D. J. (2007). *Attachment in psychotherapy.* New York, NY: Guilford Press.

Wampold, B. (2001). *The great psychotherapy debate: Models, methods, and findings.* Mahwah, NJ: Erlbaum.

Watzlawick, P., Weakland, J. H., & Fisch, R. (1974). *Change; principles of problem formation and problem resolution.* New York, NY: Norton.

Weiner, B. (1986). *An attributional theory of motivation and emotion.* New York, NY: Springer-Verlag.

Weiss, J., & Sampson, H. (1986). *The psychoanalytic process*. New York, NY: Guilford Press.

Westen, D. (1998). The scientific legacy of Sigmund Freud: Toward a psychodynamically informed psychological science. *Psychological Bulletin, 124,* 333–371.

Westen, D., & Gabbard, G. O. (2001a). Developments in cognitive neuroscience: I. Conflict, compromise, and connectionism. *Journal of the American Psychoanalytic Association, 50,* 53–98. doi:10.1177/00030651020500011501

Westen, D., & Gabbard, G. O. (2001b). Developments in cognitive neuroscience: II. Implications for theories of transference. *Journal of the American Psychoanalytic Association, 50,* 99–134. doi:10.1177/00030651020500011601

Westen, D., Novotny, C. M., & Thompson-Brenner, H. (2004). The empirical status of empirically supported psychotherapies: Assumptions, findings, and reporting in controlled clinical trials. *Psychological Bulletin, 130,* 631–663. doi:10.1037/0033-2909.130.4.631

White, M., & Epston, D. (1990). *Narrative means to therapeutic ends*. New York, NY: Norton.

Wile, D. B. (1984). Kohut, Kernberg, and accusatory interpretations. *Psychotherapy: Theory, Research, & Practice, 21,* 353–364. doi:10.1037/h0086097

Wilson, T. D. (2002). *Strangers to ourselves: Discovering the adaptive unconscious*. Cambridge, MA: Harvard University Press.

Winnicott, D. W. (1965). *The maturational processes and the facilitating environment: Studies in the theory of emotional development*. Oxford, England: International Universities Press.

Winnicott, D. W. (1971). *Playing and reality*. New York, NY: Basic Books.

Winnicott, D. W. (1975). Through paediatrics to psycho-analysis. In *International psychoanalysis library* (Vol. 100, pp. 1–325). London, England: The Hogarth Press & the Institute of Psycho-Analysis.

Wolff, P. H. (2001, June). *Why psychoanalysis is still interesting?* Paper presented at the Annual Meeting of the Rapaport-Klein Study Group, Stockbridge, MA.

Zeig, J. K. (1985). *Ericksonian psychotherapy*. New York, NY: Brunner/Mazel.

Zinbarg, R. E., Barlow, D. H., Brown, T. A., & Hertz, R. M. (1992). Cognitive behavioral approaches to the nature and treatment of anxiety disorders. *Annual Review of Psychology, 43,* 235–267. doi:10.1146/annurev.ps.43.020192.001315

INDEX

INDEX   279

Values, 29–30, 202–203
Variability, 23–24, 52–54, 61
Vicious circle(s)
    anxiety in, 93
    evolution of, 100–104
    and integrative theory, 54
    necessity of breaking, 156–157
    and patient behavior, 20–23
    in patient's daily life, 255
    perpetuation of, 172
    processes of, 95–96

    systemic, 152
    and viewpoints of all parties, 81, 98
Videotaped sessions, 65–68, 128, 186, 226
Vulnerability, 161

Wachtel, P. L., x, 14, 43–44, 47n6,
    48n7, 214
Wait-and-see attitude, 204
Wallerstein, R. S., 19
Westen, D., 30–31
Winnicott, D. W., 40

ABOUT THE AUTHOR

Paul L. Wachtel, PhD, is a distinguished professor in the doctoral program in clinical psychology at City College of New York and the Graduate Center of the City University of New York. He did his undergraduate work at Columbia University; received his PhD in clinical psychology from Yale University; and is a graduate of the postdoctoral psychoanalytic training program at New York University, where he is also on the faculty. He is internationally recognized as an innovator in the field of psychotherapy and for his contributions to the application of psychological theory and research to the pressing social problems of our times.

A cofounder of the Society for the Exploration of Psychotherapy Integration, Dr. Wachtel is the author of many books on psychotherapy, personality dynamics, and psychologically oriented social criticism, including *Action and Insight; The Poverty of Affluence; Family Dynamics in Individual Psychotherapy; Therapeutic Communication; Psychoanalysis, Behavior Therapy, and the Relational World; Race in the Mind of America: Breaking the Vicious Circles Between Blacks and Whites;* and, most recently, *Relational Theory and the Practice of Psychotherapy.* A number of his books have been widely described as classics in the field.